Letters from 500
Amen

Robert Lee Potter

BrightWire Publishing
Warren, New Jersey, USA
To contact us about this book, please visit our site and blog at www.lettersfrom500.com

ISBN 978-0615694184
1. The Future. 2. Consciousness. 3. Spiritual Life. I. Title.

2 4 6 8 11 12 10 9 7 5 3

Contents

Acknowledgments v
Author's Note vii
Poem Three xi
Letter Fifty .... Gathering 1
Letter Fifty-One .... Look to the Sky 7
Letter Fifty-Two .... An Invitation 15
Letter Fifty-Three .... No One to Greet Us 23
Letter Fifty-Four .... Galactic Embrace 31
Letter Fifty-Five .... Being Space 39
Letter Fifty-Six .... Golden Pyramid 47
Letter Fifty-Seven .... Ability to Respond 55
Letter Fifty-Eight .... Evigilatus-Sapiens 63
Letter Fifty-Nine .... Expression of Service 73
Letter Sixty .... New Reverence 81
Letter Sixty-One .... Hierarchy of Conscious Expression 89
Letter Sixty-Two .... You Are the Unknown 97
Letter Sixty-Three .... Three Last Suggestions 107
Letter Sixty-Four .... Playground 117
Letter Sixty-Five .... Spirit into Matter 125
Letter Sixty-Six .... Place of Knowing 133
Letter Sixty-Seven .... Hole in the Heart 141
Letter Sixty-Eight .... Essence of Eternity 147
Letter Sixty-Nine .... Source Gazing 153
Letter Seventy .... Cœur Sacral 161
Letter Seventy-One .... Scryer's Pool 167
Letter Seventy-Two .... Soul Talk 173
Letter Seventy-Three .... Un-Formation 181
Letter Seventy-Four .... Return of Mars 187
Letter Seventy-Five .... Mars in Paris 195
Letter Seventy-Six .... Apollo's Palace 201
Letter Seventy-Seven .... Invoke the Void 209
Letter Seventy-Eight .... Surrender to Oneness 215
Letter Seventy-Nine .... Open Opportunity Essence 221
Letter Eighty .... The Future Now 225
Letter Eighty-One .... Wealth..229
Letter Eighty-Two .... Linear Fashion 235
Letter Eighty-Three .... So It Might Seem 239
Letter Eighty-Four .... Intrinsic 245
Letter Eighty-Five .... Vesica of the Gods 251
Letter Eighty-Six .... Adieu 255
Letter Eighty-Seven .... Destiny Well 259
Letter Eighty-Eight .... Open Space.......................................263
Epilogue .... Why Souls Love the Earth 269
Who is the Scribe? 281

Acknowledgments

Stefan Bright and Judy Welder are the most excellent collaborators. They have persistently offered their advice, support, and hard work throughout the production of the *Letters*. Our partnership undoubtedly spans many lifetimes. Of course, I recognize them as members of the group of twelve in 500 who originally launched—who *will* launch—this project. Thank you Judy, Stefan and the group.

Once again, I render sincere appreciation to the nine muses. Their leader is the inimitable Musagetes, or Apollo—poet and prophet, riddler and charioteer for the Solar Logos. In particular, Clio and Caliope have been the two muses most closely associated with our project. Their inspiration and guidance is very clear to me when present—and so obviously missing when they're away.

I credit that inexplicable person, Peter Kingsley, with triggering my sensitivity to Apollo. I wish him much gratitude for his periodic instruction and guidance. I met him in Asheville and was inspired in one of his lectures for the title of our final volume: Considering the 'end times' we're living in, he asserted, there's nothing left to say but "amen." After reading his book, *In the Dark Places of Wisdom* in Paris—I quietly placed it on a shelf at the Shakespeare and Company bookstore as a gift to the future.

Of course, I'm always thankful to Eckhart Tolle for being *here,* on this planet, and holding the space of Now for us all. In one of his silent pauses there is wisdom that no quantity words can convey. Given his initials, ET, I wonder just where he *comes from,* and who might have sent him. Be that as it may, his teachings have motivated much of my ideas and writing.

Closer to home, I credit my friend, Felicia Hueber, for inspiring the poem of this volume. Over many conversations and cups of coffee or tea, we have a true meeting of souls. Loic Barnieu is another influential friend; he comes, from Auxerre, France—by way of Paris. Although he is steadfastly skeptical of my 'spiritual' interests, he inspires me in a paradoxical way. Opposites do more than attract; they provoke revelation. He offers the humorously surly attitude of a successful entrepreneur in the so-called 'real world'. It keeps me grounded—as much as that is possible.

Now especially, I wish to thank those who have never met me and yet have found some resonance with the *Letters*. For you, the test is clearest for whether or not the message has a place in our time. I would appreciate hearing from you.

Author's Note

Writing these letters has been a wild and exciting ride. Beginning four years ago, they came out of thin air—as a totally unexpected opportunity. *Letters from 500* took on a life of its own immediately, from the very first day at Assateague Island (see Author's Note, Book One). From that day, I became a scribe and a participant in the events of 'Orange' and her cohorts. And this adventure has opened me up in surprising new ways. In particular, I've found a much clearer access to the simple voice of inspiration deep inside. This voice is, of course, within all people who would listen. It does not use words though; nor does it literally *speak,* not even in thoughts. Yet it *is* a living presence, seeding forth the essence of all we ever know or say in our lives.

The transition years around 2012 are living up to their billing in so many ways, both negative and positive. They are a potent metaphor for the turbulent evolution going on inside us as individuals: As above, so below—as within, so without. From ourselves collectively, we are projecting out all the great Earth dramas onto the canvas of time in these days. We're each involved—wholly and deeply, right down to our *holy* roots. I believe the fiery battles of ego we witness coursing around the globe and through society are the evidence of human DNA in its throes. *What will become of us?* That is the basic question for our species and our selves.

One answer to that question can be found in these *Letters.* The messages tell us our species is ending—and yet *beginning* too—transitioning into a new universe of *Conscious Evolution;* we are involved in nothing less than an awakening and quickening of our bodies and souls. Hearing the truth of the soul can *make us free,* the prophets have promised. Our species is remaking itself—in the form of freedom. These *Letters* portray, symbolically, the process of re-forming and re-divining our future.

When the soul speaks its truth, it whispers. It comes through the 'still, small voice', resident in our hearts. This whisper has been called the 'voice of the silence' or simply 'stillness' itself. It does not come from ego or from any form of separateness. It is never a *raised* voice. To hear it we must *descend* to its level. In meekness and subtlety, it reports our innate connection to Source. There, we know *who we really are*—our true foundation for communion. Sinking deeply within and listening intently, we hear the noiseless sound our soul makes. The experience is at once intimate and infinite; for the ego, it can also be intimidating.

The essence of any inspired writing is to put *words* onto the empty space of stillness. Shakespeare called it the "airy nothing" (see his verse, quoted on page 115). After four years of writing the *Letters,* I've come to a better understanding of how the process has worked: I feel the still, small voice produces all my core inspiration. It rouses the *muses*. They whisper with their thin, fine vapors, offering the fragrance of ideas to my mind. With sensitivity and respect, I have found ways to place these ideas into form, namely as *writing*.

To produce worldly expressions out of the stillness is a tricky business, however. A multitude of words or images might be chosen to describe any formless impression. Words and pictures can show the way; but they can also mislead or beguile. We must be careful when we use symbols. At best, they are pointers to reveal the living emptiness within them; at worst, they distort and manipulate the mind. Through all, we must be discerning.

Now this project of *Letters* is coming to a close, at least in its writing phase. The publishing of Book Three is completed. Other stages will open from here: connecting with a growing audience; there will be more seminars and gatherings; through Stefan's blog, we have reached hundreds of people around the world. Through both Judy and Stefan, we have had meetings with many enthusiastic supporters. These meetings with readers have proven to be uplifting and engaging. I guess I shouldn't be surprised. After all, what topic could be more stirring to any of us than the awakening of our species?

Regardless of the content or impact of the *Letters from 500,* the way they were delivered still amazes me: They basically dropped out of the ethers into my lap—literally into my *laptop*. In the manner of the first two volumes, the third was written in exactly *five* months. Writing began on January 1, 2012 and ended on June 1. The 'one' and 'five' numerology is again evident. The reason for this remains somewhat a mystery to me. I know in numerology that 'one' symbolizes *beginning,* wholeness and Oneness. It can also mean *initiating* new projects. 'Five' symbolizes the five senses, the imagination, freedom and exploration. It also connotes progress and *growth*. Together these two numbers seem to represent empowerment of the whole trilogy project—its inception, generation and outward presentation. 'Three', as in the 'trilogy', connotes *manifestation*.

In this installment, the adventure story continues, with twists and turns I could not—and did not—imagine before I began writing. It's a bizarre way to compose a book, I know. Critics may certainly agree, and I couldn't blame them. All I can say is, it *is what it is!* This process for me was rather like chauffeuring a car on dark, unknown streets, to unfamiliar places. Even though the adventure story carries the dialogue and adds color, it's what lies beneath and between the lines that is most vital. I personally feel the stories have been provided only as a way to facilitate deeper understandings.

We find in this book, the usual characters. But I meet some delightful new ones; and they have *names:* Mihelo, Gavrea, Omis, Invm, Breanne, Krotos and Treema. A seven-year-old Parisian girl, Phileina, from 200 years in the future, made the deepest impression on me; the reason will be obvious when you read about her. When I finally leave Phileina, it is with a deep sadness of parting. I'm sure it's not unusual for writers to love the characters they describe. In this story I feel they have loved me *back,* and have become real friends and teachers. By them, I have been truly blessed. May you, too, find those blessings as you get to know them.

Late last year I saw Woody Allen's movie, *Midnight in Paris.* In it, the protagonist decides to live in Paris and write a book. That idea resonated with me deeply. During the same period, my friend, Loic, was coaxing me to spend some extended time in France to hone my language skills. The two influences converged, and before long I was off, renting an apartment in Montmartre. It's a kind of dream come true, I guess—writing in Paris. That magical city certainly inspires such activity. Not surprisingly then, the place worked its way into the unfolding story.

In spite of the inspired surroundings of the city and the presence of the muses, I worried at times that inspiration might dry up and leave me stranded. In fact, there was a period in March when the muses went silent and I *couldn't* write. I needed *recalibrating.* I somehow managed to accept this as part of the experience; it ended up giving me more confidence in the mysterious 'unknown'. It also enabled me to focus on studying French and exploring Paris more deeply.

The muses did finally return in full force. They swept away my worries and I got right back to work. Upon my return to the States, in a huge burst of enthusiasm, I wrote the last eight chapters in only six days. The Epilogue, after that, curiously, required a full three weeks of work. Now that the writing is done, I feel the muses are receding again. There they go. *Au revoir.* It always happens; it's part of the cycle of things. Though it's difficult, I accept it. I needed the break anyway.

Beijinhos,
R. L. Potter,
Chester, Pennsylvania, Spring, 2012

Poem Three

Sweet fields of peace and grace are
sweeping up around thee,
sweeping inside through.
The whisp'ring essence is adrift
in hearts of passion everywhere.

There is a poem without words.

◊

So let it be

in spaces without words
and in between the words.

Our space becomes our words,
our forms, our times on Earth below.
Therefore,
become the Word.
To be *and* not to be.
To feel. Reveal.
This timeless moment
we will be.

There is no catch or hook,
no way to lock the door of ever more.
We're going in between the particles
of matter
to the spaces in the locks
of all the doors that ever were.

We speed down through the portals
to the Space
that is itself a portal,
only infinitely so.
We ride its presence
to the gentleness.

We're riding, riding.
Stillness rising.
Crying out, we fly.
We're free of all
that ever we have been or done.
Our flight, our exclamation,
is the punctuation to an age
that time revealed, surrounded
by the timeless One.

This punctuation
is a pointer
to the boundless Point of Source.

We live in thought—in form.
Yet we are not
what thought believes itself to be.
The mind of thought must fall away at last
and leave us free.

As light as that, we float.
Just smiling. Tiny smiling.
like a Buddha, Mona Lisa,
or a Sphinx.

We, within our deepest, inner knowing,
find the essence from it, form it,
open up it.
Flower to a Butterfly.
Caterpillar to the chrysalis.
It is a treasure true, this wonder,
if our eye will only see.

And that, my friends, beloved ones,
is where we're riding—
into Oneness, as our own,
away from fear
and far beyond alone.

— R. L. Potter, January 1, 2012

Letter Fifty
Gathering

To All Concerned,

"This is it. The time has come again, that we may sit down together and reflect on the grand future."

I hear your voice in a distance, a kind of fog in my ears. *I don't think I'm ready for this.* I say these words in my head. Then I repeat them aloud.

You speak directly now, emerging out of the mist of my mind. "You are ready. We know better than you—here, on this end of the timeframe. Allow us to draw you out, dear friend. We draw you out of your slumber, your cocoon and chrysalis. Come out of your fear. Let your ego rest now. It has fought the good fight. It has won its share of victories. There's nothing for it to be ashamed of. No shame. No blame."

I wriggle in my chair and squint, whispering against a wind that seems to sweep up inside me. I realize I'm harboring a strong resistance. It is a fear that I've allowed to gradually build up over the months since I last wrote for you. *All those writings seem like something someone else did.* I voice my fear. "I'm afraid maybe it just won't work this time, O. It's not a huge fear, but it's very well-entrenched. It has grown roots deep into my subconscious."

"I know. I feel those roots all knotted up around you. But it does not matter; they will dissolve as we begin to pour the elixir of awakening into the soil. Simply allow. Allowing is so simple. There is no obstacle, save the image of obstacles you have created in your mind. And that is merely a thought. Replace that thought with this one: *You are free.*

"By the way, your roots go much deeper than your human mind—a kind of 'mud' on the surface of awareness. They go all the way down into essence. Slide down beyond the ego world, toward the core of you, to the well of the Earth. Source. So simple!"

"Easy for you to say," I grumble. But I do notice that my resistance is softening, ever so slightly. I try once more a delaying tactic. "O, the world is so full of fear and negativity right now. It seems to be building up, not diminishing. The freedom movements around the world seem to be descending into chaos and conflict. Economies everywhere are on the brink of collapse or upheaval, or both. Corporate mentality still rules politics. Wars are still waging and being dreamed up in faraway lands. It is so hard for people to break free of that past. Evolution seems too slow to save us!"

"Stop!" Your voice is firm and unyielding. "That's enough. Tell me something you appreciate about your world, your time."

I bow my head and realize my words are, themselves, generating resistance as I write. I listen to what you've just said. I stop and ponder. Silence. Then, hesitantly, I begin to turn toward your light.

Slowly, I answer, "What is good and wonderful in my time is what has always been good and wonderful for all time—the beauty of nature, the warm sunlight on the first days of January, the inspiring teachings that are coming up around the planet, even amidst turmoil and despair. I am so fortunate to be healthy, to have shelter and food and opportunities in great abundance. I have resources and great friends, family. Exciting projects! We are all moving, together, toward a cleaner and clearer destiny. I can feel it."

"Thank you. Now we shall begin. Relax. Take a very deep breath. Hold it for few seconds. Let it out slowly until your lungs are very empty. Hold the emptiness. Count 'one ... two ... three'—*emptiness*. Feel the timelessness within that time. Right there, in the center of time, lies eternal *no-time*. You are the being who lives there in the center of eternity. It is now. Forever. Feel it in your arms and legs and hands, in your eyes and heart. See through it—*with* it. This eternity is your vision.

"Welcome back, one and all, to this window on the way you will evolve. We are so delighted to have the opportunity to speak with you again. You are very dear to us, humanity. We love you deeply. We *are* you, in a very direct sense. To speak now, amongst ourselves, is to strengthen our bond, our realization of the Oneness within our two species."

I sit up and take myself in hand. I stammer, "I'm glad you're back, too. It has been a long dry spell since we last spoke and wrote. I have crusted over during that time. But I feel that crust breaking up. Thank you, O and Black and OM, and all the others in the group. I think I'm ready to begin. Please, lead on."

"We will take you on a journey in this volume of *Letters*. 'Buckle your seat belts,' as your culture used to say. It will be an enjoyable, enlightening ride, we believe. There are seats for everyone in our vehicle. It is grand and wide, large enough for any passengers who would climb aboard. It is the vehicle of Oneness. We are one being. The more we ride together, the more we shall all feel that shared sensation of the whole. Come."

With that, I feel I am being lifted up, swept away in my imagination. There are clouds passing in a deep blue sky. The Earth is turning below. I feel a thousand hearts surrounding me as I fly. What a wonderful sensation. And unmistakably, you are here with us, O. I *sense* you more than I see you. For the humans in this throng, we are a growing body of souls, assembling by the thousands and now millions, eager to rise up and share the sky with you. We are all angels for this moment—winging to God-knows-where. It doesn't matter. The sky is our home. It is a sunrise, sunset, full noon and midnight all at once. We are experiencing your 'endless abundance.' *Akasha*—space—empowers us.

"May I ask, O, what is this about? Where are we heading? Who are all these beings?"

"They are the future of humanity, being *born again* right now, and they are being *borne up* through the air by their emergent appreciation. You are gathering now, this year, in your true time. Your sensibilities are rising on the tide of clear aspiration; you all understand that the time is now. You are the seed generation of genetic transformation. Embrace your blessing. You have been given this great gift by none other than your grandest Self—Source."

We are floating through the stratosphere, feeling no fear or concern. There are uncountable numbers of us, streaming as far out as I can see to each horizon. I sense they are coming from all the corners of the Earth, from all continents and islands. *Ah!* I realize. *My mind has been placed on hold.* I'm not asking the obvious question about how this is happening. Instead, I'm simply accepting it.

The more we fly, the more real it becomes. I look down and see lights shining up from the land in small clusters. Far below, there is a harbor with buildings and cars along a narrow street. Boats, appearing tiny, are moored in the water along the edge. We sweep down for a closer look. I recognize this is France. I know the look of the village, this style of buildings and roofs. We move out again, over forested hills and pass along a wide river. Here's another village, and another. I see no cities, and not many people.

"O, are we in *your* time or mine?"

"As we fly, the time is changing. You are witnessing the passing of 500 years as we go."

Time-travel and travel-time, I amuse. As we sail along, it seems now that our numbers are dwindling. Some are pulling off into the distance on the sides, heading for other destinations. Some are swooping down to the Earth below, and finding their places in the settlements. And then, there's a strange sensation; it feels like our numbers are merging; we are becoming fewer individual bodies. A million have merged into a few thousand; a thousand souls are fused into a hundred; somehow, each body, myself included, is holding many other souls. I feel in my form the bundling of many minds and hearts, looking out through my single eyes. I marvel: *Strange technology of the vigilans!*

Without hesitation our composite group gathers into a wide arc to begin a descent. We're over a great, sparkling city. *This can only be Paris.* I hover in awe over the beautiful sight of it. I've always loved this city and have visited here as often as I could. I see many of the features that existed in my time, still here 500 years later. There is the Seine, of course, with its islands of *la Cité* and *Saint Louis.*

I see monuments I know well—*Notre Dame, Sacré Cœur* and the *Arc de Triomphe.* But the city is clearly much smaller than it used to be. The outlying countryside has moved back in toward the center; the sprawl has vanished. Those unsightly tall buildings are gone, even in the distance. *Hah,* I remark to myself, *La Défense is gone!* There is more forest and parkland sprinkled and woven in everywhere. *And the Eiffel Tower! Well, there it is.* But it's different.

Our group slows and gradually comes down on the opposite bank of the river. I finally see what has changed. *La Tour Eiffel* is no longer made of metal. *Amazing.* It's composed of pure holographic light, like a sculpture of light. *In the City of Light,* I note. Beams of amber, emerald and rose sweep up in the same shape as the original. It all sparkles and gleams in a dance of delight and welcome. My eyes are transfixed on it as we finally touch ground. I'm standing in what used to be the *jardin* of the Trocodéro, across the Seine from the tower. It too has changed dramatically.

The old garden is now a large amphitheater on the slope. Its grand semicircle opens out toward the river and the scintillating light-spire of Eiffel. This new arena is not large by 21st Century standards, but in the vigilan world, it is huge; there must be 5,000 seats. It's probably two-thirds full, and more people continue to arrive. Most of them are coming in through large arched doorways below, facing the Seine. But others are arriving the way we did—floating gracefully down from the sky.

You smile, standing next to me in full physical form at last. I reach out and touch your shoulder, your hands. "It's good to be back, O. Good to have *you* back." We embrace warmly, staring into each other's eyes for a perfect moment.

"OK, O. What's going on?"

"You said you would like to be invited to one of our congresses. Well, *here* we are."

"Wow," I gasp. "Yes. I do remember asking about that. Outstanding. But I'm surprised. This seems very large. Didn't you say your congresses are small, like a few hundred people at a time?"

"I did. This is the largest congress ever held on Earth. Eighty percent of the population is in attendance. Many are in attendance remotely or by proxy. I assume you felt the *merger of eyes* into yourself. You and I, and all the rest of the assembled guests, are here for others, as well as ourselves. We are acting as broadcasting stations for those others; they are tuning in silently through us."

"My God, O. That's staggering. What's the occasion? It sounds like big stuff."

"Indeed it is. But I will not try to describe it just yet. I'll let you build your appreciation in stages—with a little suspense." While you pause, the soft sound of bustling people surrounds us in a comfortable envelope. "First, for now, let's talk about this final book: Allow me to tell you straightaway what the purpose of it is."

"Ahem. Yes. I guess we've just started it."

You grin. "It is all with good reason that we have maintained our distance these many months. Again suspense is good. The unknown is good—it is *God*. We have played your ego concerns and mental self off against the emerging message we seek to deliver. The duality and tension—yes, even your *resistance*—are useful in drawing this out. But now, all must be revealed."

"So, just what is the purpose of these letters?"

"We propose to take you on a journey into the world that your species is creating. This will be your story of awakening, of what *Conscious Evolution* has wrought. It is the world you have passed on to your children's generations. This is the story of your legacy, bestowed on us—and by extension, from your own soul to you."

I pause and wonder aloud, "Will this be anything like my visit to your world at the end of the last book? It was so delightful to be with you and Green there. I felt what it was to actually *be* a vigilan. Unfortunately," I frown, "that's only a *memory* to me now."

"Don't worry. It is a *living* memory within you. It's *incubating* there. And, yes it may be something like that experience. But I myself do not know much. As to what the story will be, I may be able to intuit a bit more than you, but certainly not all the details. The unknown is just as strong a presence for me as it is for you. We will go exploring and learning *together.*"

I furrow my brow and look at you. "So in a nutshell, the purpose of these letters is to show us your *world*? Is that it?"

"That and more. We will show you *your presence* in that world. It will also empower a manifestation of forms back into your old world. In *Portal*, we established the bridge and link to the new universe; this was to open the passage between our worlds. It has acted to facilitate a mutual understanding and avenue of appreciation. What will unfold now is an implementation phase—a joyful closure for the message. We will 'close the deal' with you, humanity. We will find our own true consensus within one another, and demonstrate some of the rewards for all your struggles and suffering. Together, we shall embrace your time with *now*. So be it."

Letter Fifty-One
Look to the Sky

As my vision clears and your world takes on more solidity, I realize we are with the whole group of twelve. All the various multi-colored, robed figures greet us with nods. Black and Green are here beside us, hands touch and arms embrace in a cheerful reunion. Black kisses me on the forehead and I am filled with the most amazing, bright energy. I feel my mind opening and resonating directly with my heart. It is as though there has suddenly been a merging between head and heart—a realization of what I heard before, intellectually, that all the chakras are really only one chakra: *the heart!*

Now I notice the amphitheater more. It is composed of many distinct spaces, each open to the sky, but having low walls around groupings of seats. There is a thin film that bubbles over each compartment. We can see the whole crowded theater at will, and yet we have a sense of being in our own private living room. There are small tables between the comfortable, reclining chairs. Each table has glasses, several bottles of various beverages and a tray of snack food with it. We each take a seat and look out at the assembling throng.

I have sensed the vigilan race before in large numbers, but never have I looked upon you this way. It is awe-inspiring to witness the way you walk and interact even in this teeming venue. There is a peaceful silence under all the commotion, ready smiles on each face, occasional laughter that ripples out and touches minds throughout the arena. The serenity of the multitude is what I keep feeling most. *How can 5,000 people be so peaceful, so in tune with one another, so at one?* I ask myself.

You answer my thought, "We love to be in love with our family. It brings us indescribable joy to feel the presence of Oneness within our neighbors. Every person here, and every person participating from a distant location, is aware of that presence; and it grows in intensity the more we move together. An occasion like this gives us all an opportunity to amplify our love and appreciation."

"You're right," I state the obvious. "But what amazes me is that the feeling is so tangible. And it seems to be increasing geometrically with more people arriving."

"We are here, not only for the event that is about to unfold, but also to experience each other and the heightened presence we bring together. This is a culture of the Now, of the *presence.* We feel it and live it. When we assemble in such a way as this, we participate in what Christ called 'life more abundant.'

You can feel that abundance here now. But I must point out, you could also feel it in your day within certain large gatherings and celebrations. When the ego stepped aside in those situations, the one heart was allowed to shine forth. In lesser measure you could also feel it in small groups that came together for harmonious purposes. It is the fundamental resonance with Source that you're feeling."

The arrivals have finished. I sense that the audience is fully assembled. An air of anticipation sweeps the arena. I look around at the members of our group and feel a piercing appreciation among us; I feel it for each one of you. You are my true brothers and sisters—Tan and Gold, Red, Blue and Brown. It matters not that you are from a different age or culture or species. My heart goes out to each; each of your hearts comes into mine. I suddenly, literally, see a fine web of golden light linking each of our hearts.

Then, in a glance, I look out to the larger crowd and see that same gossamer filament spreading everywhere. There is a subtle-but-distinct form to our collective sense of Oneness. I can see it—the web. *Is this the 'inner-net'?* I chuckle to myself. My curiosity at the phenomenon stirs an experimenting spirit in me. I begin to play with my visioning, and realize I can turn this sensation off and on at will. I can choose to see the web or not. *Why doesn't it work like this back in my own time?*

"Because you are not living in freedom there yet," Black's voice whispers next to my ear. *She too is reading my thoughts.* "Here you are immersed in *our* sensitivity. This little wonder, and many more shall be added to you in the near future—in your own time. What you have not yet seen, you *shall* see. What you have not found, you shall find. What you have not yet appreciated, you shall soon appreciate—in great abundance."

With an almost synchronized motion, 5,000 seats around the amphitheater begin to recline. I look to you and you nod back. Our chairs, too, lean back to almost horizontal. My head sinks to a comfortable headrest. Our eyes—all as one—look to the sky. Stars dot the blackness. *And there's no urban light pollution,* I notice. We all just stare into the spectacle for a very long time. Appreciation of the Cosmos builds within our collective mind.

The universe is truly amazing to behold. *Mesmerizing.* The more I stare, the more *alive* it becomes for me. That Life is continuously there, embracing our planet and all creatures here below. Yet humans forget it; we ignore it, dismiss it in great measure—this profound cradle of liberty, founded on the vast emptiness of Source. This sky is with us always, just beyond the blue and the clouds and city lights, endlessly. It is as infinite, eternal and permanent as anything can be in our little world. *So many humans just ignore it or take it for granted. Why?* Perhaps we *fear* this spectacle and its depth. Perhaps it represents *too much* freedom. I read once that we can only see a few thousand stars under the best conditions with our naked eyes; and yet there are 400 billion stars in our galaxy alone!

Strange, I've never realized how much energy is coming into my senses from the sky. *It's basically just a dark dome with random points of light, right? What's the big deal?* But now I see! Now I feel. It is raw power, raining down constantly, in abundance. It synchronizes with the Earth energy, dances and dapples, lifts, then presses down in turn, animating our entire spectrum of sensitivities. *I always wanted to be an astronomer. Now*, here, I know why. I wanted to spend endless hours appreciating this presence. I still do.

Never before have I truly meditated on the Cosmos. My eyes are full open and penetrating deeply into the tableau arrayed above. Yet it no longer seems like 'above' to me. The Cosmos is simply here before and around me, embracing every aspect of my being. The energy I feel keeps building. I know intimately that it would never cease, were I to simply stay in this position for the rest of my life. Now I see the golden-web filament, rising up out of the assembled people to meet the sky. It moves off into the emptiness, into forever. The net undoubtedly continues in multiple dimensions throughout the whole Cosmos.

Along the filaments, I feel a vibration coming toward me and toward the congress. It hums in the air for several minutes and then begins to wind down into lower frequencies. These, in turn, become words that my ears can apprehend.

"Welcome, one and all, to this unique gathering—our Congress on *Conscious Evolution*." The words are coming straight out of thin air all around me and inside my body simultaneously. The voice is melodious and hypnotic. Then I realize it is *your* voice, O, addressing the entire congress. "Tonight we shall be entertained and engaged to participate in an event that has already transpired, some 500 years ago. Yet it is still happening today and tomorrow— in this sacred moment.

"We have all heard and felt the ripples of this great experience in recent years. Some of us were party to the original congress that set it in motion. Tonight we invite you, we invoke you, to own this event in the core of your awareness, for it is in fact already an essential part of that awareness—in both psychic and physical ways."

As your words taper off, images begin to dissolve into the sky above. At first they are gossamer-thin, like borealis curtains. Gradually, they solidify into three-dimensional, holographic pictures. They spread entirely across the visible sky. I watch transfixed, entertained and entrained to my core, eager to see what unfolds. To my amazement, the images are very familiar.

I gasp to see our group gathered around the Mayan calendar outside your house, chanting and singing in response to Black's beautiful vocals. The songs are literally lifting our spirits. All in the wide arena feel themselves pulled up into the imagery. We are experiencing this together—as though we are there, and it is happening for the first time right now. I see my own body dissolve in from the ethers of time. I float above the stone slab, coming in and out of focus, disappearing, then solidifying again.

Other pictures sweep through, pressing both visions and feelings into our sensibilities. I see the group deliberating in private, working to create its original project, then being surprised—even alarmed—at what it has produced. We all watch as the revelations dawn upon you and then beyond, into the world at large. There is the first congress, called to debate the virtues of the project. Some are openly opposed to proceeding any further; some argue for deeper understanding and exploration of this unique opportunity. There are many wise minds brought into the circle to ponder and deliberate. Destiny is afoot, clearly.

The story continues to unfold sequentially. Consensus is reached within the congress and oracles are consulted. These oracles are disembodied beings, I am informed, residing in spaces beyond the Earth plane. They bring into the mix a far deeper comprehension than incarnate beings can have. They speak with authority and humility, describing the process of evolution that is underway. We see these beings, now embodied for us, in the sky. I recognize them immediately—angelans! *The oracles are angelans!*

Collectively, we are clear that at every important turn in history, in the maturation of the species, the angelans are there. They stand in their timeless zone, embracing incarnate time as wizards would embrace a crystal ball. They move their hands and their countenance over the emerging events, coaxing and sustaining the emergent birth in this stormy transition. They are the ones who 'channeled' the impetus for it all to begin now, in the year 500. They announce the movement and transposition through time, back to an earlier age, back into humanity's last great crisis.

With rapt attention, the assembly in the bowl of Trocodéro follows the *'scenari'* into my own time. I am suddenly, along with everyone, witnessing myself on the Assateague Island beach, receiving the initial poem and letters from you. I find it more than a little embarrassing to have all these vigilan eyes upon me. I cringe to see myself arguing with you, O, proclaiming naïvely that I would 'put you to the test.' My feeble ego, filled with doubts and resistance, is all too obvious.

Mercifully, the story moves quickly on, into scenes of my first visit to your 'house with no roof.' Technically, this is my second visit, but it is clear that time is fluid and malleable, from the angelan perspective. Temporal sequence is a mere detail within the true essence of events. It plays a *supporting*, not leading role. From there, we move through each aspect of the journey, into flashbacks and jumps forward, around the planet and the galaxy, down into the Void and up into visionary abstraction.

The *scenari* are filled with much more than imagery. Every moment is bursting with emotion and revelation. It pierces our appreciation in an unending strain of symphonic resonance. The story builds and sways, swerves through our senses, links and wraps profound ideas that are far beyond me to truly grasp. I am a novice in the halls of masters here. The unfolding 'story' is so much more than that word conveys; it is so much deeper than I realized as I lived and transcribed it.

I witness, with my own eyes and mind, how far vigilan 'entertainment' has progressed over our human efforts. We did indeed lay the foundations. But it's staggering to see how it has blossomed. These '*scenari*' are an engrossing, holographic movies, yes. From that foundation, however, they become a complete life engagement. It is full to overflowing with meaning and disclosure and ecstatic presence. One cannot see this without being *in* it wholly with one's own being. I know in my heart that each individual watching this is experiencing it in the same way we did in the original happening of it.

Suddenly it dawns on me that these very *scenari* are the source of the premonitions and visions I had, early on, when you were first writing to me. These images were already projecting back through time, drawing me in. As each scene unfolds now, I see a kind of tracer, a golden filament, shooting back into the past, into my own time and mind, gradually revealing itself and enticing me to follow you. *Wow!*

Hours pass and we are all held within the trance of this show. Finally, after we cross through the Jaws of Hunab Ku, it is time for an intermission. The sky dissolves back into its natural state of stars and velvet blackness. I move my chair into an upright position and turn to you. You are already facing me, along with Black and Green. Smiles are on your faces, as on mine.

"Why didn't you tell me," I gush. "That was beyond amazing!"

Green speaks in his characteristic, simple monotone. "I did not know myself the extent of this production. It's the first time I've seen the whole story. That is, part one, eh? O, you have been very busy behind my back." He winks softly at you.

"I knew more than you, what was coming, yes. The elder committee wanted me to be involved in giving those opening remarks and tweaking some of the narrative. But I had no idea how moving it would all be. This may be the most intense *scenari* I've ever seen."

I interrupt, "How could they have known the whole story—and in such depth? There was much more to it than I realized—even having lived through it. It was wonderful to see and feel it through angelan eyes."

Black stands up and stretches. "Simply wonderful. But now let me take a break. You three are here in projected forms. I am in the actual physical body. I need to use the facilities. If you'll excuse me…" With that she gracefully moves through the partition of the little chamber and into a narrow passage outside.

We smile and nod. I get up and gesture toward the aisle. "I need to move around a bit, too, O. May I?"

You nod agreement without any further comment. I step outside and feel the evening breeze in my hair. A sweet, natural aroma wafts over from the nearby wooded area. *Ah, Paris. It's always pleasant to be here—especially 500 years from now.*

I stare over at the light tower on the other side of the river. Its intricate fabric of luminance duplicates the original structure exactly, in every detail. What's new, obviously, is its transparency. It had always been a delicate and airy form. This new creation seems like a *fulfillment* of the original design. At the pinnacle, I notice a pencil-thin beam of light, aimed straight up to the zenith. This laser line goes right into space, disappearing far, far above.

My gaze falls back to the crowd; many of them are milling around, visiting with friends and partaking of refreshments. The colors are a wonderful mélange of rainbow hues. Mostly people are wearing the typical robes. However, I see a few people dressed in garb from my own era. *Curious. Are they visitors from a former time, like myself?* None of them are near enough to ask.

After wandering among the bubble rooms, I amble back into our space. B has returned as well. I sit down next to you and immediately start, "O, I saw some people in human dress. Are they from my age?"

"Yes. You are not the only human with us today. Vigilans are working with many others in your world."

"That's surprising. Why didn't you tell me this before? Will I ever get to meet them?" I react.

"I'm sure you will—in both my time and yours. I didn't mention them before, because there weren't any that we knew of. When we established the portals, individuals began to find their ways through; they began creating their own portals. With passages opening, nature is taking its course. This is very encouraging. The portals are not, of course, exclusive to *our* efforts. *Conscious Evolution* is generating many openings in response to humanity's mutation. "

"What do they expect, these visitors? Where are they coming from? Who are they?"

"They're people just like you and me," you answer with a smile. "They expect what you expect. Many of these souls you have worked with or they have read the *letters*. They often bring their doubts and ego perspectives with them, I might point out." You give me a look. "Largely so far, they seem to be coming through in their dreams, or in imaginal journeys, like yours, and in subdimensions. Back in your time they may or may not recall their visits. They often do not have the whole context for understanding what's happening to them."

"So, what do they *think* is happening?"

B leans over, having been listening in on our conversation. "They sense a major shift within themselves and in the world around them. Their minds are intensely curious about with what may be coming in the future, and with what has been hidden from them in the past. They want answers to thousands of questions. They are sensing *through* the Veil and opening up to being in two universes simultaneously. Their so-called 'dreams' are giving them inspiration and instruction, as well as adventures."

You add, "In many cases, these individuals are generating portals without being aware of what portals are. They are simply pursuing the unknown. They are faced with a great unknown, and they *want to know!* What they don't generally accept is that this 'unknown' is really their friend."

B says, "It will be most interesting to meet with some of these individuals. I sense you shall—in the near future, either during this writing or shortly thereafter."

"I agree. I mean I would like that too," I say eagerly.

You look to me, more seriously. "In this book we intend to provide a context for these and other humans to begin to answer the questions plaguing them. This is a fundamental purpose for writing."

You stop and look around. It seems that everyone in the group is now paying attention. Green chimes in, with his dry, slow voice, "In the bigger picture of things, our project is injecting energies into your human society that will have ripple effects. Humans do not need to read our letters or even hear of them to be affected by these energies. Nevertheless the letters are creating a 'carrier wave' for changes and mergers between our worlds."

B now gets serious, looking at me in particular. "You should know, friend, that these Letters are not simply for you. Nor are they limited to your timeframe. They are actually intended more for the generations following you than for yours. We are planting energy-seeds—seed-links, if you will—that will begin to germinate in your time. They will sprout and bloom in the ensuing decades, and even for 500 years. And, of course, it is not the words or stories, but the energy that is important in the books."

I am starting to get stirred up inside about this topic, but before I can say anything more, the sky lights up again. All eyes lift to the heavens, and the borealis curtains pull back. I recline my seat and witness yet another scene from my own life. *How strange.*

Soon, all the assembled audience is collectively participating in the experiences of you and me, OM and Green and Black—and the angelans. We are pictured floating above the Void's Threshold, over into the Hall of Memories, down into Atlantis. I wince to recall the events associated with Levaticol, Beneth and Sarites, Allamorath and Mestiphius. There, portrayed in full dimension and color, felt within each and every conscious being here, are the happenings of many lifetimes. I realize that the entire audience is being drawn progressively into the story—as though they were there, as though it is all happening right this moment *to them.*

Letter Fifty-Two
An Invitation

The *scenari* moves even farther into deep consciousness now. Not only am I feeling and seeing from my own perspective, I'm also sensing the far-reaching connections of all things—from what can only be the *angelan* point of view. This is a rare glimpse into how that mysterious species sees the universe. It is totally beyond time and materiality. There is an expansiveness that transcends humans and vigilans and all that we have ever known with our minds and bodies.

The angelan view is comprehensive of all material forms; it reaches into the heart of matter, and into what 'matters' in every event. For them, the events of life in our world are linked and conjoined, self-evidently, with all other events. Time is one, integrated substance, almost indistinguishable from space. All is held in compassionate and omniscient embrace.

As astounding as this is, I seem to be taking it all in stride; I accept it as a natural part of our phenomenal story. My immersion is complete. The awe of this encounter does not separate me away, to regard it from the outside; rather, it unites me with the Oneness in which it is anchored.

It seems like no time at all has passed as we, in this congress, staring up into the sky, witness our descent into the blue ocean of Atlantis. There, before the Ark of the Covenant, the bridging between universes is consummated. The underwater lightning is particularly entertaining. Everyone gasps and I hear a general murmuring across the arena. I expect the story to end there. But no, it goes on.

We now find ourselves viewing the amphitheater from above. In the images spread across the sky, there I am in my little bubble and reclining seat, surrounded by my friends. 5,000 pairs of eyes, and many more by extension, are hovering over my body. I feel pulled out of myself and into the collective mind of the audience. Then I'm slammed back into my individual self. Suddenly I'm flushed with the strangest feeling yet. The larger mind and all its sensations are driven together into that body of mine. Wham!

What the hell is going on? I shriek inside, turning to you and the group. I feel like I am no longer just *me*. I'm also everyone else. I have all the eyes of vigilans everywhere looking out from inside me. *This is too much!*

"O, what is this? Can you help? Can you explain what's going on?"

You are silent, as dumbfounded as I am. Black speaks. "We are all under the influence of the angelan guides in this. I do not fully know what they intend, but we are now in the thick of our own *scenari*—along with most people on this planet, sharing our awareness. We are stepping into the future events of our lives as though they have already happened. The story is now and then and every time. For our finite minds, this is seeing the *future*."

There is a long pause as we—all the millions of us—digest the implications. Finally Green begins to speak in a very matter-of-fact tone, "I don't think it's so strange really." He coughs apologetically. "We all know of the Oneness of Source within us. I'm starting to look at this *scenari* as Source brought right out to the surface. Suddenly there is no conventional time or space. There is no separation between past and future. It's all as fluid and as shared as the air we're breathing. We are all breathing time and space in this!"

"Whoa. I was sort of with you, G, up to that last thought," I maintain. "What can you mean, 'breathing time and space'?"

B answers, "We're all in the angelan space. We must remember that they do not have time boundaries like we do. Time is malleable for them, as air is for us. What we will do next—under their watchful gaze—they already know; it is done, but never *gone*. It is always accessible to them. It's really not so different from our *subdi* travel."

You finally lift your head from the contemplation you've held for several minutes. "Whatever this is, we are being given a huge opportunity by the angelans. We must go into it with faith. If they already know what we will do, they would not lead us where we don't need to go."

Green calmly suggests, "Let's stop analyzing it and just *live* it! Let's see where it leads."

Everyone in the group agrees, with quiet murmuring. We turn and look out across the arena at the other staring faces—every one of them is turned in our direction. The sight of this triggers a deep urge in me. From somewhere unknown, a voice bursts up. I can't stop myself from suddenly saying to everyone here—all 5,000 of us, "This congress is perhaps the strangest one ever held. But we're all in this together. Let's just get comfortable with ourselves right here and now." It dawns on me that I have no authority to be telling anything to a group of vigilans, but I continue. "Come with us in this bizarre story, and together we'll make it a great show."

With that I shut up and wonder what ever possessed me to say these things. But little by little there is a stirring across the space. People begin to clap and call out agreement. Soon there is applause of support across the theater. And I feel it from all around the Earth.

As another urge strikes me, I stand and turn to you, "I have to go across the river, O. I don't know why, but I feel like I just have to get out of this place and go stand under the Eiffel Tower."

You look surprised, mouth open. G and several others have similar reactions. B is smiling broadly. She stands up next to me and finally says, "This is all taking a turn into the unknown. Clearly, you are responding to it with your feelings. Do you want some company on this little adventure?"

"I sure do. Will you come along, O? Green?" I coax. Of course, somehow we all know this is in the script.

The four of us move out of our chamber and weave along the passages toward the exit. All eyes follow us as we file through the arches at the bottom of the arena. I don't have the faintest idea what I'm doing. But I know an unknown force is leading me. *Perhaps I'm learning to trust the unknown,* I confirm to myself.

As we make our way out onto the grand bridge, *le Pont d'Iéna,* over the Seine, I feel the sense of collective eyes falling into the background. Their presence witnesses everything, but more quietly now; I'm relaxing into my own self again. Yet the other mysterious force compels me forward.

At last the four of us are standing at the base of the great luminescent monument, looking skyward. I hear the gravel crackling under our feet. Strong scintillating arms of light strike up out of the ground toward the zenith; they converge far overhead. I think of all the people in the theater looking up into their own sky and seeing exactly what we're looking at. *I've got to stop thinking of that audience. Just get on with this.*

So, we're just standing here, looking up. What's next? The power that drew me here has now fallen silent. But an idea emerges. I turn to you. "All right, O. I've gotten us this far. I need some intuitive help from *you* now. What do you feel this means? Why are we here?"

You laugh and lean on my shoulder. "You're too funny. Something possessed you and brought you over here and now it's just gone?" You pause and look me in the eye. "I'm sure you could do this. But let me see; maybe I'm supposed to help. I'll reach inside and find something."

You close your eyes for several minutes. We wait. I shuffle my feet and look around at the living beams of brightness in the tower that thrust toward the stars in front of us. There's a gentle breeze. It's summer, and my mind puzzles at how this can be. It was winter when I started writing. *Oh well, it's the angelans again.* I wonder if the audience can hear what I'm thinking. *Oh my God, I've got to be careful even of my thoughts now!* Nevertheless, there's a dreamlike space around me. I seem to be buffered from my normal ego reactions and fears.

"Look down," your voice speaks with sudden confidence and authority. We are on the *Champ de Mars* here."

Our eyes turn to the south, toward the field. It looks much like it did in my time—cinder paths and grass, with trees and dramatic Parisian buildings lining the perimeter.

"This is the 'Field of Mars', dedicated in the past to markets, military displays, and grand fairs. It was the even site of a massacre just after the French Revolution. This is one of the prominent places Adolph Hitler visited after his army conquered France. It was right there, where his motorcade stopped, and he got out." She points to a darkened patch of earth some fifty meters away. Suddenly a wispy vision appears out of thin air. *Why am I not surprised?* It's a moving image of Hitler emerging from an ancient touring car, looking triumphant and smirking around at the assembled crowd of soldiers and dignitaries. I wince at the sight of this sinister character. It is almost like a poison in this purified atmosphere of 500.

"Look," you continue, not in the slightest concerned about this materialization. "This it what is happening in the Now. The Now never forgets what is within its domain. All of the past is in this moment."

Now we see other visions form. Large crowds are arrayed on this plain—angry mobs jostling, then armies conducting drills and displays of military might, soldiers firing ancient rifles into a crowd. But then the images slowly soften. Here is the *Exposition Universelle* of 1889, and even earlier, a huge, cheering throng watches a hot air balloon rise gracefully into a blue sky. The scenes seem to be moving progressively back in time. Now there is a market scene, with carts and vendors and bustling crowds of shoppers, wearing clothes from hundreds of years ago. Finally, an image appears of small garden plots, spread randomly around what seems a country field; rabbits jump between the bushes.

"One of humanity's first manned balloon flights rose from this place," you comment. "Over the centuries this field has held an iconic place in our imaginations. By its own name, it was dedicated to the Roman god of war, from the *Campus Martius* in Rome. Another famous site in Paris began as a temple to Mars—the basilica of *Sacré Cœur*.

"This field we're standing in also has another essence that is more interesting to us today. It is also an opening to Life and abundance, where the sky is balanced with Earth energy. The destiny of this place reaches from the lowly and humble soil to the heights of the towering sky.

"Paris today is a memorial to peace and equality. The reconciliation of Mars happens here, symbolizing the return of duality into Oneness. War and peace are reunited in Paris, into the essence. Equality has its roots in the city name itself. The original inhabitants were the *Parisii*, who were prided them-selves in 'parity' among all their citizens. Your word, 'peer', is a cognate."

I look up at the night and the luminance streaming into the sky, then back to our small cluster of friends. I'm wondering where your monologue could be leading. I ask, "O, what does this have to do with the congress and our being here? It's all sounding like a history lesson to me. Why do you think I felt drawn here?"

"Yes. That's coming. Remember, I'm simply *streaming* from the intuitive fields. I hardly know, myself, what I'm talking about. But here it is, I think—your answer. This place, below and above us, is asking us to further unite our dual natures for some purpose. It is saying that sky and Earth join together here. We are being asked to participate in the fulfillment of a destiny."

Again I look skyward, to the summit of the tower. "What is that line up there, projecting from the top, O?"

While you're waiting again, Green answers, "I've recently read about that. It is the Trans-System Link, the channel for transport around the solar system. It is anchored here in Paris. It goes straight into the core of the Earth and out the other side, near New Zealand."

We all look at him with curious smiles. I ask, "What is this 'System-Link' thing? What does it transport?"

He answers softly, "Anything you want. It's a grand highway into the sky. It's mostly for projecting images, and sub-dimensional forms, however."

Now I'm starting to feel the *draw* again that I felt in the amphitheater. It is actually pulling me up from my belly, like a kind of anti-gravity. *What's this now?*

"There is some connection between this place and the transport," B offers. "What do you sense, O?"

You open your eyes with a ready answer. "We are being summoned to some other place, somewhere else in the solar system, I think."

"What?" I gasp, more confused than ever. "Why? Where?"

You are all amused at my reaction. B speaks, "Three natural questions, of course. But this is certainly an unusual way to receive an invitation, I'd say—through the emotional body of an ego being." She stares at me. "Is there any-thing else, O?"

"Yes. I'm feeling the formation of a more distinct message. We are being asked to use the Link to travel to Mars."

We all fall silent, digesting what you've just said.

"Wait," I say. "I'm feeling this force too, whatever it is, but I'm not so sure I trust it. I was quite willing to cross the river and come over here, or even the ocean. But going to Mars? Can we talk about this?"

"Of course," you assure me. "I didn't say we should automatically accept this invitation."

"Just who is inviting us to go to Mars? Are there people who live there now?" I want to know.

"Good questions," you reply. "There are many people, vigilans, who live on Mars or visit there from time to time. There are extraterrestrials also."

"You mean *Martians?*" I exclaim.

"Not exactly in the sense you mean. However, the beings who inhabit the planet today can indeed all be called *Martians*. They are not the original inhabitants though. All peoples living there in our time have immigrated from somewhere else."

"Like *where* else?" My interest is starting to build.

Green answers, "They come from other planets, from Earth and from other dimensions in this universe. Again, I've read about them and seen them in *scenari*, but I've never wanted to go out there and meet any of them. I personally, like staying on Earth. Coming all this way to Paris was quite far enough from home for me."

I smile, remembering that he is actually not really here any more than I am. We're both just projections. Still, the traveling does seem very real. I address you, "O, I remember you saying in the first book that aliens—um, extraterrestrials—don't generally mix with Earth populations. So what's happening out there on Mars?"

"You remember correctly. These beings only rarely visit us on Earth. But on the other planets and moons—that is another matter."

"Moons? You have bases on the moon?"

"We have settlements in many places around the solar system. Gravity is an obstacle on Jupiter and Saturn, so people have set up communities on the moons of these planets. Orbiting Venus, where there is no natural moon, we have constructed a large artificial moon."

I sigh, "It sounds like a busy solar system all of a sudden. What are people doing out there?"

"As in your time and in your species," Black answers, "People were curious. We are all innately explorers. In your day, you could not travel to these far planets. But you dreamed of it. You frequently sent out vehicles and robots to photograph and collect data. We have continued the curiosity and exploration over the centuries. Our industrial firms collect materials that are rare or difficult to find on Earth—'mining', in a word. It is often better to mine the depths of Titan or Ganymede than to inflict any more damage to the Earth."

"Hear, hear," G whispers.

She continues, "But far beyond the resources, the beauty of these places is… well, *unearthly*. I have visited a number of the settlements, and I can tell you the landscapes and the people themselves are like nothing here on this planet."

"I have only visited the moons of Earth and Venus myself," you offer. "But I agree, it is truly an extraordinary experience to be off the Earth, away from the familiar energy fields of home."

I squint at you and say, "What about the center of the galaxy? Aren't you including that?"

"Indeed, that was beyond extraordinary—exactly my point."

I am distinctly of two minds. I'm certainly curious at the idea of going out to Mars. That was never possible in my own time. And there is the matter of feeling drawn to 'lift off,' so to speak. But I'm not sure what to expect, or *who* to expect. I'm not sure what's right.

I ask, "O, can you find out who's inviting us? And why?"

"That is being kept from me. It is a matter of faith, as I said before, for us to proceed. I feel certain there is no danger. I do feel a presence that is welcoming and powerful; it is strong enough to keep my intuition at bay. It seems to want us to trust it and to venture into the unknown on faith."

I shrug my shoulders, pondering for several minutes. Then I slowly look at each of you in turn. "Well, what will it be? What do you think? Who wants to go to Mars?"

Green is quick to answer, "Not I, thank you. I will keep my feet firmly on this planet."

I look at you and B. You both glance at Green and smile, not surprised at his position. B puts her hand on my shoulder and nods. You look at me. "We're coming. It's written in the stars."

"So, what do we do? How do we actually get there?"

The two of you glance around the field. We're standing near one of the legs of the great tower. Off on the far side is a low structure with several arched doorways along its side. You point there.

Green follows us to the doorways. He says, "I will bid you all a pleasant journey now. I'm going back to the amphitheater. I'll watch you on the sky screen from a comfortable chair here on Earth." You step up and kiss him on the cheek and touch his hands. With green robes flowing, he walks away into the night.

Letter Fifty-Three
No One to Greet Us

I'm feeling a little nervous now, not sure of the decision we've just taken. *What if something goes wrong? Can I trust this technology?*

You reply, "Remember, my friend, your physical body is still sitting safely back at home, 500 years ago. Come over here. We will register with the clerk."

Beyond you now I see an ephemeral shape, leaning behind a counter. It's a ghostly projection of a person. Even if he were solid, there's something strange about him. You notice my reaction, and offer an explanation. "The clerk here is a robotic projection, not a vigilan. He will assign us our travel bands and frequencies, and register our locations of origin and destination."

"How do you know what destination to use?" I query.

"I don't. But my guess is that the coordinates have already been entered."

The ghost clerk nods and looks us over, processing our information. He replies, "Madam, you are correct. Your destination has been entered from the Martian Ministry of Research: For three individuals—one of whom is here in the flesh; two of whom are projections from other locations on Earth." The robot pauses, confused, then continues, "The date of origin for the gentleman is not consistent with our program. I cannot…"

You lean forward and enter a code on the screen that floats before the clerk. He looks at the code and straightens. "Yes, madam. You may all proceed now. Please step this way. Only one of you will require a 'holding'."

"What's a *holding?*" I wonder.

"It is a non-temporal field that holds the body while we are in projected form. Your keyboard serves that purpose for you back in your time, believe it or not."

"My keyboard creates a 'non-temporal' field? If you say so—I guess I can believe anything at this point."

"We've arranged that any device you use to communicate with us does the same, even a pencil and paper."

B follows the apparition toward a small niche in the wall—her 'holding'. She looks back to us with a quixotic smile. "See you on the other side."

The thought gives me pause. I turn to you and ask, "What was that code you entered? By the way, I love the holographic screen technology."

You smile. "What? You don't have *air screens* yet? I thought you did. Well, they'll be developed soon in your time. We've had those for hundreds of years. The code I gave the clerk told his program to override our temporal anomalies."

In a moment our ghostly host returns. He leads us to another alcove nearby. I hesitate on the threshold, a tight feeling in my chest. The clerk looks at me curiously. *I guess he's never seen* fear *before.* I gulp and follow you into the recess.

I don't know why I'm suddenly fearful. *I thought I was making such progress in trusting the unknown.* I close my eyes and try forcing my mind to relax. I'm aware instantly, this maneuver simply adds more resistance. I pop open my eyes and look at you.

"Take a deep breath. You'll be all right."

As I stare out into the square under the ancient tower, a buzzing rises in my ears. My body starts shaking. My breaths are coming faster and faster, and not so deep. Then we're off. It feels like a roller coaster in free fall. *Or free rise*, I guess. We are soaring swiftly above Paris suddenly, following that thin, vertical laser beam into the dark. I envy Green sitting quite contentedly in his seat below, watching us fly away.

Strangely, I'm sensing we have become as thin as the laser itself, occupying one of innumerable channels or 'lanes' inside the beam. Still I can see all around, as if in a space capsule. The Earth is now a bright ball dwindling below us. Rapidly, it has become just one of the round lights in the firmament. Now we approach another light. I can only describe it as a long 'diamond' floating in space. It has innumerable tiny spikes around its surface.

We shoot into the diamond and hover within it for a few moments. Lancing out from the spikes are many other laser beams, aimed in different directions. *I guess this is a relay station.* One of the beams must go to Mars; the others go to other destinations in the solar system. It makes sense. I try to speak, but apparently it's not possible inside this beam. *I don't seem to have a voice in here.*

But then I hear you inside my ears. *"You still have your inner voice. We can communicate this way."*

"All right. Am I correct about this being a relay station? Which direction is Mars? How long will it take to get there? Where is Black, by the way?"

"Too many questions, friend. You will know soon enough." It is B's mind-voice; she has obviously joined us. *"Yes, this is a 'relay diamond'."* You don't say anything more, and I decide to keep my *mind-mouth* shut. I see that my questions

are largely irrelevant. My mind drifts off, contented to guess which beam we'll take next.

A slight shudder, and we're suddenly off again. I guessed wrong—different beam. *Irrelevant!* Surely, we're on the laser line that connects the red planet. My fear has subsided for now, and I'm feeling a sense of elation at the adventure. I'm not sure, though, how I'll feel when we have to zoom down toward the ground again. A worry begins to grow again.

One of the bright lights ahead becomes larger. *Is this it? No, just another 'relay diamond'.* We wait for a time in silence, and then go forward again. A ball of light in the distances grows; it has a distinct orange-red hue. Soon it fills our view. And we're not slowing down. My worry is justified; a queasy feeling storms up. *We're clearly falling out of the sky!*

Before I can register real fear, however, we stop. Our bodies are released from the laser and we stand on firm ground.

What a trip! It took only fifteen minutes—all the way to Mars. That must be the speed of light, I realize. I breathe a long sigh of relief and look around. I'm inside another arch, like the one in Paris. You two are already moving out. I lag behind, staring hesitantly into the open space outside. *I'm on Mars!* The thought of it staggers me.

Before us in the distance is a cluster of buildings under a pale blue sky. A rolling, dry desert stretches out beyond. The sun is not as bright as on Earth. All is still. *The air is breathable. We must be in some kind of air bubble.* Mars' atmosphere of is largely carbon dioxide, I recall.

"Exactly," you reply aloud to my thought. You have returned to escort me out of the archway. "Domes protect these settlements. The temperature outside is very cold by Earth standards."

We're on a low promontory; there is a town below. The settlement has winding, narrow streets weaving through it in a Mediterranean way. I see palm trees, large cactuses and other desert plants, tucked in among dome-roofed buildings. The structures are simple, low stucco, all the same dusty pink as the landscape. There may be fifty buildings altogether, in an area of about ten acres. In the center, a few structures rise above the rest. The tallest of these has a kind of steeple. The whole scene looks like it was sprouted up out of the ground. *But I see no people.*

With you escorting me, I walk out to a covered platform that has two small benches. I feel as light as a feather here. *Less gravity.*

"It's about one-third the gravity of Earth" B's voice comes in from behind. "It's interesting, is it not, to feel the difference in this energy field?"

Of course, I had not felt it. But now that she mentions it, I *do* feel it. It's a kind of *thinness* of vibration compared to Earth. It's not just the gravity or the air. The energy is truly different. In a word, *alien!*

Again we wait. There's no one to greet us. In fact, there's no one to be seen anywhere. I'm starting to feel a little creepy, like this is a well-kept ghost town. *Is this just another robotic projection?* Sitting next to you, I ask, "Where are all the people? I thought someone would be here to greet us. Didn't you?"

"On the contrary, I had no expectation. This is a meeting with the *unknown*, my friend. We are in its midst. Why not just relish the flavor of it."

B offers, "I think I'll take a look in town. You two should stay here, in case someone comes."

I watch her walk down the dusty hillside and disappear around the corner of a low building. "I'm feeling uneasy, O. What d'you think we're waiting for? Why wouldn't they just be here for us when we arrived—whoever invited us here?"

"Because it is our part to *wait.* Whoever it is will arrive at the right time. It is all within the same moment, in any case."

"I don't understand how you can be so complacent. Where's your curiosity?" I get up off the hard bench and begin to pace. When I've walked all the way to the transporter station and back, you look up.

"It's not that I'm not curious. I am indeed. My awareness is exploring this waiting period—the deliciousness of the unknown. Let me help you with your impatience, friend. Please sit beside me. There. Now, look out into the desert and tell me what you see."

"Nothing. I don't see anything but dust and rocks."

"Look again."

I squint and peer more closely at the scene. It's empty and desolate. There's nothing to see. Wait. Now there *is* something. "O, I *do* see something out there I didn't notice before."

"Yes. Remember it's all about *noticing.* What do you see?"

"I see a faint sparkle on that slope. The more I stare at it, the more it looks like something." I try to focus all my attention, but it still has no definition—just sparkling desert.

"Keep looking. But this time relax. Let go of your resistance. Fall back into the formless, into your authentic being."

I shrug. *That's what I thought I was doing. But no, it's not about thought, is it?* I stop my impatience. It just evaporates as I sink into noticing. I observe my mind, squirming and asking for understanding. I feel my body, tense with frustration and anticipation. I relax, sink back into myself. It feels like falling into the Void, except I'm staying right where I am. The Void is coming up into me. It embraces my awareness, filling it with fresh energy from Source. Calm. Peace. I look over to you and see that you are in the same space of peace.

"All right, Madam O. You talked me into it. I'm finally in the moment."

"I sense it finally," she says. "Now I will ask you again to notice what's out there."

I turn my gaze back to the desert. The sparkles are brighter now. The pink earth of Mars seems to take on renewed definition and life. Suddenly I'm shocked to be looking straight at a shape that's been there all the time, only not for my eyes. It's a glistening oval-sphere of pink, dusty metal, the same color as the sand. And it looks for all the world like a *flying saucer*.

You laugh out loud when I've finally seen it. "I saw the ship some time ago. But I'm convinced they were waiting for *you* to notice it too; the ship can now truly *be* here."

"What do you mean 'truly be here'?" I murmur.

"That object is the source of the messages you and I have been receiving. It has not been fully in this dimension until now. We needed to complete the circuit through our recognition. It's the same principle that kept many humans from seeing off-world ships in your time. Now that we *can* see them, they will become visible."

"They?"

"Wait and watch. Be still."

My gaze is fixed on the oval object; it is about half a kilometer away, I estimate. Slowly it begins to shimmer. The dust slides off and reveals a totally polished metal surface; it is still the same color at the rocks around it. I doubt that I would be able to see it even now, had I not stopped resisting.

Out of the shimmer, a figure appears. It is a single person, walking steadily toward us. He or she is moving very quickly, with great strides. In a very short time I can see a man, wearing metallic clothing—a kind of platinum jumpsuit. He reaches a point on his trajectory and pauses. The atmosphere shimmers around him. It seems that he has passed through the wall of our bubble. He proceeds directly toward us.

"Welcome, friends," he recites in a rather raspy voice. "Thank you for coming all the way out to Mars. It is more convenient for us to meet here than on Earth, I'm afraid. We are still observing the interstellar protocol. Had you not been able to see my craft over there, I would not have been able to meet you."

I'm busy looking over our host. He appears human, but I'm guessing he's not. He stands a few inches taller than me and has a normal face and body. Yet there's something unusual. The proportions are a little off. His ears are too high; his temples are too wide. He has a very narrow waist, with long, thin legs. The clothing is also not quite like anything on Earth. *I will keep my mouth shut.*

You say gently to our host, "Thank you for the invitation, friend. I take it you are not from the Earth system."

"Indeed not. I am from the star system that you call Sirius. Nevertheless I have lived on Mars for two hundred years. This planet has become very much my home. I *am* now a Martian indeed."

I offer to shake hands, in the manner of humans. Then I remember the vigilan gesture of touching fingers to the palm. Immediately, I get flustered and make a clumsy twisting movement with my hand, resulting in nothing but whimsy. "Excuse me. I was just trying to introduce myself. That was awkward."

The man nods and reaches out his hands to me in the vigilan greeting. "Nothing lost. We use the customs of Earth while we are here," he says.

"Yes. Thank you." I mumble. "You know who we are, I guess. Would you mind telling us who *you* are?"

The tall Sirian pinches his lips in a kind of smile. "My name is Invm," he says with a slight accent, rather like Austrian. *Ah, he actually has a name,* I note. At a noise behind me, I turn with a start. *God, I'm jumpy!* It's only Black returning from her reconnaissance. As she approaches Invm, she stops suddenly and stares, as if she had an instant recognition. She quickly resumes her normal, placid demeanor. Whatever she has realized in this moment, she's keeping to herself.

Our new acquaintance motions us to follow him into the town, beginning an explanation along the way. "Ostraness is the name of this place. It is virtually empty at this time of year. Almost everyone moves south for the winter games. You see, our town has a rather nomadic culture. Many settlements on Mars are like this; we are always running off chasing the flux of energy fields. It is what many inhabitants occupy themselves with here—for business *and* pleasure."

I haven't the faintest idea what he's talking about, but I feel it would be more polite not to launch into my usual barrage of questions. Then Invm continues speaking, as we lope beside him. "I know you must be curious about all this, why we invited you, and what it might have to do with your congress in Paris."

I look at you and get the feeling you'd like me not to speak right now. I stifle my questions again. It hadn't actually occurred to me that there might be a connection to the congress. Invm seems to be ahead of me. He continues, "My team of Sirians has been working with your solar system council, in a long-term project. It is not unlike the project your group has been developing—that is, the project being celebrated in Paris right now."

I think of the holographic screen-dome above the amphitheater, and all the eyes that must be on us. We turn a corner after a few minutes and enter an open square. The tall building with the spire is at the center. We march on toward it, a small cloud of dust rising in our wake. I take note of the spire as we approach. It's unlike anything I've ever seen on Earth—*or anywhere else for that matter.* I chuckle at myself, *Of course. I haven't been on any other planets!*

The tower is composed of alternating, spiral rings of metal and stucco. Each layer is a fraction narrower than the lower one. At the top, some thirty meters high, sits a strange crystalline ball, perhaps two meters in diameter. The outside of it is a smooth sphere, but inside are many facets of pastel, transparent colored plates. It's quite beautiful. *Is this art? Religion? Technology?*

Invm, turns to us as we come to the obvious entrance way. "I must alert you that the air inside is a little different from what you're used to. It is composed for the Sirian metabolism. It's breathable for you, but it may take an adjustment on your part. Please come in."

With that, the wall gives way to a gaping oval hole that opens like an iris. It's very dark inside. It's eerie. Sudden apprehension rises in me. An ominous hissing sound stabs into my ears.

I hesitate. I can't see anything inside that doorway. *This is all so, so alien.* I cringe. But you and B have already disappeared inside. I look around at the empty square and the streets of this dusty 'ghost town'. It isn't any more inviting out here. In I go. The darkness envelops me. It's suddenly cold and clammy. The air is thick with the aroma of some strange-smelling flower. I sniff deeply while my eyes adjust; they water with a slight burning sensation. At last I see a large cavernous space ahead. Faint glowing lights dot the blankness, swirling, wispy ribbons of color sweep across the view. Indistinguishable shadowy figures move in the midst of it all. What am I looking at? *This is so...*

I feel you at my side touching my hand, now *holding* my hand. And then I'm inside your mind. You whisper, *"This is strange for me too. But isn't the* unknown *so delicious! Can you feel what I feel?"*

I look at you in the dimness and my heart swells. Your eyes glisten. I reply in thought, *"You are such good friend. You really* are *on my side, aren't you. Thank you for that burst of energy and confidence, O."*

Invm is standing before us, his tall silhouette blocking my view of the interior. "Please step this way. There are some seats on the side here, where we'll be more comfortable—and out of the way."

Letter Fifty-Four
Galactic Embrace

The Sirian leads us to a small glass cubicle. We are offered seats around one side of a long, low table. It is made of glass. Now that I look around, all the walls seem to be made of some transparent material. Sitting, I glance at B, then you. You're both still smiling softly, while I'm feeling a little uneasy, even suspicious. In the open space beyond our room, other humanoid shapes move in the light streams. They appear to be interacting with the mist.

Our off-worlder host sits down in a chair at the end of the table and then he looks out through the window-wall, at the activities of luminance, incomprehensible to me. He turns his gaze on each of us, silently. At last, he looks directly into my eyes. There is a rare power in those eyes. I haven't felt this since the first time I looked into Black's face. I sense a deep and inscrutable presence.

He says to me, "I will speak first to you, the human. I am aware of the feelings you have. But I also know you are able to work within yourself to change and evolve. The suspicions you feel right now are not without foundation. There were, in your time, extraterrestrial species in the solar system that did not mean well for your race. They were a distinct minority in the overall scheme, but they had significant impact on your development. This minority had its own egoic agenda that participated in manipulating you for many millennia."

He points through the glass at the twisting beams of light and blinking globes. *It's all so science fiction,* I think. That hissing sound, I notice, accompanies the swirling, iridescent ribbons as they wind across the space. To my astonishment, the room is much larger, here on the inside, than the building is on the outside. The darkness, with its points and ribbons of light, stretches off into a hundred meters or more. *A sub-dimensional field?*

Invm says, "Right now we are re-creating a pattern in space that has not existed for 500 years. These beams you are observing represent energy fields in space that were dominant then."

B volunteers, "I feel what you're describing. You're taking us back to the Great Storm that raged throughout the solar system at that time. It's actually visible in these patterns of light. I can see the conflicting forces spread across the entire field."

"Precisely," Invm replies. "Those were uncomfortable times to say the least. And not only for humans, but for many off-worlders and other local species as well."

B continues, "We recently learned of the galactic *Ark of the Covenant,* buried in the Atlantic Ocean. I imagine that the off-world interference you mention was kept at bay somewhat by this."

He resumes, "The ark—and its powerful protection—is well-known to all off-worlders. We are compelled to respect it, regardless of our intentions. Even the extraterrestrial groups who manipulated you had to respect its presence. Nevertheless, they managed to find ways around the protective field and around the interstellar protocol as well. They achieved this by negotiating agreements among certain exclusive human institutions and their family lines. They were thereby able to achieve separative and destructive ends. Thus, humanity was controlled and directed by its own kind—not a violation of the Covenant—under the influence of the galactic interlopers."

I can't resist a question at last. "Invm, excuse me. But what is this 'interstellar protocol' you've mentioned twice?"

"The protocol is a set of spiritually-binding parameters for behavior across the galactic social field—the grand network of civilizations. The Authority of One created it in our galaxy thousands of millennia ago. Some have called it the 'prime directive'. Fundamentally, the protocol guides the manner of general species' intercourse, respecting the disparity in spiritual and technological development between them. It is a galaxy-wide mandate governing those with the means to voyage abroad among star systems. In short, it is the rule of 'non-interference' with evolving societies."

'Star Trek' was onto this. I make a mental note to ask about the *Authority of One* later.

You've been silent while the others were speaking. But now you interject with intuitive clarity, "Nevertheless, was it not always part of the grand design to allow a loophole in the protective framework?"

B answers, "Yes. I share that view. Humanity needed to be put through its torment in order to grow, to remember its true Self and Source. That torment reached a crescendo 500 years ago during the Great Storm."

Invm responds, "Indeed. The Authority has its inscrutable purposes in all this, guided by its own destiny and relationship to Source. The Ark reached its apotheosis 500 years ago as well. It became reinvigorated by the galactic cycle, and by the upwelling of awakening within the human species. The Ark itself was seminally responsible for ending the interlopers' involvement, and for bringing in your avatars of that period."

I recall standing on the floor of the ocean looking up at a towering obelisk with the fiery blue vesica all around it. I mutter, letting my thoughts drift into words, "We, uh, know its power first-hand. What a mighty force... "

A question rushes up to me, as if from the ocean abyss, "Wait, Invm. Our visit to the Ark was 13,000 years *in the future*. It was *not* during the time of the Great Storm."

He gazes at me tolerantly. "On the contrary, your experiences were all of the same *moment*—your moment. And all the cycles relating to the Great Storm are within a singular, 'galactic embrace', if you will. I will try to explain: The vast star wheel, that is our greater home, projects its attention upon us during such an epoch—not just for a year or two, but for many, many more. Within the continuum, events occur according to *patterns of destiny;* this is the essence of what you call history. The galactic embrace spans 26,000 Earth years—forward and back. There is also another approximate 26, 000 year period that has its center at point zero, in your time.

"Our science now knows that space-time geometry is basic to manifested evolution. Geometric forms are *energy portals*; the purer they are, the more efficient and transparent they are—and the closer they are to formlessness. *The purest geometry is a bridge between form and formless.* The 'galactic embrace' creates two spherical fields in time around your Earth projection. One intersects the other, overlapping as I said, at your zero point—the transition between Great Years of 25,620 solar revolutions. This intersection generates an enormous vesica piscis in time. Under these influences, time can even appear to be ending and *rebooting,* as has been thought by certain students of the your Mayan calendar."

I nod with a faint glimmer of understanding. "I've read a lot about this calendar and other long cycles of civilization."

B interrupts, "The ancient Egyptian and Indian understanding of this process was that ages, or *yugas,* run in long, repeating cycles. The highest awakening is in the Golden Age; around that, in great temporal cycles, are the Silver and Bronze. The Iron Age—also called the Kali Yuga—marked the end of a long passage, and the end of your species. It was the lowest and densest of all—quite contrary to what your "civilization" believes about itself. 500 years ago—your time—the Iron Age ended and the new Bronze Age began. That is where we are now, our 'rebooted' perspective.

"I can give you a little demonstration of the *energetic* patterns." Invm draws his fingers through the air, like a magician. As he does so, a small diaphanous, holographic globe appears suspended before them. "Here, this will help us visualize the 13,000-year point in the context of the 26,000-year cycle. And now for the vesica."

He repeats his hand gesture and another, identical sphere appears. The two float side by side. He pinches his fingers; the globes slide together until over-lapping by half. The space inside the overlap takes on a bright, independent glow. It's like a lens—a three-dimensional vesica piscis. Invm explains, "The one you knew as OM, the Old Man, revealed this phenomenon to you all. It is what we Sirians call the *Birth Lens.*"

I'm amazed at his simple, brilliant graphic. But I'm even more impressed by the vast and profound concept he has just revealed. I whisper, "So, you're saying time can make a vesica shape just like space can? This must account for the portal in time."

Invm answers, "Exactly. When experienced as an energy pattern, this is what happens. Recall that time is a *form;* it is governed by the laws of geometry. And portals exist within all geometric forms—both temporal and spatial. There is no separation between time and space; they are one—simply alternating formations, like waves and particles of spectral energy."

I remain silent for a respectful moment. But now that the way has been opened for me, I ask, "May I ask another, more mundane question, Invm?"

"Certainly."

I glance at you. You're intent on watching the light show before us. I follow your gaze into the cavernous room. "What is this space we're in? What are you doing here? Who are these people?"

"We are a team from the Sirius system. Our mission is to monitor the progress of your *Conscious Evolution.* And beyond monitoring, it is our task to channel energies from Source into the grand geometry of time and space around your system of planets."

"Who gave you this mission?" I wonder.

"Ah," exclaims B. "I understand now. It is all becoming clear to me."

I look at her. "Yeah, OK, B. Do fill me in then?"

She looks at the Sirian, pausing for a moment. "Invm and his colleagues here are from our sister star system, which is composed of a binary pair. What we know now, and what humans of your time were just beginning to discover, is that our sun, Sol, is also a part of that same system. Sirius and Sol are the *true* twins. They revolve around each other in a great solar dance across more than eight light years of space. There is a powerful, electromagnetic and gravitational bond between our two systems. The Sirians are here—and have been for ages—as our older siblings, watching and assisting us through our coming of age. We are all cousins."

I'm shaking my head. "Pretty *serious* stuff; no pun intended. What does it all mean though? What are you doing with those globes and lines of light out there?"

You interject this time, "I've been watching those streamers. I can see their patterns now. This is a large multi-dimensional map of energy in our solar system. The lines show a geometric grid that links our sun with all the planets and other objects in the system—and they with each other."

Invm replies, "Yes. Good observation. Allow me to explain further. Please look out there now. Notice the Earth." He points to a blue-white, fist-size ball floating on one side of the cavernous room. "The line you used to travel here is just *there.*"

As he speaks, one of the lines shows much brighter; it reaches out from the blue sphere. That line connects with a diamond; the bright line continues on to another diamond and then to a red sphere—obviously Mars. Now that you have described it, I begin to see all the planets, their moons and the sun, arrayed around the room. The space now seems to be growing larger as I watch. It is stretching out and up and down—growing in all directions. We all seem to be floating in outer space now. This room seems to be in direct resonance with our appreciation of it.

Invm continues, "Of course you recognize Saturn and Jupiter, there and there." He points, and the panoply swings around to show Mars right in front of us. "And here we are, on Mars. Part of our task within the greater project is to continuously read the geometric configurations and energy fields. They are always changing with the movements and relationships of the objects in the system. The ebb and flow of electromagnetic and gravity fields reveals quite a story. Destinies are constantly on the move—on a grand scale. You might describe what we do as energetic *astrology.* Our reference point is *outside* the solar system, however."

You ask, "So, what do you do with this information?"

"We only coordinate it—give *coordinates* to it—and report to the angelans."

"The *angelans?*" I exclaim. "You know the angelans? You report to the angelans? This is getting more bizarre all the time. Where are they?"

Invm makes a laughing sound this time, "Where are they *not?* Angelans, my friend, are *space itself.* But let's save that conversation for a little later."

His eyes pierce mine with a softer quality that I can only describe as paternal. He is revealing himself to me, one step at a time. I suddenly have a much more accepting feeling toward him. I ask, "How is it that you appear so humanoid if you're from Sirius?"

He tilts his head back. "A very good question. It has a lot of history behind it, but I will summarize briefly. Throughout all the Cosmos physical life forms are manifestations out of Source fields. Source guides the development of forms in a consistent, structured manner, respecting each stage of evolution in consciousness. Wherever in the Cosmos you find beings at the general stage we inhabit now—your two species and mine—they will appear relatively similar. It is a functional emanation; I believe humans knew this phenomenon too, as 'form follows function'.

"There are differences and variations among the species, to be sure, but it all lies within a bounded range. Incarnate forms on the cusp of awakening out of *duality*—whether from Earth or from Sadalmelik—will be bipedal, with two arms and hands, and *one* head. And they will have faces roughly like ours."

I shake my head in wonder. "Are you an awakened species, like the vigilans?"

"Indeed, we are—now. 500 years ago many of us, however, were not. There were some groups, even from my home in the Sirius system, who were still under the influence of the egoic epoch. Sirians experienced the transition over a much longer period of time, as the proportion of awakened individuals gradually increased; it took several centuries for us. When the Great Storm arrived, we felt its effects too, only more as a culmination than as a triggering event."

You finally enter the conversation again. "This is interesting to hear. My understanding is that your planet has had civilizations much longer than Earth."

"Yes. This is true. By virtue of that, we were able to know of our sun's relationship to yours, to travel to Earth, and to become aware of the galactic community of civilizations. But we, like you, were not formally invited to join this community until we outgrew the dominance of ego-mind."

Of course! This makes perfect sense. I nod and continue, "You have a name, 'Invm'. Why is that? The vigilans have stopped using names here."

"This I know. In my own culture, we have adopted the same protocol for the most part. But we have also retained some the naming function—fundamentally for situations such as this, when we visit other cultures."

B is busy looking into the expanding space before us. She asks, "How do you interpret the solar fields on this system map?"

Invm answers, "Let me show you. What we have before us right now is the system as it was in the years 2000 to 2020, human calendar."

I easily pick out the planets, moons and sun, with thin laser lines connecting them all—*yes, there's a line leading directly into the sun.* Now the space begins to fill with clouds of colored mist—blues, yellows and reds. As I look closer, the clouds are not random, however; they have three-dimensional, geometric shapes. *These are the 'fields' he's talking about.* They have moved into an arrangement throughout the solar system. They're forming a kind of funnel or torus shape, with the larger end out toward the Milky Way. I sense powerful 'winds' sweeping into the funnel from there.

Our host continues, "You are registering correctly. The fields are being impacted by energetic winds from the center of the galaxy, Hunab Ku. Notice that every systemic field is vibrating under this wind. Some are becoming unstable and breaking up. Others are emerging out of the nothingness, the Void, and growing stronger. Look at the *torus*-shaped field around the Earth. There is another such field around each planet and moon. And on the larger scale you can now see the torus field of the entire system. The channel in the center is what creates the 'funnel' you observed."

As we watch, the Earth is brought around directly in front of our chamber. I see the filmy aura around our planet, in a large doughnut shape. *This is the torus he's talking about.* Stormy, ruddy colors are sweeping around the torus, twisting in tormented swaths. They are dark, brownish and dense. Mesmerized, we witness the colors turn to fiery reds and purples.

Suddenly images from human history—my time—emerge around the torus, projected from the planet itself. I see huge crowds gathering in city squares; armies are aligned against them; images of wars across the globe erupt; they are followed by peaceful gatherings of great numbers of people.

We now see earthquakes and tsunamis, lightning and rain. We can detect the pervasive extent of toxins in the land and sea everywhere. We see smoky clouds of pollution from factories, industry and war. Suddenly the toxins are quenched down with an ethereal mist from the torus, rising up from the hearts of awakening people. The images zoom right down into individual faces; some are terrified; some are indifferent; then, finally, some are awakened faces. The images continue to zoom in—through the skin, down and down into the cells and molecules, DNA, atoms. Finally, a three-dimensional, lens-vesica appears at the center of it all. *I've seen this before,* I gasp. The tiny field is pulsing with magnified Life.

The image zooms back out to the Earth-wide torus field. And as it does, a shape materializes from the galactic stream. It is a second torus that now moves in to intersect with the Earth's field. It spins around and overlaps halfway into the field. Gradually it makes a complete circle around the Earth. As it moves, the effect is immediate. Thousands, millions of vesica lenses, spring up in the field, glistening like oval crystals. Some are small, others large. *Portals!* They seem to come and go, and roll around in random patterns. Yet I'm now convinced that nothing is ever random. The Earth's aura is literally filled with these portals. More are arriving continuously.

"Let me now progress the model to our current time," our host directs. He moves his hands in the air, into precise positions. The lines begin to shift, along with planetary locations and fields. Also, the Milky Way moves into a different alignment. The colors in the torus soften; they're more pastel—pinks, violets and oranges—rather than the dark primary colors of 500 years before.

Invm resumes his commentary, "You can see that the fields have now developed a new arrangement. They are much more stable and self-contained. The vesica portals are still here, but they too have stabilized."

As I watch, the energies take on the shape of order throughout the whole solar system. It gives the impression of a well-tuned machine. A phrase erupts into my mind and I can't help but speak it aloud. "Peace on Earth!"

Letter Fifty-Five
Being Space

We drink in the visual, archetypal image of that peace for a long moment. The images are no longer shifting through time. *We have arrived at where we are.*

"Tell me, Invm, what does the vesica piscis mean to you?" I inquire.

He pauses for a moment, looking off into the spacey model before us. All the historical images have dissolved away and he conjures the vesica *lens* we saw before. He answers, "It is a fundamental element of universal and sacred geometry. This aperture within all forms is the crossover between spirit and matter. Its presence enables communion among all levels of manifestation. The vesica brings birth and death and all creation through us and into us. It is the initiatory icon of the Source field."

Black adds, "And, thereby, it is the vehicle or portal of power within each person, and within all forms, including the form of *time,* as Invm has demonstrated. Vesica is the divine feminine that empowers and generates all form, springing forth from formless Source—that is to say, the Void. If we realize this, we are privy to the most basic of divine secrets. Power does not come from force or dominance; it rises from the humble acts of vulnerability and surrender. This is the divine feminine."

"Indeed," he agrees. "When humanity realized the feminine principle within each person, the change began; that is when ego began to pass away. We witnessed the identical process in ourselves in our own time of awakening.

"I am a *geometer,* a facilitator of *energetic geometry*—the dynamic female-male, yin-yang structure of space. For our profession this element, the vesica piscis, has always been of foundational importance."

I ask, "But why? What is it about that shape that matters so much?"

You respond, "We have discussed this in the previous book. Let me refresh the topic here. The vesica is the fundamental portal between Oneness and duality. Symbolically, it is created out of the superimposition of two circles and two center points, and it is the unification of them both. It *divides* Oneness—while at the same time, *unifying* duality."

He looks at you and nods respectfully. "Again, my work concerns the dynamic structure of space and the energies within it. Geometric forms are not simply iconic or metaphorical. They embody literal forces of Life and creation. These geometric forms are beings are higher consciousness, coming into archetypal representation. They continuously move throughout the Cosmos at every level of expression. And it all revolves around the vesica—the resolution of point and circle, center and periphery.

"The dynamic nature of spatial geometry is what I wanted you to witness in our map of the galactic winds. They were following the crystalline, web structure, integral with space. The arrival of these winds in your time, of course, resonated harmonically with the time continuum. All time and space in the Cosmos is precisely integrated, thus are all events and manifestations, when you know how to look at them from within. The end of the Great Year cycle brought it all together at once, in the oval of a cosmic vesica piscis. The circle arrived at the point."

B replies, "I was most impressed in your map by the interaction of those interstellar forces with the local framework. The galactic winds, bringing in the Great Storm, have never been clearer to me. I'd love to have a closer look. Is it permissible to go out into the model and see it from the inside?"

"Yes, you may," he says. "My only caution is, do not focus your attention too long on any specific image. You might find your mind transporting to that location unwittingly."

You and B decide to go together. Strangely, I feel glued to my seat, and stay put. Here I am, sitting alone with the extraterrestrial. *This is different,* I realize. Being one-on-one is very different from being in a group, no matter how small the group is. He gazes quixotically at me, but says nothing.

"So, my friend," I decide to break the silence, and intentionally be more sociable. "How does it feel to be living so far from home? How long have you been here in this system?"

He looks me over slowly, appreciating my good intentions. "I have never met anyone from your era—that is, a human, with an ego-mind. So, you are of definite interest to me. To answer your questions, I have been here for about 200 Earth years, and it feels quite normal—after all this time."

"Hmm. That's a long time. How often do you go back home? And what is home like anyway?"

"Actually, I return regularly through projections. I rarely go back in physical form; that is a more rigorous journey. My world is not unlike your Earth. We have land and water in abundance, with mountains, forests and deserts. My planet has fewer animal and plant species than yours, however. Such species abundance, as on Earth, is relatively rare in the galaxy."

He falls quiet. I sense he's not much for small talk, but I'm curious enough to continue further. "Do you mind if I ask why you came here in the first place? What went into your personal decision to make such a journey and commitment?"

"It was not at all difficult for me to decide on this mission. It is my destiny. We Sirians are all guided continuously by our destinies, just as vigilans are. But I understand that your human species was not like that. Let me ask *you* a question. What is it like *not* to know your destiny?"

"Hmm. Interesting question, Invm. And you're right. There are a lot of humans who do not even *believe* in destiny, I'm sure. They wouldn't think to apply it personally to themselves at all."

I try to imagine how the average person of my time would react to this question. "I think most people don't think much about destiny; it's just not part of their experience. Perhaps they think it exists only in fairy tales, or out in some far future, relating to great movements of civilizations. Come to think of it, some might even see personal destiny as a *disadvantage*, like being *locked* into a program, you know. In any case, most humans would prefer to just let events *happen.*"

Then another thought crosses my mind. "In a way, this might not be so different from how the vigilans look at their mysterious 'unknown'. For humans destiny is largely an unknown."

"Really? How do humans look at the unknown?"

"I would say that we have some *fear* about it. Most people in my time do not happily embrace the unknown."

"I see," he replies, looking at me thoughtfully. I think he sees this as more than mere small talk now. "You fear the unknown, instead of welcoming it. Strange. For us destiny is *known*, however—at least in essence. It's not at all the same as the unknown. This is nevertheless a good question. It relates quite directly to the energy dynamics I study. I am always looking into the essence of energy flowing through time. What I document and visualize on maps such as this, is the brink of the 'unknown' transitioning into the 'known'. Once it is known it is destiny."

I ask, "Surely, you must project these energy patterns out into the future. Doesn't that short-circuit the 'unknown'?"

"Not at all. It enhances the quality of what we perceive in the flow. We are cutting into the edge of the formless when we do that. It is a great pleasure. It fills us with admiration for the workings of Source."

This reminds me of the question I delayed earlier. "Speaking of Source, please tell me about the Authority of One. Just what is it?"

"Ah, yes. I'm surprised you held your curiosity off this long. The Authority of One is basically a kind of *spiritual government* that unites civilizations throughout the Milky Way Galaxy. But it is no form of government that humans would recognize; it does not manifest in ways you could normally see or encounter. It is composed of a whole race of beings, evolved from creatures like us, a very long time ago. They moved through many stages of awakening and, finally, beyond the need for physical or *mental* incarnation. They are many levels more subtle than the angelans.

"The Authority still relates to the physical universe in its own way, however. It does so as the energetic geometry of existence. I am particularly interested in its workings, due to my own calling. Its geometry is the foundation of all our functioning forms, embodying our greatest limitations and our greatest freedoms."

I squint, trying to imagine what these beings must be like. "Are they *gods* then?"

"In a way, they are. Certainly, from our perspective they possess all the powers we would ascribe to divinity. However, they do not engage themselves with our worlds directly, except through its geometry and the principles of interstellar civil dynamics. All codes of conduct, everywhere in the physical galaxy, derive from these principles."

I ask, "What happens if someone breaks one of these codes?"

"Interesting question. I would say *nothing* happens of lasting effect. The 'break' would never manifest beyond a temporary anomaly. There can be no permanent discontinuity within the universal geometry. Even aberrations and manipulations are based upon the principles, and ultimately accede to them. The *protocol* I referred to earlier is the nearest that the Authority comes to establishing explicit rules of conduct. For those who, under separative, ego influence, would desire to circumvent such codes, there are ways to do it— temporarily. But they can only go so far. And, in the end, the violations become caught in a web of their own geometry, linked directly to the Authority."

I venture, "So, even when evil happens, it ultimately produces order."

"You understand. Underlying energetic patterning always prevails. All distortions eventually fold in upon themselves and produce the next iteration of evolving form in the universe. This is precisely what happened to your species. Interlopers came to Earth and convinced weak-minded ego-dominated creatures to follow them for ages. They posed as gods and presented a twisted, secretive view of evolution. All the while they knew they would ultimately face limits, or else be expelled by the Ark."

I look in silence at Invm for a time, and then ask, "How should we relate to these beings? Do they ask for anything from us?"

"They ask only that you exist within the universal geometry and live. Breathe. Appreciate. Evolve. This is how you relate to them."

I know this topic is worthy of much more discussion, but alas, I hear B's voice nearby. "I see the two of you have found something to talk about." She has walked back into our cubicle. I've become so engrossed in the conversation that I didn't notice.

Invm looks a little startled too. "Yes, we have. To be honest, I have found it entertaining to converse with a human. Initially I wasn't sure how I would feel about that."

B adds, "I intentionally wanted to let you two men have some space. I had a notion that it would be productive."

I look at B and smile—*a set-up?* "Well, I'm the *human* again. But I'd like to ask one more question. This one's for any of you. If destiny is not the 'unknown', just what is it? And what is the relationship?"

You have now rejoined us, and immediately answer, "The unknown is formlessness; it has not yet manifested at all. It forever precedes manifestation. You might even say it *precedes* the Now, though this cannot truly be. In reality, the unknown surrounds and suffuses all forms of experience; its essence lies in the Void, the great empty foundation of creation.

"Destiny is quite something else: It is a *form;* it manifests *a priori* in us, arising directly from our own soul contract in a given moment of incarnation. It does this *in* the Now. Since it is intimate with our own soul-source, it is not *unknown*. Thus, the soul is *known*, but the Void is not."

The conversation pauses here. *I guess I've asked enough.* I scratch my head absently. You sit down next to me, taking my hand. This pulls me back from my wandering mind. Through your touch, peace and appreciation instantly flood my body. For a moment, I feel like one of *you* again.

"So, Invm," you ask, changing the subject and waving an arm around the space. "What does all this mean? What happens to the information you collect? You said you do this for the angelans. Why, may I ask, do you have to give *them* information? Aren't they able to acquire it for themselves?"

"They could, I'm sure," he answers. "But there are certain advantages to our division of labor. Over recent centuries we have developed a relationship with their species. Our information-sharing project is the way it works out— for the time being; it could all change tomorrow. Both species have chosen to participate in this approach. In terms of pure functionality, we time-bound beings have a better perspective on the geometry of motion *within* time; the ange-lans have better ability to see Life patterns *beyond* time. Our roles complement each other. We provide form to their formless nature."

I glance at Invm; my brows raise. "But angelans *have* forms. We've seen them and met them. How can they be *formless?* What do you mean?"

B murmurs and decides to answer this. "They can produce forms of them-selves when they need to, but this is not their natural state. As we have de-scribed before, the angelans are reciprocal to us in their essence. They exist to serve and support us, having already passed through the human-vigilan phase of evolution. But they are still fully connected to us, as our species of destiny.

"We exist, on the other hand, to manifest and act out our lives, destined to become *them.* This holds true, down to the very fundamentals of matter for-mation. The angelans, as OM told us, live within the Threshold to the Void. They are agents of initiation—bridging from nothingness into form. From the timeless state, they hold the space for all actions we take *in* time. Holding space is another way of saying 'being space'.

"Well," I lift my hands questioningly. "Then what *is* space?"

B pauses, pursing her lips, then continues, "Space is the context for crea-tion. It is the Now and the counterpoint to manifested 'existence'. *That* in-cludes time. Space holds, reveals and enables; it does *not* limit. The angelans know no limits and do not impose any upon us. Now here is the icing on the cake. We *are* the angelans!"

I force my gaze on Black. "Now hold on there. You're going way too far for my comprehension. How can *we* be the angelans?"

Invm answers, "It's all a matter of time, and immanently logical. The ange-lans are beyond time as we know it, right? We are evolving into them; they are our next stage of consciousness. From their perspective they *are* us, only with an illusory, temporal attribute. From our point-of-view—in time—we cannot yet realize that. But for them to help and guide us, is to help and guide them-selves."

I'm about to cry 'enough', when you add even more. "And here is more of the unknown. In the mysterious curvature of time upon itself, we both evolve into them and *out of* them. They are our beginning and end, just as space curves back on itself. We three species make a complete manifestation—the One and Whole—human-vigilan-angelan."

"All right, you guys." I grunt. "I'll ponder this later. I can't imagine what you're really talking about." I turn to look out at the solar system map. "So, where *are* the angelans in all this? Surely, you've got them depicted here somewhere."

You all three chuckle softly at my reaction and glance at each other. Invm answers, "They are most certainly here; they are the *space!*"

I roll my eyes, but he continues, "Angelans are holding it all together, passively watching and waiting for us to create action. You must have been told of the quality of *authentic action*. Am I right? The angelans embody the 'authenticity'; we embody the 'action'. It is the reality of formless space within the form."

Black offers, "I know it must sound far too abstract and mystical to your mind right now—all tangled up in words as this is. Let it all just serve as a means to *twist* you around into wakefulness. That which is beyond you is within you. This is to say, what you are evolving into comes out of the vastness within the vesica field. Awakening comes about through finding the *not-self* in your self. That is the Void and Source, space, *and* the essence of the angelan kingdom."

I shake my head and bow it down. "I just can't get it. Maybe if we were to meet up with those angelans you're talking about; I might understand somehow. Is there a chance of that?"

"Yes, certainly so." Invm slowly waves his long arms. "In fact, they are here now, all around us. Sit very still and watch. Use your intuitive awareness to look more deeply and, at the same time, more lightly. It is an exercise in light-depth. Try it now."

I don't have much confidence that I understand what he's saying, but I nod. There's something about his words, 'more deeply…more lightly' that triggers an inspiration in me.

B says, "Think of your own Source gazing and the Void. It's virtually the same. Only in this case, the Void isn't buried down deep; you won't fall through the floor. This awareness brings the Void right up to you."

You add, "It's how you saw Invm's craft out in the desert."

Ah. I think I'm starting to get it. I un-focus my eyes and notice the aura around us all. I'm looking at the space itself instead of the objects. A memory comes to mind of a college art teacher who told me to look at the 'negative space' around the objects I was painting. I didn't really understand it then. But now I do. I let go and *feel* what my eyes perceive; my vision shifts.

Suddenly I'm looking at the emptiness, the space between the planets and ribbons of light. The formless begins to *form*. Space turns inside out, gathers in, and precipitates into several tall, gossamer beings. I've met the likes of these before, in the Hall of Memories and the Threshold. They stream information into my mind; the images are illusory, for 'our-eyes-only'. Without words they say the angelan forms are *interpretations* of reality and space, not reality itself.

I was standing until now. Seeing these giant, transparent beings, I need to sit down again. The angelans look at Invm and walk toward us, then right through the cubicle wall, as though it isn't even there for them. All three bow in unison. We return the gesture. All is silent, yet I feel words around me, waiting to find receptors in my brain.

It is always a magical experience being with angelans. This is no exception. The air is alive with peace and understanding. This time I know the *space* is what is living. I look into each of the three serene faces, one after the other. They have faint smiles. Their eyes shine with wisdom. They don't have wings, but I'm sure they could produce wings if they wanted to. I get the sense that they are both male and female in each body. I wonder at that, and I realize I'm generating a question.

The nearest angelan turns to me and presses an answer into my mind. I feel it coming from all three of them. It is not really like words or speaking. Oddly, I feel it's more like 'chewing', of all things. I'm sort of 'eating' the message they're sending—*consuming* it. It tastes like this: "We are indeed androgynous. Formlessness could be no other way. There is no duality in our true being. Here and now, we're producing duality forms for your benefit. We wish to be of service.

"We would you to know that you, too, are androgynous beings—in the making. Your duality-within-individuality is such."

Once again my comprehension lags, hampered by human doubt.

The angelans respond, "Consider your mind-brains; they possess two hemispheres—male and female—yet they are one identity. Consider your lives; you bring two souls together with the innate desire for Oneness. Consider your twin species, vigilan and human; you are becoming one with what *we* are. Let it be so. Amen."

Letter Fifty-Six
Golden Pyramid

Awe is all I can feel, sinking into me and radiating out. It almost doesn't matter what these beings say or do. It is their presence alone that matters. And in their presence, I find my own presence, intimate and full, dancing within itself to music that is, well, *angelic.* But in actuality, the word 'my' is losing its meaning. To say it here, I can only feel 'our' and 'we'. I have no desire right now, other than to feel this space. It is eternal and endless. I am glad to be sitting down; otherwise, I might melt to the floor.

Our entire group is in the midst of some extrasensory, timeless communion, ecstatic. I realize that the congress, back in Paris, is experiencing the same feeling right now. *How marvelous!* No wonder humans through the ages revered angels, and sometimes mistook them for gods. *I am doing the same.*

The trance-state continues, but it is morphing into something more specific. There's a reason behind the angelans' appearance. *How naïve of me!* I had thought *I* was requesting to see *them.* But, no, I was only giving voice to *their* intention to appear before us. Out of the silence, I sense they are inviting us to come with them someplace. *It was their invitation all along that brought us to Mars, to Invm,* I know now.

We all stand up before the three glowing figures, and their glow wraps around us like protective wings. *I would follow them anywhere. But where?* In a gentle motion, I feel that old sensation. The floor is dropping away below. Instead of plunging, though, this time we *float* downward, light as feathers. Above is the dark sky of the solar system; below is the dark, electric abyss of the Void. *I know it well.*

In our hearts we feel a stirring. The sky and the depths are meeting here in us. *Space is space, whether above or below, inside or out.* I have never felt that I *was* the space before. But now I do. I'm feeling this through our angelan partners. They have taken our environment and made it one with us. I sense the Void in me, in my heart. And I sense also the entire universe there—becoming a tiny point, dissolving into nothing. It is so peaceful, this nothing. And yet it is also a great power field. All the power in the Cosmos breathes through it; and it pulses out as the heart of creation.

We fly ever more deeply into the sanctum of the Source, skimming over waves and shores of inchoate forms, opening down into fathomless mystery. *Here is your holy unknown,* I whisper to you in my mind. This is freedom beyond measure, love and compassion without end, raw power and purpose irrefuta-

ble. We fly over these archetypes and icons, or so it seems. But also these qualities are not separate from us; they are our own. We are bearing witness to our
own divinity and sanctity. As we gaze, our vision is who we are and what we
gaze upon.

Now our angle of descent shifts. We float swiftly across the silver-black
face of the Void. I know this place from eternity. *But also, we've been here before,
not long ago.* It's the *Threshold.* And more than that, we are approaching the Hall
of Memories and the Akashic Records. The seven of us swoop, in a birdlike
formation, down upon the great rainbow mountain range that is the Hall. I
spread my arms like wings, and to my surprise, they *are* wings. *Imagination works
keenly here.* I lift and bank around, gliding and maneuvering over the eerie, glistening landscape. At last we come to rest before the majestic arched entrance.
Now we reach the ground and stand silently, gathering coherence.

I have walked these halls before. But now they seem quite different. I recall
you and B telling me this place changes appearance according to the perceiver.
This time, we're seeing it through the eyes of angelans. It is a grand palace of
opulence and beauty. Huge, high ceilings arch into a cathedral-like space
above. Multi-colored curtains of light hang a hundred meters down from the
clerestory. Tapestries adorn walls between robust columns, carved in stunning
detail. Ornate stairways curve up into the heights along the sides and far corners.

Our guides direct us to follow them across a wide expanse of golden marble tiles. The tiles glow from within, each composed of pulsing cells of light. I
remember my first visit to the Hall of Memories. Here are the familiar, embedded globes—in every surface, walls, floors, tapestries and columns. Each one, I
know, represents a lifetime lived; each is a complete package of memories of
one individual's experience somewhere, some time.

I spin slowly around in awe, my eyes searching in all directions. This whole
grand chamber is composed of the globes, countless in number. *I wonder what
kind of life you have to live to imprint it here? Now,* out in the center of the open
square, well more than a hundred meters across, we are directed to look upon a
raised platform. It rises like a small mountain out of the marble tiles.

We walk purposefully out to the platform. It seems to be encrusted with
precious jewels and metals. However, on closer examination, all of this too is
composed of life-globes. I'm starting to feel almost disrespectful for walking
on them—like stepping on gravestones. We climb the grand stairs up to the
top of the little mountain; it rises ten meters.

There is no feeling of exertion, but it does take some time to reach the
platform. At last, we're all standing silently on a square flat surface at the top. I
look ahead at the iridescent platform; it is at once strange and familiar. There

are a number of chairs and couches around the edges, facing toward the center. Every object glows with its own inner light.

"We are being asked to sit down," you translate for us. "I get the impression we're waiting for someone to join us."

I follow your instruction and sit at the end of one of the couches. It too, I notice, is composed of light globes. I'm careful not to push my fingers directly on any of them. *This is not the time,* I caution myself. Again we wait. Minutes pass in more silence. At last it occurs to me enter a meditation state and turn my attention to *appreciation.* From my comfortable seat I look out and around, surveying the vast cathedral space.

Then it hits me. From this vantage, the space does not look like a cathedral. Rather, it looks like the inside of a pyramid; and the little mountain we're sitting on is also a pyramid, only without the capstone. I'm prompted into a realization: *'We are the capstone'.* It's odd that these pyramid shapes are not discernable from the floor below. *But, after all, this is a very mutable sub-dimension.*

I look over at you and see you and B have sensed the same thing. B nods to us. At once beams of golden light strike down along the four diagonals from the center point high above us. They continue until we're enclosed in a great, bright polyhedron. The air is electrified. I grab the arm of the couch in mild alarm; it vibrates under my hand.

As when the angelans first appeared, space itself is suddenly imploding. It draws down from the outer pyramid toward the inner one, then it converges on one of the grand chairs. A figure has precipitated there. It is another angel. But this one is larger, much more imposing. There is no mistaking its authority. I sense a more *masculine* nature, compared to the androgyny of the others. Its aura glows with a piercing, vibrant redness.

It looks at B and speaks, in words we can *hear* clearly. "Welcome to you all. My name is Mihelo. I come to you, as you come to me, in the peace beyond understanding. We are consecrating our relationship of species by this communion. Let all who observe or hear of this be moved within themselves to rejoice. We are One!"

Now in the same implosive manner, another angelic figure materializes, equally imposing, yet more feminine. Its aura color is a royal purple. She speaks, "In duality we manifest before you. May you be blessed. This being, named before you, is Gavrea. It is *I am.* I wish you sweetness and adventure here in our realm. I bestow upon you this opening in your hearts. May it so be. Amen."

I glance over to you, smiling. I'm finding this stilted language amusing, yet at the same time, enormously fresh and energizing. I glance at the other three angelic beings. *Nameless ones?* I wonder. If they were awe-inspiring, these two new presences are awe-*personified*. And I wonder how close 'awesome' is to 'awful' in these godlike creatures. I can tell they are extremely powerful, not to be trifled with—high masters of realms both material and ethereal. Gavrea stands at least four meters high; Mihelo is the same.

A vision streams into me of these two beings in action, in some ancient place and time. A wide-open vista embraces what I can only describe as a 'heavenly host'. Gavrea and Mihelo appear to be initiating a vast throng of 'lesser' angelic beings in some important ceremony. The event takes up half the sky over a great canyon land. Enormous red and orange rocks jut up from deep rifts in the earth. The ravines plunge into far darkness below. Above, glorious sunset light shines all around. Joyous music fills the air. The Earth herself is joining in the celebration. 'Glory' is the only word that could describe this. But there is no further explanation or streaming.

Then the image shifts. I recognize a smaller, very localized experience of Mihelo. My own consciousness flows right into it, because in fact it happened to me. I am sitting, meditating with stillness, on a sunny morning at Judy's farm in Asheville. All is utterly peaceful. I feel the warm rays filling my spirit and I can't help but smile and sigh. The peace is so real. I just want to stay this way forever. Then my appreciation deepens in a rush. Eyes closed, I'm aware of another presence hovering and standing at the end of the deck. It is directly in the sunlight. The figure is very tall, fiery. It has wings and a great sword of red-gold, flaming light.

It must be an angel, I remember thinking. *It has wings!* It was here as part of the peace I summoned, part of the presence of this sacred land, part of the sunlight itself. I welcomed the being into my heart and opened fully to its blessing—whatever it might offer. In a flash, responding to my invitation, so fast that I had no time for alarm, the great etheric sword swung up far above my head into the sky and then swept down upon me, driving straight through the top of my head, through my body—crown to root—into the Earth.

Transfixed. I could not move. I was pinned to the ground by this light saber. But I would not have moved if I could. As challenging as this was, I knew it was a wonderful thing. *What could it mean?* In that timeless moment I was given an inspiration without words. I knew, at some future time, I would understand what had been given to me. At last, now I realize who this being was—Michael, Mihelo, archangel.

I pull away from that vision and enter another one immediately. This time it's Gavrea. She is embracing the space around a small group of people. It is a ceremony. Again, I am thrust into the picture. I am hovering in the air over the people; it is our group of twelve, as it began the first transmission of the *Letters* project. Gavrea has no body, *per se,* except that a great aura of energy surrounds her and sweeps back and forth through the scene, very like wings. It alternately enfolds and liberates the consciousness below. Again, a bright sun shines overhead, seeming to be within the angel's very aura.

As I float, I recall my experience at the start of the last book, witnessing the entire Earth in a journey that lasted only minutes. At the time, I had no idea how it was happening. I just took it for granted that this was what *you* had conjured up for me. Now I see that it was not you, but Gavrea who had orchestrated it—and indeed she is one of the initiators of our entire project. She is doing so even in this moment. Through her eyes I sense *no-time;* All these events are simply facets of one jewel of timeless experience, spanning many thousands of time-years. For her, it is as we might hold a book in our hands, fingering the pages, turning from one place to another and back again. The actual *sequence* of pages may be of secondary importance.

My visions fade at last and we are all sitting together on the platform. The golden pyramid is still vibrating around us. I look at each being here —nine of us. We are distinct, and yet fused. We are one being with nine faces. What streams into my mind is a kind of 'tracing the Oneness'. I start from my own individuality; then I sense the nine—each persona, one after the other in the trace. I sense filaments, branches, linking and weaving in and out of the Oneness and back through each individual. I know the feelings and understandings of everyone here. Through each simultaneously, I'm drawn deeper into a soul presence.

Now my senses plunge into deeper levels of the tapestry. These are ranges of awareness beyond separation, yet still with distinct presences. Onward I descend. There are levels of the World Soul, the Galactic Soul, and others. Then I'm at the depth of the One Life, with its pure, animating vibrancy for all creation in the Cosmos. Finally, still much deeper, I find the Source itself. It glows with unspeakable splendor and mystery. But this is not the end. Below the Source I sink into the Void. My mind reels. I promise it a seed-link. *Prior to the Source is the Void.*

I snap back into my mind in an instant, still looking around the circle of nine. *Nine precedes the one.* I ponder the numerology. Part of me wants to ask a question. But what question would it be? None comes to mind. Any question I could ask would be answered before it was uttered. Shaking my head, I'm content to wait. *Patience has at last found me.*

Mihelo speaks. "We are gifted to have our friends in this presence. Let it be said: There is no time when we will not be together, having gained this invocation. We are most appreciative of your endeavors in the transition ages of Earth and space."

He looks at me. "You have fulfilled our eternal desires. We speak here for Source as well as our species identity. Take heart that we are one in manifesting the message to humanity. Let this message be seeded in the young and burgeoning generation who are now bringing our desire before the world. Thus shall you become the *evigilatus* race. Let it be. Om."

I think I understood what he is saying. I wonder why the language is so awkward?

You hear my thought and reply in kind, *"It is not awkward, my friend. It only seems that way. Rather than listening to the sentence structure, we must listen with the heart to each word. I'm sure you're already doing that."*

I nod and smile at Mihelo who has been listening to both of us. He returns the smile and raises his great arm toward me, palm down, fingers spread. It is a gesture of acceptance and power. By it I am invited to partake of his power in this moment. Automatically, I lift my own arm into the same mudra. As I do, there are sparks jumping from both our hands, meeting in the middle. Now *I get it.* This communication is all about energy, not thoughts or words.

Gavrea begins, "We are here to invoke. Consider the energies implanted in being. They will arise into your structure. It is done. Find your depths therein, our friends and partners. Find your souls. Thus it begins, even now, as it has begun ever before. Eternity is expanding."

She pauses, and it feels like the space itself is breathing, long slow draughts. "Now we are bringing to you one of *our* own, who is one of *your* own. May it bless your understanding. Amen."

Suddenly, all the angelic beings disappear. I say this, but it's not quite accurate. Their already-transparent bodies grow lighter and brighter, more ethereal and spacious. Then they expand and disperse into the entire space of the golden, glowing pyramid. They have returned to their natural element—negative space.

The four of us sigh collectively. I look at Invm who has taken on a very playful appearance. He no longer looks *alien* at all to me. His face is clearly smiling and excited. He whispers to us, "Are we not blessed, my Earth friends? Never have I had such an audience."

B also grins, looking at us. "Do you know who these beings are?"

You answer, "I do indeed."

"What do you mean?" I inquire. "They were Mihelo and Gavrea. Right? That's what they said."

You chuckle, "Yes. For here and now, that is who they are. But they are much more as well. We'll talk later." You say nothing else. I will know more as time goes on. *If time can 'go on' after such a timeless encounter.*

All is still. We wait. The golden walls around us are still vibrating softly. The air is full of peace. As I slowly turn my head back to the chair where Mihelo had sat, something grabs my arm from the inside and lifts it, beyond my control. It is raised, palm down, as when I communicated with the great being. Sparks flow out of it toward the empty seat. The air quivers there. Then the cavernous space in the room begins to quiver with it; the space flows down by degrees toward the chair where my hand is still pointing. A form is condensing in the midst of the sparks.

Lo and behold. A man is suddenly sitting before us. It is someone we know well—OM. My face lights up. He looks serenely at us, but does not speak. He's waiting for something. I sense he's waiting for each of us to register his presence in a certain energetic way. A look from you tells me I'm right. I concentrate on finding the frequency. To connect, I must resonate. *There it is— this note!*

"Hello, old friends," the old man finally starts. "And greetings to you, Invm. Our recent work together has been most rewarding." We all bow our heads slightly in unison. The normal vigilan greeting seems suspended for the moment.

"I am delighted to be called upon by Gavrea and Mihelo. This incarnation is still very new to me. I am so young in it."

Your eyes open in recognition suddenly, simultaneous with B's. "OM, you are an *angelan!*"

Letter Fifty-Seven
Ability to Respond

OM smiles, signifying 'yes'. Turning his attention to me, he gets straight to business. "Mihelo spoke of blessings rendered to you, in this space of angels. In the past, vigilans have urged you to 'accept your blessings'. Indeed. In order to truly accept these blessings, however, you must also accept your responsibilities. True appreciation comprises alertness *and* your 'ability to respond'—on two fronts: One, the joy of presence welling up within you, and two, the challenge attendant to that joy, as part of the duality system. To realize the full blessing, you must complete the circuit in your awareness."

I shrug and acknowledge, "Sure, of course. But wait, OM. I just want to say, it's good to see you again. You don't seem to have changed a bit."

He laughs, "You think not?" Suddenly his form shifts radically. He stands and reveals his true angelan height—several meters and glowing like a torch. His aura shines with vibrant hues and radiates the same presence of peace that all the other angelic beings do. We are struck with awe. Then just as quickly, he shrinks back to his old familiar form. He winks.

"Sorry, OM. I guess I miscalculated," I sigh. "I just wanted to say 'hello'."

"I understand," he says, quietly. "And I do appreciate your gesture. It's just that now I must represent my authentic being in a new way. For instance, I do actually have a name in this new incarnation—at least when I am in the formal world."

I ask timidly, "And that name would be?"

"Omis-Oristinabo-Jesuvium. Call me 'Omis' for short," he chuckles as he always did, at his own simple humor.

Looking at you, I see surprise on your face. This turns into a question. "Omis, would you please explain why angelans have names at all. This seems curiously like the old form-world."

"We are not truly in the angelan world here, though it is indeed angelic *space*. That is the *Akasha*. We are in what we call the *bridgework*—a portal region between our natural state and the form state. This is where we conduct our *work*. As I now recall, vigilans used to call this the Threshold. Naming, for us, is also a matter of power dynamics: Our names invoke particular forces for our work. They are precise formulations, mathematically designed to represent our essence. Rather than a step back, these names are a step *forward* in the ability to manifest power."

Hesitantly, I interrupt, "Omis, it's wonderful to see that you have moved on to the next species. May I ask a question?"

"It would be out of your character not to ask, my friend. We are all here for that purpose—to allow you to ask questions." He smiles.

"Well, I guess the first question will be about what you just brought up. You say we must take responsibility in order to accept our blessings. What responsibility is this?"

He answers, "Words are mathematical formulae—especially here, so we must be precise. I think you noticed this in Mihelo's use of words. It is not that you 'take' responsibility; it is that you 'use' responsibility. That is to say, you *use* your ability to respond. 'now, what are you responding to?' you will ask."

I nod. You, B and Invm look relaxed, just sitting back and watching the dialogue. I get a flash of the greater audience in Paris, and indeed around the whole Earth watching as well. This suddenly makes me nervous. *Is this my reaction to responsibility?*

"You may 'react' to responsibility or you may 'use' it. I would recommend the latter," he answers my thought.

I shake my head. "I guess I don't understand. How do I 'use' my responsibility? And what am I responding to? Yes. What? How?"

Omis replies, "You are responding to your own being, your one destiny. This is *authenticity-in-action*. From this perspective, *accepting* your blessing is identical with *using* your responsibility; it is a full circle. I will make it simple through an example.

"You are writing these letters, back in your world, in your time. It is a joy to you when you are resonating with the inspiration. You are *accepting* the gift of the muses, the flow of their energies into you. At the same time, you are *using* your ability to respond and to be responsible. The message is being transmitted into your world, as we have desired. Thus are you resonating with your authentic being and acting upon its impulse. This is destiny. You are both blessed and responsible."

I counter, "In the human world, the word 'responsibility' often comes with some negative baggage. And you mentioned the 'challenges' of the duality world. I assume you mean we will encounter difficulties?"

He studies me for a moment, shifting in my chair. "Yes. You are capable of making responsibility into a negative energy field. This comes about through resistance to *authenticity* in you. For humans who do not know how, or who do not wish to engage their authentic nature, there can be much negativity around responsibility. These humans are the dense, encrusted, dying ones. However, for the new child of awakening, the benefits much outweigh any potential difficulties."

I press on. "So what is it that humans in general need to feel responsible about? And why is this what we're talking about right now?"

"I will let O or B answer this question. I'm sure they are tuning in to this topic," he suddenly turns to them.

You look to Omis for a moment with surprise and nod; then you begin, "We have talked about blessings before. Yes. These letters are all about that—the wonders that await your species as it begins its trajectory out of time, into the Now. Responsibility is about how to make this move with more resonance and resoluteness. It's natural to speak of it at this time because this is the *beginning.*"

"The beginning?" I wonder. "How is this the beginning?"

You answer, "The other two books are about the 'setting' and the 'readiness'—that is, establishing the field of awareness and the portal. This book initiates the 'action'. It is the beginning of your destiny as a new species. The ability to respond is the mother of action. As you look into your own being and appreciate your essence, follow-through becomes a natural progression. The blessings begin to flow from your authentic being."

"All right. I see. But let me play the devil's advocate for a moment—or maybe it's the *'ego's* advocate'. I hear you saying the word 'authentic' a lot. But how do we know if we're really tuning into that? What if we're deluding ourselves? What if we *think* we're being authentic when we're not? I mean, after all this time and writing these letters for you, I honestly don't truly know *who I am!* The essence of 'me' is still a great mystery."

Invm swivels his chair and speaks. "We spoke of the 'unknown' earlier, you and I. Your *essence* lies within that realm. It is natural *not* to know, with the mind, *who you really are.* If you could pin it down and say it in words or thoughts, it would not be the real essence anyway. Truth is like that, as you've heard. It cannot be spoken, nor can it be truly known to the mind. In this way, the mind is a perfect foil for the unknown: Its 'not knowing' is one face of the unknown."

B now adds, smiling, "Yes, I agree. The mind reflects the unknown by virtue of its *not knowing.* But I would say, let the real 'unknown' *live* in you, beyond the mind. This Life is who you are. Allow it to be the ever-moving presence that animates your outer world, including your mind. And it is not really true that you don't know this aspect of yourself. You *do* know! *Who* you are is your *awareness.* You do know your awareness.

"The mind can receive hints and metaphors about essence, and can actually be satisfied in its world. But to do this, its understanding must be put in terms of *thought*. Within thought processes there will always be unanswered questions. This is the nature of mind. Mind must come to accept that there is a deeper reality. It must allow the heart to lead in matters of depth. Thinking can be used on the surface to great advantage, when it plays its role *responsibly*. That is, when it does not overstep its authority.

"Each aspect of our expressions in this world has its own worth and validity, not to be discounted or diminished. This applies to mind as well as heart. But likewise, the 'ability to respond' means that you *act* with appropriate awareness for any situation. So much of human history was a distortion of that. Humanity departed far from its true being; but for a purpose: to invoke the depth of transmutation required."

"Indeed," Omis says. "We will speak of that departure in a moment. But first, let me explain why we raise this subject now. You are writing this in your year 2012. *This is the year of responsibility for humanity.* It is the time when you will face your authentic self—or not—in very profound ways. Those who deny, or refuse, will be casting their lots with the old universe. They will go *that* way. Those who awaken to the still, small voice, 'crying in the wilderness' inside their minds, will be 'baptized' in the stream of those blessings we speak of. These souls will come *our* way. They will become vigilan and angelan."

"Whew," I gasp. "That *is* a great responsibility. I get it. Please tell me what more I can do. What can any of us do, after hearing what you say?"

"It is not about *doing,* as you've heard us say before." Omis smiles. "It is about *being.* Using your responsibility is an action, to be sure. But authenticity precedes this act. Action is only as good as its impetus, its *being* nature. This comes first, in terms of appreciation. But to realize that blessing, to stream it into the world, it must be accompanied by an your ability to *respond* appropriately."

"Yes, yes. I do agree. Forgive my impatience, but I'm feeling the *need* behind what you're saying. I want to know what we can do—that is, once we've got that 'being' thing in place. If you know what I mean."

This draws a humorous reaction from all. I smile back, looking at my own spiritual youthfulness and, yes, naïveté. "But seriously, folks. This seems like the occasion for you all to tell us what to do, how to take action, how to 'use' our responsibility."

"All right," you answer. "Here's what to *do:* Spread out your presence upon the world. Once you have reached deeply within, look around you; reach out to your friends and acquaintances. Carry the energies of peace everywhere—

into your own minds and hearts first, then into others' minds and hearts. This reaching will *build* the new universe: Some of you will build physically, others psychically and socially. Still others will build cosmically and intuitively, out of essence.

Black chooses to speak now. "Open your souls to the flow of inspiration. It abounds in your world right now—even amidst dark and divisive times. So many are moving into awakened actions, creating benefits for humankind, inventing new technologies and new ways of relating, new ethics, new appreciation. It's all happening right now all around you. Look to the 'developing' countries in your time, where the need is greatest, for some of the most profound innovations. There you will find fresh, 'developing' portals to the new universe. That ground is very fertile. Be aware, however, that negation may erupt in advance of affirmation. This is often the way of nature. Look beyond that for emerging destiny. Negation and destruction may be necessary to clear the way for creation. Shiva is that."

You take voice again. "Recognize those around you who are generating the way. It will come in myriad forms and places. Build the new universe in yourselves and in others. This does *not* mean starting a new religion, or becoming a self-styled guru, or *destroying* the old world by fighting the crumbling systems. Let the old ways destroy themselves. It does mean acting upon your readiness as an awakening being. It means dissolving the fears and resistance that many of you still feel. All that is required is that you *notice* these resistances and feel your destiny through them.

"Fighting against a thing gives it strength, and wastes your energy and power. Accepting it draws its strength into you. Be ready to accept and *forgive;* then release any resistance you find in yourselves. *Forgiveness is simply releasing your* identification *with resistance.* See yourselves already alive and well in the new universe. Practice being there—even before you think you are. For this is what the new universe is: It is the practice of itself. This is the authenticity of it all."

I am breathless after your speech. *"This is what I love about you, O,"* I whisper in my mind. *"You rise to so many occasions for me. You are the foreshadowing of what I want to become, will become, in every way. Thank you."*

You reach over and lay your hand in mine, looking in my eyes as only a future incarnation can. There is a powerful jolt of electricity there. I sense mystically that our two, seemingly separate lives, will one day be remembered—by us—as just *one* incarnation, spanning 500 years.

Invm now directs a comment to Omis. "Let me say that it is an honor to be serving alongside the angelans as they bring out these changes in humanity. I had only known of this as 'history' before I arrived on Mars. Working here, with you all, I now know that the 500 years is very brief, very immediate, still resonating in us all."

Invm turns to me and says, "The energies of the Cosmos are still focused upon your era, my human friend. The time frame of 1,000 years around you is that period—from your 'Renaissance' and Leonardo da Vinci to your awakening and the passing of the ego. We here are all speaking in unison to you. All vigilans, angelans and Sirians speak to you of what you are in process of achieving."

Omis starts again. "And so, take this message back to your time, dear human. Plant the seeds for those who follow, to build their new Earth. Innovation will literally grow out of the ground from these seeds. It is the power of creation we would engender and encourage. The systems of your time must change from *within*, as *you* must change from within. It is the only path of truth and heart.

"Nevertheless, here is a word of caution: I know that many of your compatriots wish to engage in the destruction of the oppressive systems that currently dominate your world. I would urge them to refrain from such violence of mind. Do not undermine your higher intentions with this kind of resistance. The time of destruction *will* come—brought on by those outworn systems themselves. This will happen in the appropriate time and manner. Those systems must play out fully their roles in the dismantling of the old forms. It is not the part of authenticity to reject them or deny them their place. I say, do not reject your shadows. Dance with them in the light.

He smiles comfortingly. "Lastly, let me give you an example to help quell your fears. Your friend, Felicia, recently shared her concern that the oceans of Earth are now so polluted that they will never recover. What is written in destiny, however, is that all the toxins on the planet—in the oceans *and* the lands—will be nullified as the transition progresses. Healing is already at work in the spaces between molecules, everywhere."

Listening quietly, I absorb the message, agreeing mostly. *But...* "Omis, this sounds right to me. And yet it also sounds so passive, like we can't really *do* anything to hasten the dismantling of the old forms. Are we to sit by and let ourselves be *abused* continually? Is this using our responsibility? Are we to do *nothing?*"

He answers, "My human friends, you are living in one of the most electrifying and dynamic times in the past 200,000 years on this planet. You may feel, as an individual, that you are being passive when you simply observe and align your intentions with the forces of evolution. But look again. By your observation and simple noticing—more and more, deeper and deeper—you are adding vital energy to the process. By opening your hearts and minds to the new Earth being born in you, by continually heightening your sensibilities, by sharing your messages of truth among your compatriots via worldwide communication networks, you are acting from your authenticity. This is the most powerful action you can take.

"Furthermore, by simply looking into the underpinnings of control exercised by the dominant forces in your politics, religion, military and corporate hierarchies, you are gaining true power over them. They are not invulnerable; they are becoming *transparent* to you all. But their ultimate weakness is not outward; it is *inward*. This is where they have no protection. This is where truth lies—within *them*. It is the same for each of you individually, as you transcend your own egos—as above, so below. In the past, I recall, Green advised you personally to approach your ego this way. Ego has no defensive perimeter at its center. This is where it is most vulnerable—whether we speak of the collective ego of an international institution or the simple ego of a man or woman."

I try to absorb all he's said. As I glance at the glowing, golden lines of the pyramid, they seem to come alive for me. They are somehow channeling coherence into my mind. As all this sinks in, you intervene with another perspective, "I would like to answer your question about 'doing nothing': We are not saying, 'take no action,' just that authentic action must be based on your deepest realizations from Source itself. And most importantly, such realization arises out of the Void! The Void is *no thing*. So, in more than just a semantic way, 'doing *nothing*' is a profound spiritual act, possessed of essence."

Your voice softens. "Your times—the Great Storm—are moving so swiftly, dear friend. It may certainly be difficult for you to discern the correct action to take in every situation. It is an existential dilemma for your race. But be assured that, even when you are taking no action, there are, within your being, momentous changes occurring—on all levels."

I respond, "Well, I certainly know the feeling of those changes inside me. My emotions are like a rollercoaster sometimes, while outwardly I appear calm and collected. I know I've complained about this before, but my inner world is in turmoil, *often*. Just when I know I should be moving ahead with my awakening, I can feel the most unenlightened."

Invm offers, "From an off-worlders perspective, I see the whole Earth process with a little more detachment I think. In your time, under the influence of gargantuan energetic impacts on all your systems, it is remarkable how strong your species remained. It is a testament to the preparation that had been forged and tempered in you over tens of thousands of years of suffering and struggle. This is where the dark forces, the so-called evil forces, have played their parts well.

"From the higher dimensions—which I am allowed to visit from time to time—this all appears differently. It is like an enormous, multi-dimensional chess game, orchestrated in the fabric of vast astronomies and physics. At every level of manifestation, the pieces are moving according to inner, invisible patterns and dynamics. Each star and planet and culture and individual being has its part to play—whether for darkness or light—in any given time. This is the dance and music of the spheres. It is also the very substance of the inscrutable unknown!"

You say, "And yet, what is unknown to us, is *known* to Source. This is the delightful aspect of mystery. Faith determines for us our comfort level and confidence with the unknown. While we may not *know*, at the same time, there is the *substance* of knowing the unseen. The patterns that Invm has worked with for centuries reveal a level of trust in the relationship between Source and the manifested world. We are part of that trust."

B adds slowly, "This is what you can take back with you, in your heart, body and soul. Know that whatever your inner being tells you to do, as an action through heart knowledge, you will be following one of Invm's laser lines to destined connections. You will be operating on behalf of Source itself, in large matters and small."

I gulp. "But where is freewill in all this. This is starting to sound like predestination to me."

B answers, "This is the mind's interpretation. Yes, it is a perspective you may take if you identify with resistance. But 'negativity won't pull you through,' to quote your poet, Bob Dylan. Resistance will slow you down to a crawl, halt you in your tracks and dump you in the ditch. It is the 'braking' of nature. The reward for following its lead is to be left without any path at all. Freewill gives you a path. That is *its* function.

"The alignments you make with dynamic patterns flowing in space, throughout the Cosmos, are your free will. The Void is 'free'; Source is 'will'. It is the locus of truth for all creation. To resonate with its 'dictates' is our greatest opportunity and freedom."

Finally, Omis raises his hand, standing, and extends his form into the angelan shape, fiery and tall, glowing with the power of peace. He suddenly spreads luminescent wings behind, and looks down upon us all. His voice is soft and yet deeply penetrating. "Come with me, my friends. There is something I'd like to show you."

Letter Fifty-Eight
Evigilatus-Sapiens

Omis sweeps his great wings around us in the angelan sort of way and proclaims, "We have come full circle. Source is the origin and the end—alpha and omega. Source is inviting me to bring you into the angelan realm. This is a journey I dreamt of for lifetimes as a vigilan. Now a glimpse will be offered you without your even asking. The times are indeed changing!"

I look at you with amazement. We are all feeling the same wonder and apprehension. Omis bundles us up, *en mass,* off the pedestal and into the air—in a force field of angelic resolve. A sudden *streaming* whispers to me that greater powers are guiding Omis in this mission. Is it Gavrea or Mihelo? *Omis says it's Source. But what can that mean?*

Assembled and moving as one, we swoop over the glowing marble floor toward the rear of the pyramid. There, in the far back, is a small archway, virtually invisible until now. Under it I glimpse an ornately carved door. We careen at high speed straight at it. I cringe involuntarily, anticipating a crash. But the door swings wide open at the last second, and we are through.

I turn my gaze to you and send a thought, *"I think we just left the Hall of Memories through the back door!"*

You chuckle and whisper inside my head, *"I have a feeling we've just learned a secret. Maybe that's the only way into where we're going."*

Omis advises, "Please simply watch for now. There will be time for comments and questions when we arrive."

The swiftness of our passage makes my head spin. On the other side... Well, there is no other side. It is as though our discrete existences have been wiped clean. We are still conscious, but there's no separation among us. We're in some kind of limbo—both with and without physical form, still moving rapidly. I can speak for us all in this moment, because that's all there is... the 'we' of 'I am' embodied. *What does this mean?* There is no way to tell, except to slap some words on it, like this. Maybe they will make sense, and maybe they won't."

We must be right at the cusp of the Void; I feel it bleeding through, as we skim along. We are just enough outside it to be conscious, but not enough to have any distinct form. The silver blankness weaves through us and around us, along with whorls of tiny crystalline orbs. They glitter and shine, charting the path we seem to be on. They spiral away into a forever distance.

Now, suddenly, there is red light everywhere. Yet is a entire spectrum within a single color. Thousands of shades and hues of red luminescence flash past us as we move, ranging from crimson to rose to ruby and scarlet. Then we're surrounded by shades of violet, amethyst, purple and plum. Next, we're on to indigo, blue, green and yellow. Finally we slide into bright orange, with thousands of fiery variations on salmon, copper and vermilion.

At last we rise into something more comprehensible—liquid of some sort. Bubbles and coursing streams, infusions of bright and dark surround us. Then we're on into steamy clouds, swirling in spirals of opalescence. Gleaming light ahead envelopes everything. All is brightness and fiery swirls, so intense there is no way to use our eyes to see. Some other faculty has taken over. This is like no other place any of has ever been or seen; we are experiencing in a way far beyond our kin.

I slowly realize that, for angelans, this perception is normal and natural. For us, it is beyond the 'species code' that grants us our powers of comprehension. But nevertheless, pure awareness is clearly what we *are*. We seem to be able to embrace vast schemes of information and order, endless hierarchies of evolution, relentless, eternal timeframes and super-spatial dimensions. There is no way to put even a fraction of it into thought or word. Together, we four non-angelans are at a loss to be anything but awestruck.

At last, a stupendous mountain slope juts up above the rampant clouds. We rise ever higher alongside it. The surface is like an earthly landscape, with forests, cliffs and great stone façades. Yet the scene is painted in yellows, oranges and gold. As we climb along the amber escarpment, we discover this is part of a colossal mountain range, spreading far into a gilded distance. Other ranges appear behind them, rolling in gargantuan sculpted swells, as far out as our senses can comprehend. We can see for thousands of miles before a crystalline horizon cuts across our vision. The ethereal indigo-black sky contrasts exquisitely with the color of the land below; the land—and not the sky—provides the illumination.

Together we cruise over this golden mountainscape, range after range. We're passing enormous distances. Sweeping vistas precede us and stretch out in all directions. Finally rising over one last enormous swell, we confront a deep valley, filled with strange and magical shapes. Long, glistening tubes stream down the slopes. Spiral towers arch up and touch one another high in the sky, spinning grand cascades of sparkling light around them. The whole is woven into a scintillating fabric of natural forms. *Clearly intelligence has been as work.* A vast, gossamer web hovers just above the treetops, and cliffs, undulating slowly to a faint musical presence. It's like a giant ethereal spider has constructed it all.

Centered in the panorama is a sparkling city. The tubes sweep down and become grand boulevards, weaving toward a convergence. The buildings are low to the ground, but they radiate towering forces. They are all transparent, though not made of glass or metal. The material of construction is like an ethereal fusion of matter and light. Steepled monuments punctuate the many open spaces of golden-green parkland. In these spaces, rivers meander and lakes shimmer. Some of the structures seem to have actual *wings!* The brightness in each building increases toward the top, until it dissolves into simple, shining luminance, beaming skyward. *This is the ultimate evolution of Shangri-la,* I muse.

Now we begin to slow down and make an approach for landing. There's a flattened ledge—like an aerie for angels—on one of the peaks. A huge structure rises up on it—a cross between a temple and a castle, five stories high. It is a style of architecture none of us has seen before. The beauty is astounding; ornate spires above and carvings below in the walls; windows of various sizes are scattered across every façade, almost haphazardly; there are deep, triangular recesses at regular intervals that disappear into dark, mysterious interiors. In front of this manse we are let down, out from the wings of our angelan host.

We are individuals again, standing completely dazed on a great porch next to the edifice. Omis condenses himself again into vigilan size and spreads his arms open. His smile is almost as wide. He exclaims, "Welcome to my home!"

We look around at each other, bewildered. I ask, "Where are we, Omis? O, do you have any idea?"

You slowly nod your head and answer, "I do. But you're not going to believe it. We're on the surface of the sun."

"No! How can *that* be? There are mountains here. And we're not being incinerated."

Omis laughs, "She's right, you know. Let me explain. This is a dimension of the sun that is habitable for angelans. Fire does not daunt us. We live on the edge of formlessness and so intensities of all kinds are much more transparent. We create these mountains out of golden fire and do dearly enjoy being in such a precarious environment. You are our guests, and so are protected from the dangers of the denser levels of the sun."

Invm walks up to a stone balustrade, a little unsteady on his feet, and peers over the edge. A very deep canyon falls precipitously below, perhaps dozens of kilometers down; beyond that the great city sprawls. He shakes his head. "I don't understand. Why have you chosen to form mountains if we are on the surface of the sun? You *are* forming these, correct?"

Omis looks at Invm, unspeaking, yet communication is flowing to the Sirian nonetheless. He motions us all to join him around a small table where there are a number of chairs. We follow and sit, still mystified. You hazard a guess. "The sky and the mountains are the homes of angels in many legends. I assume that the form of the landscape could be anything you choose, even here on the surface of a star. But I wonder why you would have such a place for your home."

Our host looks at you and grins simply. "We like to be close to the power source. The sun is that for our solar system. It is the ambassador for Source to all our physical lives—and the physical and etheric Threshold to space. It is likewise the gateway to your own star system, Invm, Sirius. There is a unique Life energy that flows between our two suns.

"I believe you have all experienced angelans at some time or another. You may recall seeing us in bright sunlight. This is not uncommon. We are messengers for the light, and we ride upon it to perform all our various duties. Sun energy infuses us and we embody *it*. The more fire, the better. This place is also an icon of purification—an important function of our kingdom.

Gazing off at the dazzling, gilded, alpine view, I reflect on my memory of Mihelo with his flaming sword. I turn my head back and look into Omis' eyes. They are still a dark red, vigilan color, but they have a new depth and transparency now. That depth reveals an inner flaming nature. He gazes back into my eyes and I feel a piercing of my mind. He is wasting no opportunity and no time; he suddenly uses this opening between us to send a searing pulse of light into my body. I feel an inexorable burning throughout myself, as though I'm being cleared and cleansed of built-up emotional debris—and human, mental nonsense. I reel in my chair, speechless. The echoes of this blast reverberate through me for some minutes. It's a dose of fiery, angelic bliss.

Black, always her own, unique individual, seems to have entered a meditative state. You are sitting next to her and decide to follow her lead. Omis watches intently, as if somehow guiding you both to do this. I look at Invm. We both shrug and close our eyes beginning our own meditations. Instantly, a shared vision comes forward. The mountain landscape is gone and I see the surface of the real sun. It is a radiant churning inferno of liquid fire and light, erupting and hephaestian sprays.

Massive electric flames arc high overhead. The solid mountain shapes have turned to an ocean of fluid fire, rising and falling to terrifying heights in slow undulations. They are like slow-moving mountains of golden lava. An energy of passion lies within this vision that is beyond human sensibility. The meditation is 'fervent', to say the least. I persist in it for a time, but the intensity inevitably drives me back out. When I open my eyes, the hard mountainscape returns. Omis is serene, sitting in a wide halo of orange.

I wait respectfully until he looks at me. Then I say meekly, "May I ask a question, Omis?"

He says nothing for a minute or so, waiting for the others to rally their attention. Then he nods affirmatively to me.

"I am astounded by all this, old friend. It's far more than I can take in. Is this the way angelans have always lived? I mean, here on the sun?"

He chuckles, "No, by no means. Angelans are not limited to just this. We have the run of a vast multitude of physical and etheric dimensions, everywhere in the solar embrace. But we still focus primarily on the Earth, and upon the human and vigilan species. This is our heritage and destiny."

"You have mentioned your work several times now. Would you please tell us about that?" I inquire.

"Yes, indeed. That is why we're here—that you may be introduced to what I have learned since we last met." Omis pauses and considers what to say next. "I must say that there is some confusion about angelans and angels. You may be surprised to know that we are *not angels;* we're not the same."

I look surprised and glance at you and B. You don't seem to share my reaction. I ask Omis, "You're not angels? Please explain that one. I was operating on the assumption that *homo angelicus* was the name of the *angel* species."

He clears his throat and responds, "There is much overlap between our races, so the misapprehension is understandable. I will explain only briefly. We, *homo angelicus,* are the species that follows out of *homo sapiens-sapiens* and *homo evigilatus.* I, for example, completed my last vigilan incarnation in your year 13,000, give or take a few decades. My soul was ready, at that point, to move into a vehicle that would afford greater awareness. It is a natural progression for most souls to eventually make that choice. Some few leapfrog into other systems beyond angelan, but that is another matter entirely.

"Service is what primarily distinguishes our species from yours, and this is the source for understandable confusion. Angels, *devas* and *elementals* are also incarnations in this domain, devoted to serving the denser physical realms. But we go about it very differently."

You interrupt, "Omis, excuse me, but it might be useful to define what you mean by 'service'."

"Gladly, O. Glad to be of *service,"* he quips, after his old pattern of humor. "I will start with your favorite method. The origin of the word, 'service', comes through the Latin, meaning 'slave'. And before that, in Indo-European, *sar,* meant 'to protect'. The way we apply the term, though, far exceeds either of these root words. Nevertheless, those roots account for the difference between angelans and angels. Angelans have freewill, being based out of the hominid strain of evolution on Earth. Angels, devas, archangels and other beings, while capable of very advanced awareness, are *not* granted the same kind of freewill. They are more directly bound to the impulses from Source in all their thoughts and actions. In manifestation, they are purely, direct extensions of Source.

"Angelans, like angels, serve the human and vigilan races, but not because this role is dictated to them; rather because we *choose* to do it. We understand that our own being is inextricably tied to yours. We are one essence, in three temporal phases. To serve you is to serve ourselves—the whole species, *angelicus evigilatus sapiens*, to put a scientific name on it. 'Service' then means that we look after our own wellbeing on a species level. We determine what your evolutionary status is, within given timeframes; we look at the ever-changing energetic configurations in the cosmic network that constitute your galactic environment; and we compare that with your intrinsic destiny. Our need to understand the configurations is why we partner with your Sirian counterparts."

He nods to Invm, and resumes. "We need to keep track of the progress of your civilizations, and test their alignments within the physical-temporal planes. If there is a misalignment, we must make adjustments."

I see Invm react to this information; apparently he's learning something new. Omis continues, "It was just such an adjustment that generated your 'transposition project' in the first place. I guess I should say 'our' project, since, obviously, I was involved during my last two vigilan incarnations."

I interject, "Involved! I thought you *created* the project. And, by the way, what kinds of 'adjustments' are you talking about?"

"I will come to that. The 'who' and 'when', the actual origin of creation for anything in these universes is ultimately a great mystery—property of the *unknown*. Yes, I was the incarnate individual who sponsored a linkage between humans and vigilans. However, now that I am an angelan, I see that our so-called 'project' is only just beginning in *this* incarnation. It exists far beyond time, in a sphere that cannot even be called 'timeless'. It is simply non-temporal altogether. It has to be, in order to oversee functions in the lower spheres of time manifestations.

"And behind me stands Gavrea, the high initiator, whose impetus sets it all in motion. From her perspective, however, there is yet another chain of exalted beings—whose names and presences I only know from inference—who inspire and motivate all angelic beings. There is a never-ending multi-dimensional hierarchy of consciousness, stretching above and below and beside each rung in the evolutionary order."

I shake my head, bewildered. "I thought this was all supposed to get *simpler*, the deeper we go into awareness. I remember, way back at the beginning of the first book, you said it was so 'simple'." I point to *you*.

"And you believed us?" Omis laughs. "But yes, as complex as creation seems at times, it is simple still. The stillness is simplicity, and the stillness governs and suffuses all. It is *paradox* to be sure, my friend."

You add, "The simplicity reaches within; complexity radiates without. It is the unending mission of conscious awareness to balance the two. Complexity is the mask, the gateway access to move behind the illusion. Always look through the mask. It is the first clue."

Black stirs for a moment, contented mostly to sit in the background and watch us all. She says, "This is why we meditate, eh! Source gazing! We are always in need of reaching within, *especially* when we involve ourselves in exploring the outer dimensions. Am I right, Invm?" She looks to him, and he nods in agreement. *His work must take him into serious complexity at times.*

He answers, "I would even venture to say, we need to go just as deeply within and we do without. This is the balance to be struck."

Omis gathers up our minds again and continues, "Now, back to our topic of 'service'. Let me say that what we do is not limited just to large-scale enterprises. We also have very personal roles as so-called spirit guides or guardians. It really doesn't matter what you call us—with names or not. But if you do sincerely *call* us, we respond. In this area, we work very closely with the angels. They have their *angle* on service. And we have ours." He winks again. I shake my head. *OM humor!*

I ask, "What kind of service do you provide then? I know, personally, I've often asked for assistance from my 'angels'. And I've gotten a lot in return. But I never really know *who* I'm talking to exactly and what the limits to my requests actually are."

Omis purses his lips and brushes back his long white hair. He looks just like he did all those years ago. *Or are those years yet to be?* I puzzle. He replies to my question, "There are many of us answering your requests at all times. And you may ask for absolutely anything you wish—no limits. You may ask under the influence of your soul or you may do it from ego. There are infinite possibilities. Some people call this prayer. However, as you know, there are no guarantees that you will receive what you're asking for."

"That's the rub," I exclaim. "People often get the answer 'no' to their prayers."

"That's not totally accurate. The answer is never an absolute 'no'. But it may seem that way to the petitioner. When we determine that satisfying your request would result in harm to you or someone else, we *modify* the request for you. It may be that what you're asking for would violate your authenticity or be out of resonance with your soul's intentions. The answer, however, in this case is not strictly 'no'; we have converted your request into another, more appropriate form—realignment.

"For you humans, being out of resonance most of the time, I'm sure it seems like we're denying your wishes. If you were to go within and find the resonance, you would find the altered form of your request. You would then ask for what is truly resonant with your own being. Even this, you see, is one of our services—realignment of requests. We can also, at times, help you without your asking us. But an active, sincere request has much more power behind it."

I continue, "It seems like an enormous burden for you to be listening to people's prayers all the time; I imagine it would be rather boring. How does that actually work?"

"That would indeed be tedious. We do not sit around listening to you personally. It is all energetically arranged in patterns. Our minds are geared to a broader 'band-width', as you might call it. And we can monitor many more channels than you could have dreamed of in your minds. Remember, our evolutionary state is based on the need to receive and distribute such data streams. And also time, for us, is very different. We use your timeline like a highway—a 'service' road, if you will," he chuckles at this little joke.

He continues, "I may be working in the human era in one instant and the vigilan next. Or I may move my focus thousands of years into the past or future in the scope of one single transaction. Often I am working in many different time-spaces simultaneously.

"Having this capacity for time-maneuvering gives us the ability to see the consequences of actions and events over great ranges. For instance, on rare occasions, we may move the response for a given request to an entirely different lifetime. From the individual's point of view, the answer did not seem to be affirmative. From the soul's perspective, however, it's all happening at once, and the response fits in where it's most suitable."

Invm asks a question. "Omis, seeing now the scope of your abilities, I am wondering what is the difference between your species and the soul itself. Aren't you functioning very much as the soul does?"

Our old friend smiles and answers, "From where you are, I can see how you might think that. It's a good question, Invm. Our incarnations are indeed closer to the soul than you. But they are still embodiments. The soul is *not* that. The distinction comes down to functionality. Angelans have their roles and destinies. The soul has its own, different from ours—different functions. The Cosmos, as you well know, is arranged in infinite dimensions and levels of evolutionary acumen and functionality. There are those who have evolved far beyond our species. They appear totally formless to us; and yet, from their soul's perspective they are incarnate nevertheless."

I ask, "When does it ever end? Where is the line between soul and incarnate form?"

"The soul is always the essence, the center being. All creations maintain such a center, or soul, within themselves, even when they incarnate with a minimum of form. What constitutes 'incarnation' becomes increasingly more ethereal as one moves on through the stages of Life. The soul itself also evolves into finer and more elegant textures. There is truly no end to this unfoldment. All is relative: As above, so below."

A thought pops into my head, and I can't stop from asking, though the words seem rather naïve as I speak them. "Omis, I always thought that evolution was eventually going to turn us all into gods, or God—Source itself. Just *what* does evolution intend for us in the end?"

"That is not a naïve question at all." He smiles sympathetically. "It's very deep. It might also be asked in a different form: 'what is the difference between us and Source?'"

"Uh, yes," I stutter. "I guess that's a good question too. Thanks for the 'adjustment'."

"The fundamental answer is, there *is* no difference. We are already Source. What we become, through evolution, is what we already are now, in this moment. Source. However, another valid answer to your question—taken from the perspective of incarnation—is that there *is* a vital difference. I will not give you the glib explanation of saying, 'it's a paradox', though it certainly is that. The *difference* is what our incarnating and evolving is really all about.

"We are the fragments *of* Source that are differentiating themselves *from* Source. That is our job, all of us. Source has set us on this path with its great, prime intention, the one that comes from the deepest destiny of all. There is no beginning or end to it, because time is not real. We—and Source—just keep moving in endless, interlocking spirals and vortices within the Oneness.

"What does evolution intend in the end? It intends that there *never* is an end. It uses time as a pointer toward endlessness. We turn and grow and live and die—cyclically—within the Life that breathes us all, every one, eternally.

But only Source can *know* this in truth; it is our part, in evolution, to acknowledge and accept it as the *unknown*."

Letter Fifty-Nine
Expression of Service

Omis pauses and breathes long and deep, looking out into the distant brightness. He shrugs. "Now, in a more practical vein, let's take a look at some examples of what I'm talking about. Place your gaze upon the space over the table."

Our eyes turn to the small surface in the center of our circle. A holographic hole opens just above it, about a meter in diameter. Immediately there is an image of people on a street; they're wearing 21st Century clothes. It's a scene from my time. We seem to be following a man in a tan suit; we're looking over his shoulder. He weaves his way through a crowd up to a busy street corner. Cars and trucks are speeding past on his left. We are suddenly privy to his thoughts. He is on his way to an important meeting. His thoughts are projected out before him—worries about entering the meeting late and being embarrassed.

The man reaches the corner and looks up at the crosswalk lights. In his distracted state he confuses the direction of these lights and steps off the curb. We all wince as a taxi slams into him and his body goes flying into the intersection. People scream. Cars screech and swerve around him. But the man's twisted body is clearly dead; blood seeps out from his shirt collar and stains the pavement and the tan cloth of his jacket.

I look around at you and the others uncomfortably. Omis comments, "Now let's watch this same scene with a slightly different outcome."

The image winds quickly in reverse to where we first entered. The man is still in a hurry, weaving among the throng. This time, however, amidst his worried thoughts he pauses and looks around, taking a deep breath. He realizes he's not in balance. He shakes his head and relaxes his resistance. A brief request goes up to his 'spirits'; he asks for assistance in getting to the meeting in good time. From there his course is identical to the first vision. However, when he arrives at the corner and looks up at the lights, there is a difference.

The air around the man suddenly shimmers and condenses, as we've lately observed with the angelans. An invisible form swirls and funnels down into a woman walking next to the man. She looks around at him just as he begins to step in front of the on-rushing taxi. She grabs his arm and pulls him back. His life is saved by inches.

"You used the woman as an *angel!*" I exclaim.

"It was convenient. We always ask permission on deeper levels, however, before we do such a thing. The woman's soul agreed to participate."

I gasp, "How could you have had time to ask her about it?"

"We need no time for such negotiations. However, if we did need time, we could simply rewind the clock and start from an earlier position. In this case, our request and the woman's agreement all took place between the pulses of time."

"What is a pulse of time? Do you mean like between one second and the next?"

"Yes. Only it's a much shorter measurement than that, called Planck time in your physics."

I continue, "All right. I think I've heard of that. You're saying you can transfer information back and forth very quickly. So, what was the real difference between the two events you showed us? Was it as simple as the the man asking you for help in the second version?"

"Almost. For the human mind, that answer is sufficient. However, the deeper reality is that in the second scene, the man was opening a channel within himself for acceptance of our presence. He did not have to think about it, so much as *accept* it, in a timeless way. As you observed in his thoughts, he was anxious in the first version, while in the second he let go of his resistance."

"Were these real events?" I ask. "If so, which one actually happened?"

"They were both real," our angelan answers. "Up until that short walk down the sidewalk, the man's form expression had largely existed in one dimension. Given the radical split at the choice-point—that is, when he faced imminent death—his soul generated an alternate dimension. It gave him a 50/50 chance of survival.

"Some, in your time, have called this phenomenon an alternate 'universe'; however, that is not accurate. The universe stays the same. It is only a subdimension of the prevailing universe that slides in an altered direction. In the original dimension he died instantly; in the second, he decided to relax his anxiety and be open to us."

B interrupts. "I assume you had 'alternate' methods, as well, that you could have used to save the man."

Omis answers, "Yes, of course. We could have manifested a form of our own and intervened. However, we prefer not to do that, because it creates karmic ripples when a body suddenly materializes before a group of people, even if no one consciously saw it. We could also have entered the mind of the taxi driver, except this would not have been productive; the taxi driver's mind refused to accept our interference with his own destiny. We in fact contacted several people on the street during the Planck moment."

B asks, with mounting curiosity, "What about entering the man's own mind and just warning him of the danger?"

"Good idea. We tried that first. But once the man invited us in, he entered a very 'slippery' state of dismissal toward his own thoughts; he actually registered our advice as another form of his own mental resistance; he dismissed it."

Invm mutters, "Very tricky technical work. Is there that much going on in every such encounter between angelans and people?"

Omis grins. "Yes. In fact, it gets much more complicated than this in most situations. In the event depicted, we were standing at the ready to intervene if other people or automobiles had reacted badly to the danger. Of course, the people must always allow us to intervene before we can act. Preferably, they *ask* for our intervention first. And we must always respect the destiny of each relevant person on the scene."

I ask, "By saying 'preferably,' you imply you can intervene at times without being asked?"

"Yes. We monitor patterns of destiny at all times, everywhere on Earth. When we detect potential breaks in resonance, we gather our forces and apply readjustments. Sometimes there is no local request for our help. In these cases there is a decreased chance of success because the 'service roads' I alluded to before are blocked or defective."

I continue, "You mean you can fail to make the needed readjustments?"

Omis answers, "Indeed. Human history is full of such failures on our part and yours. In the original scene I just showed you, early death would have thwarted that soul's intention; it would have resulted in pushing certain important life lessons off onto another lifetime. Such things build stress into a soul's incarnational system."

"I get it. Apparently you work with destiny all the time. What about the destiny of the man who died? Did he have two destinies?"

"It seems like two, but that splitting sub-dimension wove itself quickly back into the original one not too much after that. And in any case, the event itself is *not* the destiny. Destiny is the energetic pattern of conscious growth woven into the incarnate expression. Whether the man lived or died may or may not affect this inner pattern."

"Whoa." I murmur. "What does all that mean?"

You decide to field the question this time. "Destiny is the reality of the moment as it emerges from the soul. It is always now and not in the future. We've told you this before. The single, underlying energy pattern of presence can manifest in a multitude of events or even sub-dimensions. The presence is one; the forms that are generated out of it can be many. In other words, this man's destiny was to die and to be saved simultaneously, as strange as that may appear. The destiny was generated in the moment of living interaction with his environment."

"Whew," I sigh. "I *guess* I understand."

Omis leads our attention back to the hovering globe above the table. "Now let me show you something a bit more complex."

As if that weren't complex enough, I mutter in my mind. The image clouds and swirls into another 'human' scene. There are tens of thousands of people gathered in a large city square, obviously protesting something *en masse.* I'm used to scenes like these on the nightly news back home. On the perimeter, all around the protesters are military personnel and equipment—tanks and guns, shields and helmets. But these images are not like on television: In this holographic projection we can read the thoughts of the people.

There are several levels of perception to this. On the collective level, we sense the over-all feeling of the crowd. It's like a churning ocean of emotion. Waves rise and fall, crash and rebound. There is fear and courage, restlessness and anticipation, all mixed with other strong emotions. At any given time one particular sensation rises to prominence for a while; then it is surpassed by another, different wave.

In a second level of sensibility, we register small groups of *leaders,* scattered amidst both the protesters and among the soldiers. The people know some of these individuals around them. However, we can see that other 'leaders' are present that no one recognizes outwardly. They are silently holding the space and channeling energies into those around them. Some are conscious of what they do, others are functioning without fully knowing their role; many of the individuals, supposedly in 'authority' are *not* true leaders.

There is then a third level of awareness in this event: Each individual's mind is open to us, but only when we actually focus on the eyes of the person. Our individual vision has expanded inside the hologram to the point where we can wander out over the crowd at will, examining any detail. I look into the faces of a few and sense their thought patterns. One woman is concerned for her family, left at home. Another man is anxious about what may happen here, but is proud of his participation; he senses this is a moment of destiny; he is looking to the future, and knows this moment is the start of that. In another face I find an attitude of prayer; this woman is standing still, watching the flowing movements on all sides. She is asking for peace and protection for her assembled compatriots.

"Now watch this," Omis directs, almost gleefully. At the wave of his hand, we see something that had been invisible before. An orange-golden cloud is hovering above the scene. At first it seems only a formless, gently flowing mass. Then as we look more closely, we see that each individual has her or his own small cloud. This includes the soldiers as well. These orbs of mist follow the people wherever they move; some hover lower and closer than others; some are bright, others dim. But in every case, there seems to be a subtle interchange between the mist and the person.

Another wave of our host's hand produces further clarity. Each cloud condenses into the form of an angelan—towering, transparent figures. Around the angelan there are other small shapes—beings of various sizes and forms. They seem to come and go from visibility, at times even diving down into the bodies of the individuals below. These little ones are apparently being directed from above to perform particular missions.

Now apart from the individual angelans, other winged beings come into view. They float aloft, surveying and sending energy into the groups below. Finally, above them, faint images of a few others come to us; Gavrea and Mihelo are among those. They remain completely stationary and firm, holding the space together.

I ask, "Omis, I'm amazed to see what is going on undetected behind the scenes here. But the angelans seem to be supporting both sides in this conflict. Is this true? Are they indifferent to what's really happening here?"

He answers, "Not at all. All the spirits are well aware of the import of this event. That's why they're here. In fact, they are more attuned to it than most of the people are. They are acting in accord with a deeper purpose. They guard the clarity and destiny concealed within the event, resonating on multiple levels. What guides them is not the personal trappings or actions, but the is resonance with destiny or not. The angelans look to the soul and Source first in whatever assistance they are asked to offer."

I inquire, "I'm a little confused. Who *asked* them to do this? It appears to be a well-orchestrated mission. Are angelans always this attentive to human affairs?"

"We are always attentive, yes, but not quite this active. What is going on here, is part of the awakening of humanity 500 years ago. We are summoned in larger numbers to such gatherings. The same was true in most of the wars that

humans created. Any large-scale calamity or natural disaster affecting you or
your vigilan siblings draws our concerted attention. Still, we must be *asked* before we can marshal such action on your behalf. Sometimes the greater destiny
itself makes the request, taking on the attribute of an individualized entity. It is
the *shared* soul. The event you are witnessing here is exactly such a case—hence
the gravity of it. Now observe how it unfolds."

We continue to watch and sense the thoughts and feelings of the crowds.
We see that certain members of the military want to attack and put these 'rebels' down. They are ready to shed blood, perhaps slaughtering thousands in
this square. But other soldiers are sympathetic to the people. They are standing
against their commanders—in spirit, if not in action. This has actually come
about while we've been watching. The numbers of sympathetic souls in the
military camp has grown in this short time. They seem to be *waking up* to the
deeper quality of the event, in significant numbers. *This is perhaps* because *we're
watching!* I realize.

Omis catches my sensing and interjects, "You are correct, friend. Our observation has in fact played a part in making the awakening. *Any event, sufficiently
observed, will be turned toward the essence of the observers. The more authentic the observation, the greater is the effect.* In the time of this particular uprising, the world communication media of your day were monitoring it closely. Hundreds of millions
of people were pouring their empathy into it, helping it to resolve in the most
beneficial manner. It also planted seeds that matured a number of years later,
into a permanent shift in consciousness and governance—both in the lands of
these protestors and beyond, in the lands of the observers.

"What we are now here to teach you is that our role is much greater and
more connected to you than you have ever dreamed. It is time for you to know
this."

My mind begins to race to other events, similar to this one, that did not
turn out so well. "But, Omis, while this protest may have ended peacefully,
there were many others that ended in violence and massacres. What was the
difference in those?"

"Simply a different destiny working itself out," he replies, a little too casually for my liking. "Do not misunderstand; we are not *peacekeepers.* Our role is
to assist the unfolding true destiny of Earthly actions and events, whether they
be collective or individual. Each event in history has its own inherent destiny,
just as each individual does."

I scowl, knowing he's reading my thoughts. He continues, "Not all destinies involve tranquil outcomes. Some events are intended to produce growth
through trauma. As the soul, you know this to be true."

"Yes. I understand. My own soul has tolerated much adversity in my life. I guess to teach me lessons," I respond.

Omis explains, "This is true for all individuals. The soul is not just 'warm and fuzzy', as you say. If you personally must suffer or die to learn a lesson, the soul grants it—within its *dispassionate* compassion. Nevertheless, I have chosen to show you this event because it was particularly seminal in your species' awakening."

"So, you're saying that this one had more lasting impact. Was that because it turned out peacefully?"

"Yes, and particularly because it generated peace within both sides of the conflict. The fulfillment of inner peace evokes peace on the outer planes. You may look to that outer expression as an indication of inner success."

"Well, old friend," I react. "It certainly is helpful to know you angelans can pay so much attention. But I still have to ask 'why?' You said that we're all in this together; we're all one. Yet that can't be the whole story."

"You are correct, brother. We are, indeed, conscious of the whole greater being when we perform our functions. But the answer to your question is *service* itself; this is the key. It is our essence. And it is, likewise *your* essence, if you only knew. Service is much more than 'protecting' our investment, as it were, or being subservient, or even 'helpful'; it is a quality of transcendent authenticity—which is to say, 'authority'. To *serve* is to pour grace from Source into the world. Service is a portal for grace and empowerment to the giver and the receiver. He who truly serves, reveals God in form and brings spirit into matter."

"But wait," I protest, being admittedly dense. "*Why* is this so? Why would God itself want to *serve*? Isn't God beyond this?" As I say these words, an understanding streams into me. I know it's a silly question.

You catch my inner reaction and ask, "What did you just register?"

I pause—not really ready to put words to my senses. But at last I say, "Sorry. I think I finally get it. Divinity, Source—whatever you call it at the center of the Cosmos—creates *by means* of service. That's what makes the whole thing happen! Service *is* creation. The Creator is the Great Server." I chuckle at a sudden thought. "It's kind of like 'serving' in a tennis match. It gets everything started."

Omis enters. "You've got it. That's exactly *why* we serve. We are moving our whole race—including you all—toward the divine essence of creation—the active instant of creation called destiny. Service is simply another word for 'making it all happen'—the entire cosmic manifestation."

Black looks us in the eyes, scanning all around, and says, "Another way of looking at it is that destiny is the expression of service to the soul, for each incarnate individual. It is why we are each here now, and why all those souls on Earth are engaged in following us, through the congress. Each action we take—by anyone in any time—is an act of service to the whole, when taken from authenticity and authority."

Omis bows his head to B, acknowledging the truth in what she says. "And each authentic action taken by the whole is an act of service to the individual."

Letter Sixty
New Reverence

I continue with my inquiry, "Please tell me about etheric guardians and spirit guides. Are they angels or angelans?"

"They may be either, or both. Each situation dictates who will be invoked. For direct assistance in matters of form and manifestation, you call upon angels; they facilitate creation and manipulation of forms. You may give them names, such as you yourself have done many times. Your religious traditions have generated many angel names. The names you choose may be formal and noble or familiar and amusing, reflecting the function you wish them to perform—such as 'Parky' to help you find a parking space for your car. Yes," you smile knowingly. "We *have* paid attention to that. We are much amused."

"It was not *me* who coined that name; a friend of mine did that. Do you think it disrespectful?"

"Not at all," he replies. "It is playful. Angels and angelans love to play. We would prefer to play with you more; it's humanity that is so serious! Besides, you would not ask for our assistance at all if you did not respect us."

"So, angels are basically invisible creatures around us who help us in various ways, in daily life. And we can give them names. Do they have names otherwise?"

"Not as such. But their presence allows a name to be generated; this is in keeping with their predisposed functionality. Angels exist purely for the manifesting of functionality. Strictly speaking, it is not accurate to say they are 'around' you. It is more accurate to say they exist in dimensions *beside* you."

"And what about angelans then?"

Omis stares into my eyes in a most disconcerting way. Obviously, he means to make an impression here. *"You* are your *own* spirit guides, your own *guardian angels!* This you must know."

"I must? I am? Just what do you mean?"

"You serve your *self* throughout all evolution and the recursive nature that is built into our three *species-in-one*. From your perspective within the time game, the guardian seems separate, a distinct 'other'. But think about it for a moment. Feel about it. You will realize in this revelation that there really is no boundary. You and your guardian guides are on the identically same 'wavelength', so to speak. You resonate completely, eternally. You can know this. The guide is a parallel expression of your own being, returning like a mirror presence to provide the other half of your manifested life—the other half of the sky."

I respond, "You know, now that you say this, I remember having that revelation many years ago, during a spiritual, inner journey. I met my so-called 'guide' and *she* told me her name—Bernadette. I called her a 'guardian angel' at the time—a distinctly female presence. She explained that we had been generated from the same divine spark, from the very beginning, and that she was the etheric version of me. She said she mirrors me on the other side of the Veil; she called it a 'circular rainbow', half on her side and half on mine; I was her 'feet' and she, my 'wings', she said. I assumed she was talking about two distinct worlds in one timeframe. But given what you're saying now, it was the other way around—two distinct timeframes in *one world*."

"That is not incorrect. Timelessness brings it all back together—in one world. However, there is another aspect to angelan culture. It is the evolutionary one. We move through *Conscious Evolution,* just as you do. It is not from the same sense of time and timing, but it is with the same purpose and momentum, the same destiny: To return to Source. We are continually expanding our own awareness, as are you. We in fact do it together, with our species on the higher, nearer turn of the spiral; we link with you at the center point of forever."

Then it dawns on me. "You are *Green's* spirit guide! Correct? Why did he choose not to come with us on this journey? Why isn't *he* here, if *you* are?"

Omis laughs in response. "I am serving him now, by allowing him *not* to be here. He hears our words, along with all those watching; and he is realizing a few things for himself. Let it be so.

"Bear in mind, however, that we are not assigned, as guides, to only our own previous incarnations; we serve at will, anyone we choose, anyone who chooses us—including beings in the animal and plant kingdoms, if they are individuating. There are those among the vigilans, and even in human times, who would become etheric 'guides' during their sleeping hours—pre-cursors to moving into an angelan incarnation. Human dreamtime was a great training ground for awakening, as paradoxical as that may sound."

There is a natural pause suddenly. We all gather in our senses in response to it. I feel unbidden energies swinging up from within and below. They rush into my mind, demanding recognition. Something 'other' is coming.

In the hologram our view begins to lift above the gathered protesters, above the angels and angelans, above the whole Earth. We see great storm clouds and turbulence everywhere. Violent bursts of lightning and thunder rock our foundations. We can't help but be disturbed by this. The holographic sphere reaches out into us suddenly. We know, in this moment, that we're witnessing the energetic essence of the Great Storm. It is at full fury before our eyes and inside our minds.

Down we plunge now, through the crashing, churning etheric rain and wind. Great, violent whorls of mist turn into tornadoes and strike the trembling ground. Thousands of these vortices pound the Earth in every quarter. We recognize it is not a *physical* happening we witness. This storm is within the collective psyche of humanity; it is happening within each individual in the race. We have arrived at its pinnacle of tumult. The mist shatters and our vision abruptly races down upon the forms of a space—a man and a woman, sitting alone together in a room. All the vibrant electricity crackles into stillness.

The twin avatars! A 'streaming' tells us they have temporarily retreated to this private space, out of the focus of those many people who would claim their attention. It's a small living room. A fireplace is lit in front of them. Comfortable chairs and a couch face the fire. A few paintings adorn the walls near long drapes. The two look quite normal, carrying on an ordinary conversation; one is sitting on the couch, the other on one of the chairs; there is nothing about their appearance to indicate an elevated spiritual mission. But we are afforded a deeper understanding from our privileged perspective.

We sense a fount of compassion and character within them. Nevertheless, there's conflict here. We see that they are embattled by constant anxiety, from within themselves and pressed upon them from others—many others. Their natural inclinations of heart would be to withdraw into a simpler low-key lifestyle—the one they had lived during their *last* incarnation. This is not to be, however. Still they maintain a profound stability and confidence amidst the pressures and tensions. I feel in them, more subtly, the same peace and power the angelans have.

The precise faces and identities of these two are, once again, obscured from me. I understand it is because you don't want me to say, in this writing, specifically who they are. I sense that I *do* actually know these two, just as most people would. Yet, for now, a veil descends upon my mind. We listen in on their conversation:

The man smiles bleakly, sighing, "What is it they want this time? Why don't they let us do our jobs?"

"You know," the woman sighs. "It's *their* job to put us to the test—*every* test there is!" She chuckles grimly. "These are the times that try men's souls. They're putting themselves to the same test."

He does not reciprocate the humor. His eyebrows furrow and he asks, "When does it all end? I'm getting weary."

"You're not allowed to be weary. Not yet. Too many people are counting on you, on us. This is our job: to be counted on by many; and to be reviled by *just* as many." Again, her sardonic humor makes her smile.

The man smiles back this time. "I wish I had your sense of calm resolve."

"You do. You have *me!*"

He looks into her eyes deeply and whispers, "Thank you. You know, I keep having these dreams. I can't quite remember them, but I remember the feelings. They're inspiring and wonderful. I wish my waking life were like that."

"In those dreams we're truly awake. I have the same dreams. And I *can* remember them."

"Why can't *I*, then?"

"I've told you before: It's because we divided our labors. It is my task to remember, and to be the *grounding* for us; your task is to be the lightning rod."

He chuckles. "Well, I'm doing that part pretty well!"

They both smile. She reaches out and grabs his hand; then the smile falls into a serious stare. "Together we must hold the center point. This is where we are, and where we must remain until the end. Go ahead and have your doubts. It's the way this is supposed to play out; you know that on a deep level. Doubt fiercely, if you must. And then rise above it—in the same measure. You are setting the grand example for many people who feel similar doubts and fears in themselves, everywhere. Show *me* your doubts, not them. Show the people the way to *rise,* to wake up into inspiring dreams."

"I couldn't do this without you, not for one second."

"If you could remember the dreams, like I do, you would know the *real* truth of that statement. Of course you can't do this without me. I am you; you *are* me. We are *one being!* This is not for our rational minds to know right now. But I trust in my heart that it's true. I remember the dreams. They tell me this every night, every morning when I wake up."

He stands up, dropping her hand and turns away, toward the window. "I've heard you say that so many times, I'm starting think I *do* remember the dreams. Well, at least I remember the *feeling.*"

She continues, speaking to his back, "The day is coming when the arrows that target us will fall short; they will fail. Then, we will lift up our own arrows!

This battle will dissolve into history—along with those who attack us. Mountains will fall. And we will live up to our destiny."

The man frowns away from her against the glass. "I'm so worn down." He stares out at the night, the city. There are a thousand blinking lights across the black expanse. A fire siren wails from the distance, calling his senses into the dark. *Is there a fire there? Is there light?*

The woman moves quietly up behind him and lays her head on his shoulder; tears are on her cheek. The fireplace crackles softly. "We've been put here for a reason; it's what we must have signed on for. And I know we're protected by unseen forces; we are blessed and guided by angels. Were it not so, we would already be dead."

Silence hangs long in the air like overripe fruit. We are so drawn into the drama of the holo-image that we're startled when Omis breaks in. "This is the surface only, friends—a little, personal peek behind the scenes. Now, please look with deeper sensitivity at the next level."

Inside the bubble, our view expands beyond the room and its occupants. We see angelic forms, but not as many as in the last vision. This time there are only a few, standing like commanding guards around a fortress—a fearsome energetic image. The unbendable power of these beings is evident. They are *armor* incarnate. This is yet another face of angelans—the *warrior!*

Now we see other elements of the scene. Streaming and spiraling from beyond the energy fortress are two long channels of electricity, casting off small sparks all around, as they twirl. These sparks are not random. They have lives of their own, following the direction of some intelligence within the light beams. These lives are the same small creatures we saw around the protestors and soldiers before—sent out at intervals by the angelans. Judging by their intensity, there must be a great need for readiness.

I wonder why we don't see the same host of angelans as before. At once I receive a streaming answer. *This is the center of power for the Earth at this time. A direct intervention is demanded here. The host you witnessed before was a dilution. This is full strength engagement in* Conscious Evolution!

Our view now follows these electric spirals into a parallel dimension. To no one's surprise, we find Mihelo and Gavrea there, as resplendent as ever. They're filled with an immaculate luminescence. *The avatar was right to ask his question,* I think. *There* is *fire here*—and *light!* The high angels are standing in the center of two flaming vortices. Many colors spin through their auras. Barely visible webs of energy appear and dissolve. The two are busy, moving rapidly. Their arms and hands fly faster than we can see, in great mudras, reaching out; then in upon their breasts; then down into the space before them. Occasionally, the hands seem to grip invisible forms and hurl them aside, accompanied by brief squealing sounds.

All this is happening at blinding speed. The two incredibly powerful beings still maintain complete composure in the midst of it all. It is a feat of profound agility and elegance. They are drawing upon invisible forces and projecting strains of luminance and sound into the beams of light; they're like two synchronized conductors directing simultaneous symphonies of staggering intensity. We're afforded glimpses of the mudras, only when they pause amidst the swirl.

Suddenly the dynamic pair divides—each in two forms. The new duplicates project out toward us. While the original ones continue their symphonies, the new figures come straight out of the holosphere at us. Instantly they're huge, standing right here. They glance at Omis, expressionless; and yet we *feel* their expressions. Contrasted to the busy movement of their other forms, these two radiate the familiar peace and stillness we felt before.

Mihelo speaks in a soft-yet-booming voice, like someone talking low into a microphone. "You have been witness to the center of the Storm and the beings who hold that center. They are the avatars of your age, dear humans. We are compelled to say this: Respect their mission or perish! Hark! Many of your compatriots *will* perish out of their chosen blindness and disrespect. Honor and respect are due. Cast off your ego chains and let go the old ways.

"You may not understand the exact place of these two emissaries, nor the meaning of their actions, but do no harm to them; they are grand beings, who sacrifice for you, who are benedictions to your race. This we say with the authority granted. New ways demand new reverence; divinity lies in this. Your world has an unparalleled choice before it now. We stand at your sides and *at your back*, to propel you—those who choose their divine destiny. Come with us—into our new universe of light. Or regret your decision in profound darkness."

Gavrea allows a reverent silence to rise up for a time; then she follows it with her own message. "Welcome now to the new Earth. We are the beginning and the blessing of it into you. We are at one with your avatars. Sufficient numbers, there are, among your race at this time of apocalypse, to make your passage manifest. Know that *we* are the portal you seek, and the *newness* your destiny demands. Come with us now, before you allow another moment to fall away."

While the thundering of their two voices still echoes, the two figures sweep their arms in unison into the air. Sparkling ribbons of brightness follow the motion. The sparks hover for a moment; then they rush out into our auras, each of us; there they orbit for a time. At last, the swirl of sparks turns and dives straight into our hearts. I'm ecstatic, flushed with emotion. Reverence and desire rise up in me; I seek only to create and *serve* the new path. Then the two august creatures vanish, as swiftly as they arrived, back into the holosphere, back into their original forms.

We watch them re-merge themselves; the work of 'conducting' continues apace. Now our vision moves farther away; we see the entire Earth again, and the Great Storm. The sparks and beams shining out from Mihelo and Gavrea, are weaving a web of lightning everywhere through the Storm. It has become an intentional geometry around the planet. The sparkling web has myriad filaments and nodes at many different levels. I think of Invm. *He must love this.*

"I do," he whispers aloud at once.

The web in the holographic sphere finally connects around and into the Earth, ever increasing its intricacy. *And in many dimensions,* we are told inwardly. It tightens and releases, in a vast pulsing movement. The web seems to be absorbing the negative, turbulent forces of the Storm, and converting them into its own essence—force into energy, form into formlessness, rage into reconciliation. It seems to be feeding on the negative forces, growing its total self as a result. My mind reels at the realization: *This is my immediate future!* It's the energetic portrayal of my species' transformation—*yet another face of the portal.*

I begin to ask a question before I know what I'm saying. "Omis, are the avatars holding the center of the Great Storm?"

"Indeed, they are. There could be no other. Look around your world. There is truly no alternative to the leadership they provide. Even if you cannot guess their names, it does not matter. You know their presence by the gravitational and magnetic forces around them, and around those who stand with them. You will know them, as your scriptures all have said, 'by the *fruits* of their labor'.

"I will? What do I look for?"

"A word to the wisdom in you: Attend to the 'fruit' and not the labor itself—labor yields the growth of blossoms; blossoms wilt and fall away to make the fruit. Seeds and generations ensue. The sweetness shall be the key to your 'tasting' and comprehension."

I think, *He's sounding more like an angelan all the time.*

He doesn't respond to this thought, but adds, "And, strikingly, you may also know these gifted ones by those who oppose them. Watch carefully the divisions in your societies around the globe, around *them.* This is offering you clear choices for your future."

You touch my arm and add, "As we witnessed in the metaphorical 'Ends of the Earth', these avatars are truly, only ordinary humans. But they have returned to Earth from a state beyond human in order to transform your species. They are immersed now in *being* human. But they carry within themselves the seeds of profound evolution: your death and rebirth."

Black adds, "There is a center for any storm. The *Great* Storm needed a great center on Earth. This vortex manifested in two parts because of the extreme duality inherent in such a transition. All the amassed division, divisiveness and separation demanded it. Two was the perfect number for the end of your species, and for the end of the Dark Age. Your destiny and your *density* called it forth. These two exalted humans suffered massively for your race. Honor them."

Omis speaks in a low but powerful whisper, "In a time of great planetary and galactic stress, they led us through the Jaws of Hunab Ku."

B concludes, "Even their followers knew not the full import of their gift and their sacrifice. Such is the lot of being human, I'm afraid—ignorance and unconsciousness. Even at the heights of your appreciation, you miss so much."

Letter Sixty-One
Hierarchy of Conscious Expression

I look at Black and nod my head in agreement. "I know exactly what you're saying. I'm keenly aware of the value of appreciation, and yet I often catch myself not practicing it. When I realize I've lost it, I immediately pull back into the moment. That seems to work well; I always find something to appreciate."

You reply sympathetically, "That's only natural while you're incarnate. It's about living in duality. For humans, perception is an *on or off* situation. Humans needed to monitor themselves in order to be appreciative; they needed objects to focus their feelings. The more often you 'catch' yourself, the more aware you become—the less 'dual' you are. But it's not about quantity, it's quality that counts. Once you can appreciate something—a *thing*—in your environment, take the next step: Appreciate *without* an object. Feel the quality of the moment and hold *that* in your heart. Then when the object is removed, the appreciation will remain.

"When you look at others, appreciate the wholeness in them, not the fragmentary and temporary aspects. Allow their formlessness to shine through their limitations. It is for this reason you are enjoined to not judge others. When you judge, you're looking at a person's ego, the mere surface; and it's your own ego making the judgment. When you perceive more deeply, you open yourself to an immensity beyond the measure of ego-mind's understanding."

"You're so right, O," I reflect. "I recall sitting at a café recently, watching a street scene here in Paris. A stranger was on her cell phone, pacing back and forth, speaking loudly; it was an ordinary thing to witness. Yet in that tiny moment I had a transcendent realization. The woman was arguing with the person on the phone. But then, suddenly for some reason, I could feel her soul—just for a flash. I felt it as appreciation without an object, as you say: The issue was not *her* personal limitations, but the embrace of wholeness. That was enough to free me from my *own* limitations. Her soul was radiating all around her and within her, despite the surface ego. My making any judgment of her in this context would have been ludicrous."

Black responds, "The ego is entirely on the surface. This is what vigilans learned as we moved beyond the human stage. Your shallow surface reactions hid the real depth you possessed within yourselves. That depth was simply blocked—by a *thin* veneer. The depth is where appreciation lies, whence it derives. Once your genetic, ego blockage is removed, you will freely dive into the wellspring of your own being. This is what appreciation is, this *diving in*. It can happen at any moment for you. It is the moment that offers revelation. The Now. The diving platform is here."

Omis smiles and looks around. "And for you, Invm? What has been your experience of appreciation, coming from the Sirius system?"

Invm leans forward and nods acknowledgement. "We had the same revelations, of course. The soul knows no boundaries from one system or planet to another. We too had to overcome the limitations imposed by our egos. For us, it was even more entrenched, for a much longer period than for the Earth experience; but everything was more gradual for us.

"Our development was less dramatic. Even though it had great longevity, we realized in the end, how very thin the illusion of ego was in ourselves—a mere patina over true *being*. We did not have the Great Storm to aid us in sudden evolution, like on Earth. And yet, the Earth is enviable in its depth of feeling and emotion. While it obviously created many problems, emotional resonance with consciousness greatly aided the human transformation 500 years ago.

"From a purely technical perspective, the process on Earth rapidly drew *up* more karmic completion and drew *down* more intensity of grace. The interface between karma and grace was so powerful and focused that it brought unprecedented speed to Earth's transformation. It was truly unmatched anywhere in the galaxy that we know of."

Omis replies, "And I suspect you know the galaxy well. On Earth, we have experienced rapid acceleration indeed. Your course of ego transmutation was more the norm, from my understanding."

Invm replies, "Yes, but ego is ego—the same everywhere."

"Curious, is it not," comments Omis. "How similar each expression of ego is. Yet expressions of the soul are *unique!* Ego has no uniqueness, yet strives for that above all else! It seeks endlessly to be *special*, but never quite succeeds. That is, until it meets its own soul and surrenders. That which the ego has always sought was its own soul!"

I ask, "But egos certainly *think* they're unique, don't they?"

"They pretend they are," the angelan replies. "It's all on the surface. Uniqueness comes only from the depths. That is why the avatars were so misunderstood by most humans. They came from the depths, and people were looking mainly at the surface."

My mind returns to the avatars. "How did they manage to be at the center of the Storm, Omis? What did that all mean? What was their mission?"

"Your avatars were tasked with a simple assignment. It was to bring *simplicity* itself into awareness. Their job was not to accomplish great works of human ingenuity or to solve weighty problems, pressing on the minds of men. It was difficult for many around them, who wanted *performance* to be dominant. They thought all the injustices should be overturned—at the waving of a hand. They wanted to see the course of history reversed in a moment. It was wishful *thinking* superimposed upon insistent emotions. I emphasize the word 'thinking'.

"Power resides in *simplicity*—not in the complexities of thought. Here is an example: We can, in one *simple* streaming, understand all the problems of humanity as a complexity mask, generated by the collective ego to keep the soul at bay. What the ego sought—its own soul—was being held away by ego's fear of surrender. The simple, inspired presence offered by the avatars was thus a threat to the grand ego."

I sigh and ask, "Were the avatars ever in a position to truly satisfy the demands of humanity? Did the world really look to them as figures of power and influence?"

"Yes and no," he smiles. "They were popular at times and very well known, but they were also a disappointment to many. For some humans, they did not provide enough; for others they were doing too much, in the wrong direction. People knew there was something vitally important here, yet the ego structure refused to allow them to apprehend it.

"The heart of humanity sensed that these two were offering them a way *out* of the world of form. They presented themselves within the context of human enterprise and thereby disguised their true roles. They were seen to take action on many fronts, with many different types of people and organizations, and were generally at the hub of many projects and challenges. But their true gift lay within the heart of the human race, not on its surface. In the end, they fulfilled their mission entirely, masterfully; and they were eventually honored and loved as the transcendent beings they were. Mihelo's injunction was at last observed: the avatars were respected."

I squint and stir inside with a new concern. "Omis, *who* is Mihelo?"

I expect the old man to be evasive. However, he speaks directly. "Many knew him as the archangel Michael. He has gone by many names throughout the ages. By whichever name he is known, it is a manifestation of his power in that station. He is not, I should point out, an angelan. Neither is he an angel. He has a rank of reverence higher than the angels, lower than the Christos in terms of the spiritual, multi-dimensional hierarchy."

"Hold on for a second. May I ask what you mean by that? Many people in my time have an aversion to the word 'hierarchy'."

Omis looks to Black. She feels moved to answer this question. "It is understandable they would have an aversion. Throughout the ages many abuses were laid down upon humans under the label 'hierarchy', right up to your present time. It was a spiritual form, hijacked by dark forces, and turned into a force for coercion and constraint. However, there is a *spiritual* hierarchy of consciousness. It is not the linear, imprisoning form you see in your male-dominant, command-and-control paradigm.

"The spiritual hierarchy is based on a natural phenomenon of nature—that *each* is composed of the *other*, in endless cyclic turns of evolution, in endless levels of experience and expansion. It is the power of freedom and expression in ever more generous and proficient adaptations. When we use the word 'hierarchy', we understand by it the greater reality that energizes us."

"I'm sorry to digress further, B," I interrupt. "You mentioned the 'dark' forces, and it just occurred to me that I've never asked you about the colors you wear. Why do you wear black?"

"These are the emblems of my station in a progression of learning and exploration. I have not spoken of this to you, for it will not be brought to bear until your next life on Earth. You have sensed the relationship that Orange and I have had. I have been her mentor in the explorational field. I will be *yours* in your next lifetime. I will be your mother in that time."

My jaw drops. *I'm glad I thought to ask!* B smiles back and continues, "Your talent in Source gazing has been revealed to you, and to us all. In your next incarnation, you will begin your *training* under me." She raises her hand to halt my next question. "Enough of that subject for now. The colors I wear represent the work I do; they do not represent the dark forces; they often wear any *other* color, by the way. I concentrate on the Void, the exquisite, holy darkness of the depths. This will be *your* color in that next life. These robes are not simply black, however, as you have labeled them; there is much more to them than that. Take a closer look."

I'm surprised at what she says. *They look black to me.* But no; as I stare into them, as if for the first time, I see their depth; it's like holographic cloth. In it I can feel the Void. *I can see it.*

Suddenly, I slip into the emptiness. I'm gone and falling free, into another dimension. B is with me, holding my shoulders from behind, guiding my descent as though I'm a little child. *And as though she is my mother,* I realize. There on the Threshold, I *see.* I cannot yet describe it in this writing. There are no words for the essence that envelops me—from the inside. It is my future incarnation, welling up into being, straight up out of the Void, through the Threshold, *into* me. It's thrilling, wondrous and, again, indescribable. This upwelling basks in the light of a divine lineage, granted from ancient ages. I am at one with the Source. As usual, everything goes blank. I return, some infinite time-space later. I realize, *I will be able to put words to it before long, but not now.*

When I look up, Omis bows his head slightly and resumes the topic that has been interrupted. He says, "The archangels are direct manifestations of Source as it radiates its hierarchy of conscious expression into the world of forms, layer upon layer. Thus they are the embodiments of great energy. Their power is never surpassed in our realm, though they are very circumspect about applying it; they do not interfere unless firmly prompted to do so. Their missions are always directed from the center of peace and truth within themselves, within us all."

I'm still trying to process the Void experience, staring at B. She smiles serenely, but says nothing more. I look away and gradually shift back as best I can; I *have* heard what he said. "Um, so how do the archangels relate to angelans then?"

He answers, "They are our role models. And, mysteriously, we are theirs. Beyond the realm of time and form, we are merged with them. In duality expression, we have two distinct functions—and directions. Angelans represent *e*volution. Archangels and angels represent *in*volution; it has been called the deva kingdom. We occupy the same plane of being, embodying two interwoven *vector* fields. The angels express outwardly, downwardly from Source *into* the world. We, angelans, move inwardly and upward *toward* Source, *out of* the world. We meet and join in one overlapping cross-dimension."

I shake my head and let out an audible long breath. "You're the same-but-opposite? This is very unclear to me. Why am I so often confused by what you tell me?"

You, O, answer this time, "Everything in duality is either the same or opposite, or both simultaneously. You are confused because what we say is very new to your ears. It's only to be expected that you would not have the vocabulary yet to process many of these concepts. Just *allow* it into yourself. The vocabulary will evolve alongside your awakening. All of you will find this happening as you *allow.* The more you '*allow*' in your collective world, the more fully will the 'all' of Allah be manifested."

"Nice, O. Nice. I like the idea of 'allowing Allah'."

"I didn't make that up. It was inherent in Mohammed's message from the very beginning. The Arabic word 'islam' means 'submit', or 'surrender'; this is fundamental 'allowing'. This message was intended for *all.* But as with most prophets and avatars, a form-based—inauthentic—hierarchy captured the message and forced *it* to 'submit'. Spirit never acts by force, of course. Alas, under the regime of the human ego, it was inevitable."

Omis turns back to me. "Any further questions, my ego-friend?"

"Well, since you asked…" There are smiles of amusement at my eagerness to question. I too chuckle, but continue, undaunted, "OK. I'm curious about what kind of protection the angelans and angels gave to the avatars? Why did they need so much protection? How did that work? Oh, yeah, and were the avatars aware of the angelic interventions?"

Our host leans back in his chair and crosses his legs. *He looks just like a real person,* I'm glad to say. I find his angelan form rather intimidating. He grins and begins, "Their mission needed great assistance. This is obvious. The Storm demanded it. It was inevitable that they would end up at its center, and that *we* would end up pouring our attention into it. This is destiny. It was also destiny—in *density*—that the dark forces would focus on the same vortex. They were drawn to the Great Storm, like air is to a vacuum, as an opportunity to play *their* role."

I interrupt, "And just what *is* their role?"

"The dark forces are the duality reflection of the light. Underlying reality—Oneness—is composed of both, as you know. During the Great Storm, they assisted in bringing full attention to bear on the moment of transformation. You required a grand choice-point in *Conscious Evolution* in order to engage the mechanisms of awakening. Without the dark forces, you would not have been sufficiently stimulated to make the shift. It requires an enormous energy focus to propel an entire species across such a threshold, and to carry out the sweeping genetic mutations that developed. Such energy! You might profit to ponder the way the Earth holds onto her atmosphere, surrounded as it is by the infinite vacuum of space."

Omis takes a long breath and closes his eyes. He waves his hand toward me. "I will answer your other questions briefly before we move on. The protection we afforded to the avatars was all part of the grand scenario. The darkness was always threatening, from every quarter. They would indeed have destroyed and killed the avatars if they could. They certainly tried, and there were some close calls. Mostly, however, it was a concerted psychological and social assault, maintained over a long period. It gave all human souls the option to choose the old or the new universe as part of their process of awakening. A critical mass eventually made the choice to come with us.

"The way our protection worked was directly through the archangelic auspices. Their power was marshaled to the utmost around the avatars for an extended period; such an action had not been undertaken for 26,000 years. A sphere of energetic shielding was continually maintained and constantly reconfigured by Mihelo and Gavrea in order to counter the shifting directions of attack. This was the 'orchestration' you observed in the vision portal.

"Archangels are multi-dimensional beings, as are angelans. We are able to consciously manifest our forms in many places simultaneously, performing numerous functions at once. Thus, Mihelo and Gavrea were able to continuously attend to the protection and support of the avatars while fulfilling their voluminous other duties. You would call this 'omnipresence' from a time-bound perspective. However, we are operating free from those time constraints. From our view it is simply the one-presence in many forms. Time-space is one of those forms.

"As to whether the avatars knew of all the protection being offered, the answer is 'yes and no'. On the mental level, they did not. They only knew that they were in a dangerous situation and that they had faith in their destiny; they believed in potential spiritual interventions. They knew that if they stayed true to their course of working for the good of the whole of evolution, their mission would be fulfilled."

I interrupt, "If they were avatars, why wouldn't they know what was going on? Why didn't they have full knowledge of their predicament?"

Invm surprisingly answers this question, "The physical planes don't work that way. There is an exchange principle governing them—requisite within duality. The dynamic structures, themselves, channeling energies into the mind, create these limitations. The *constraints* in place are precisely equal to the *openness*. The soul has a choice, of course, about how to maneuver and balance within these constraints. My observation is that the avatars chose certain limitations in order to have freedom to act more powerfully within the physical dimension. This meant that they relinquished some awareness in so doing. Am I correct?" He looks to Omis.

The old man agrees, "Exactly. They were thus unaware of the specifics and magnitude of the operations. But they did not need this awareness to do their work. They needed focus, firmness and faith—which they possessed in great measure. With these attributes, the archangelic and angelan forces could perform their functions without inhibition."

Now Omis flexes his shoulders, revealing briefly his energy form—bright wings extended, aura cascading around us. Then he returns to the smaller, denser version. *I guess we needed that little refresher, as an energy boost.* He speaks again. "Now let us look into the portal one more time."

The sphere glows brightly and settles down to another image. It's one familiar to me. Before us, I'm sitting with a friend in a restaurant. The place is bustling with youthful energetic forms. People are enjoying themselves, talking, eating, drinking. Music plays in the background. I remember being there recently; I was commenting to my friend that the young people around us are subtly different from my own, older generation. He is young himself and does not quite understand my observation.

I try to explain, looking around at various faces in the room. There is a softness and humbleness to them that was not yet evolved fully in my own youth. He shakes his head and replies, "I think you're just imagining things." I don't persist in trying to convince him. He has grown up in the new context. He can't resonate with mine, the one from the older age. *Evolution is happening right before my eyes,* I realize.

As we look upon the scene in the bubble, our view is directed toward many of the individual faces around the restaurant. In each one we see a unique expression of the unfolding consciousness. Each is fresh and uninhibited by certain ego structures of the past. While these individuals are not actively aware of the change they represent, there's a presence in them moving forward into the world. To a person, they have an *uncertainty* about their role. This is not surprising. Yet along with this uncertainty comes a feeling of newness and wonder. They are releasing their fears by feeling them in the presence of others, sharing the open unknown before them.

We pull back from the holo-globe and look at Omis. He explains, "Your observation was true. You were seeing clear signs of the mutation happening within humans. These young individuals are on the very verge of shifting beyond human, though they do not even suspect it. As you have been told, many early vigilans did not immediately realize they had changed. The world required a different vocabulary, a new, full generation before its significance could be understood. Nevertheless it was happening. Evolution was and is becoming conscious in your time!"

Letter Sixty-Two
You Are the Unknown

Omis stands ceremoniously, and assumes his angelan form; he raises his arms high above us. In a simple sweeping gesture, he draws a glossy membrane down, dividing you and me from Invm and B. He says in a theatrical voice, "I will now divide my time presence in two parts, and take Black and Invm on a little journey. At the same time I will take you two on a different journey."

I manage a little humor, even amidst the drama. "Are you trying to show off, Omis?"

He laughs and agrees, "Of course. I'm *playing* with my newborn powers, and *practicing* them too. We will all come back together in a bit and share our observations." He then dissolves swiftly into the air around us, and transforms into our environment. *Fascinating.*

I'm suddenly not there anymore; I'm back in my own time and space. I look around hurriedly, not quite sure what to believe about where I am. "O, what's happening?" The two of us are sitting in a café in Paris, in my own, present time. I speak low, across the table to you, "That was sudden. Did you know this was coming?"

You look relaxed, your auburn hair glowing in the low lights of the restaurant. Large windows reveal the sidewalk full of passing strangers around us. Your silver eyes meet mine before you speak. You look like a trusting little girl, open to any new adventure, as you answer. "Not exactly. Omis is now more angelan than ever. And, you know, angelans have always been unpredictable. This shift doesn't really surprise me. I knew you were in Paris; and I knew you needed a break."

I nod. "How do you mean, I 'needed a break'?"

"You've been *doing* a lot—that is, 'doing' more than 'being', if you know what I mean. That's understandable in your situation, what with moving to a foreign country and all. Your translations were becoming a little erratic and uneven—like your French," she chuckles. "Your friends who are reading these draft letters have noticed it. Have they not?"

I feel a little ego twinge, not wanting to admit to any shortcomings. I smile at the knot in my mind. I reply, rubbing my forehead, "Yeah. They said something about it. And I guess I knew too. It's just that I wanted to keep on pushing through, and get this done. You know, I'm in Paris after all—for only three months. I'm here to write. Right?"

"You don't have to *force* it." I sense that you're realizing this is just another little example of how the ego clings to its sense of importance. "Let's have a glass of wine. Relax. It's good that you've taken a week or two off from the writing. With all your travel and arranging and adapting, *c'est normal, alors!* [It's only natural!] "

I look around the charming, dimly lit restaurant. It sits on a sloping corner in Montmartre, not far from the apartment I've rented. It's one of my favorite places in the neighborhood; it looks so *'Parisien'.* A familiar song is playing on the radio. We decide to order *un demi-pichet*—a half carafe—of the house *Côte du Rhone.* It's a simple, delicious wine.

You lift your glass and take a sip. "I've observed enough of the way ego performs by now, to know that it takes much vigilance for you humans to slip out of its grasp. I did not mean 'vigilance' as a pun," you laugh softly and stare into my eyes. "Well, perhaps I did."

You continue with a clear expression, "One can look at this ego problem as a 'battle' if one wants to, or else 'play' with it, like a game of hide-and-seek. Either way it's quite a challenge, I'll admit. My 'vigilant' pun, of course, reveals a truth behind the human dilemma. Basically, it's a reminder of the need to be alert and watchful of your individual evolution. Your persona is gradually being unmasked.

"Yet the ego knows all your secrets. It flows along with your conscious-ness everywhere you go; sometimes it seems to sleep, sometimes it jumps into an opportunity to 'defend' you. Your human insecurities—not trusting the un-known—leave you vulnerable, available to be *defended.* When you feel uncom-fortable, stressed or lonely, for example, ego looks around and sees a chance to *help* you escape and *separate* your mind from the moment. It wants you to keep relying on *it,* rather than just accepting 'what is'. It offers you a distancing mechanism."

I sigh, "I know this all too well, being here in this beautiful-but-sometimes-lonesome city. There are moments when I'm delighted by just being here; and then there are others when I start to be depressed by all the challenges. I'm not all that comfortable in French, yet I insist on immersing myself in the local situation, in cafés and bistros, and in the language itself. It's a lot of work! It always has the risk of pushing me to feel not accepted or different."

"Precisely. That's the role of the ego. For you, it is not a character that ris-es up and storms around boastfully. Yours is a more subtle stage in ego-evolution. Your *persona mask* is gradually growing thinner as you begin to awak-en. The thinness is what enables you to notice the ego more readily, say, if it tries its more aggressive behaviors. The ego, in turn therefore, evolves and learns to become subtler. It learns from your own conscious presence, stride

SIXTY-TWO: YOU ARE THE UNKNOWN

for stride. That's very good in the end, because this subtlety makes the mask even thinner.

"The ego cannot win ultimately. It strives to imitate your true presence, in order to hold your attention—or perhaps to fool you. It sincerely does want to protect you and to be of service, as strange as this may seem. It desires to be more and more like the soul. It has always wanted this. In reality, consciousness is the only model it has for its behavior.

"For generations ego has been in control, while your awareness slept. But it was always unconsciously imitating consciousness. Within its limitations, defending you was the only form of assistance it could imagine. It recognized that *power* exists for the soul; the imitation of power is *control*. This was ego's option of imitation."

I nod and take a slow swig of wine.

You continue, "Now, as your need for defenses dwindles, as you awaken to the fact that defensiveness itself is keeping you from the full blessing of awakening to the unknown Source, ego has to change. To keep pace with your expansion, the ego too has to expand; it has no choice."

I interrupt, "An expanded ego sounds like a more *dominant* ego."

"It sounds that way. And indeed the ego may dream that it will be so. But it can no longer generate enough of its old substance in the new, evolving atmosphere of consciousness. As it expands to compete with true awakening, it only grows thinner, like the surface of a balloon that is over-inflated."

You move your hands wide apart to simulate the expansion of a balloon, then continue, "To follow this analogy, you are left with two possible outcomes: Either the balloon bursts, or it gradually deflates through the thinner membrane. If you *battle* the ego, as some would have you do, you create hostility and tumult; alternately, if you *play* with the ego, it will gradually dissolve—a much gentler approach. I advise the latter."

I nod, exhale audibly, and set my glass on the table, feeling a light buzz from the alcohol. "Me too. I would definitely choose that too. But I'm always nervous about not catching myself quickly enough before an ego explosion."

"A little nervousness isn't a bad thing. Feel it, and let it stimulate your attention. Just don't let it *feed* your ego. The idea for you, and those at your stage of awakening, is to stop feeding the ego. You do this by vigilance, by continuously catching yourself and by *playing* instead of battling. By vigilant, I do not mean a strict disciplinary attitude. Strict discipline moves you away from awareness. Awareness is not discipline!

"Whoa. Come again." I lean back in my chair. "I thought it *was*. Don't many spiritual, uh, 'disciplines' advise otherwise?"

"Yes, they do. This is an ancient model that worked well at earlier stages of development. And it still works for some today. But as humans begin to actually awaken—that is, when the Veil of Illusion begins to fall—you are ready for a more mature and integrated method. You are ready to allow the soul itself to move through you. This is *vigilance*. It is wakeful allowing and acceptance. Vigilance replaces discipline."

You sip casually from your glass and continue, "Discipline is ultimately *divisive*; it separates you from essence. It creates a 'structure' that you must climb over to get to where you already are. It relies on the notion that you must *learn*. The root of the word, discipline, is 'to learn' in Latin. This practice assumes you are inadequate to grow without the imposition of additional knowledge and obedience to some external authority structure."

"Wait. What about *internal,* self-discipline? That's not an *outside* authority."

You counter, "The thinking *mind* is what I'm talking about. It is indeed 'outside' from the perspective of the heart and soul. Discipline is a *mental* function, linked to the external world; it is basically a kind of resistance and constraint. How can this serve your awakening? Learning happens in the mind, not in the heart. The heart lives only in the Now, where *knowing* exists, outside of time.

"The soul needs no learning. It only needs revealing and experiencing. This is the Apocalypse, remember—the Revealing. The mind, yes, needs discipline and learning. Any physical, form-based function requires discipline. But we are moving beyond form now, into the formless, the unknown. The mind and *its* needs will not serve you here. To move forward now, you must release and allow—from your heart. To attempt to discipline your heart will only defeat your intentions toward soul maturity. It will only place reliance back into the province of the ego."

I scratch my head and look briefly around the room at other customers arriving. "But I still think of being vigilant as a form of discipline."

"The mind will see it that way, yes. If you choose to do battle with the ego, then discipline would be right up your alley. But beware, and be aware. That alley is where ego lives; it is a dark alley, full of mistrust of the unknown. It is the passage where force wants dominance over power and freedom. 'Yea, though I walk through the valley of the shadow of death, I will fear no evil.' These beautiful words from the psalm, from Source itself, lead one to let go, to allow and release, not to grasp and struggle.

"Is that the *alley* of the shadow of death' you mean?" I laugh, rather irreverently. But you join me with a grin. I quickly add, "Sorry. Yes, that psalm is incredibly beautiful and full of grace. In fact, I've often thought of it as one of the greatest pieces of counsel ever written."

You continue, "For the heart, *vigilance* is being alert *without* discipline. It is allowing the moment to guide you, while staying centered in your own deeper presence. It is relaxing and appreciating; this is the opposite of strictness and obedience. There is no force or difficulty involved. The word, vigilant, comes from Latin too, meaning 'keep awake'. Is this difficult for the mind? Indeed it is. Awakening is *not* for the mind. It is for the soul that is being born inside you, in the new species."

I look around again at people arriving for the typical late Parisian dinner. The noise level is rising, fueled by various beverages. Amidst the clamor, strangely, I find a space to ponder. I am silent for some time. Then I ask, "O, tell me about the new species again. Everywhere I look in the world today, I see the same old tired ego games. I'm afraid I don't see much 'evolution' going on. I just see a huge distance between the average human and the *awakened world* of your people. How can such an enormous gulf be crossed between you and me? How can there be enough time?"

You sip and ponder now, savoring the noisy space. "This is the great question, isn't it? As I sit here in this sub-dimension in your time, I too can ask that question. How can I even exist? Will there be enough time for evolution to work? Where did my race come from?"

I look up into your gaze, a bit surprised. Then you reply to your own question, "Of course the answer to the last question is simple: We came from *you,* from the *heart* of you. What existed already deep within your being, came forth and cast off its accumulated, encrusted ego baggage. Vigilans are, in a real sense, merely *stripped-down humans.* With ego removed, your essence was revealed in us: And your essence *was* us! You were carrying us within you all along."

"Go on," I urge with growing interest and order another *quart pichet.*

"The upheaval and struggle you witness in your world is, in fact, the birth of *our* world. The bitterness, divisiveness, the fear and violence that seem to go on ceaselessly, is a statement that the evolving ego is making to your broader awareness. It is saying 'Look at yourself. Wake up.' Like the script in a science-fiction movie, the bad monsters from the past have to have their day—until they *don't* anymore.

"Unwittingly, the collective ego boasts, 'See what I can *still* do? Do you think you can awaken while I'm still alert?' Ego challenges us with this taunt, because it truly wants to be the enlightened presence, to be vigilant. But it can achieve that goal only through its own sacrificial *death.*"

I frown. "The ego wants to be *vigilant?*"

"Yes. The ego wants that, to be sure; but it interprets vigilance as *defensiveness.* Over its lifespan it repeatedly copies the soul's ways—without knowing where this is leading! It imitates the soul, hoping to preempt natural evolution. But this is the end for the ego. It rushes ahead, driving and conniving, unconscious of deeper processes at work within the human soul; as a consequence it moves, unsuspectingly, toward its own dissolution. That dissolution brings in the *era of consciousness.*"

"It sounds like you're saying the ego *reincarnates,* along with the soul."

The bustle of the café continues around us. You slowly nod. "That is a curious phenomenon. The natural evolutionary state reasserts itself in the progression of human lifetimes; it does produce a renewal of the ego imperative life after life. This can be called a form of reincarnation, I suppose. But the ego does *not* have a life after death, in the spiritual domains. Technically, it generates anew in each lifetime—until it *doesn't* anymore."

I respond, "Very strange. I do sense a lessening of my own ego. But it keeps reasserting itself. It doesn't want to stop. Is there anything I can do to hasten its passage?"

"Simply retract the *independence* of your ego. Own it again. *Notice* it fully; do not *resist* or fight it; and make your presence truly *authentic* within it—*within* the separated self. This is tricky business; so be alert: Unconsciousness can sneak back, if you unwittingly allow its *independence* to return. It can even re-enter through your intuitive revelations, at the threshold where you begin *thinking.* This is how religions were formed, creating *dogma* based on revelation. I advise: Make ego *dependent!* Say this to your little self: 'Ego independence stops here. Now *soul* rules!'

"I know that, across your world, you are witnessing insane wars, the actions of greedy corporations and ego-bound dictators clinging to their illusions of independence from Source. You see people dying and suffering in cruel and horrendous ways. What appears from your timeframe to be a hopeless, endless rehash of hatred and recrimination against your own species self is really the *breaking* of the mirror of illusion. The jagged, dangerous shards of glass fall all around. But in so doing, they reveal what had, up to now, been hidden—the *emptiness* lying behind the self.

"The secret, silent awareness abiding within all of your kind, has the presence, at last, to recognize what it could not see before—the *emptiness.* All that you needed was this final burst of shattering, exploding, deflating ego to trigger your *presence* into the world. This is what you now see on the collective, global stage."

I bow my head and shake it. "I don't know, O. I sure hope you're right. I guess most souls have opted to *battle* the ego; that's the Great Storm, eh? Even the most enlightened spiritual teachers of my time are saying we may not make it; humanity might not survive."

"I've told you before that humanity does *not* survive these times. It will indeed *perish* amidst the wreckage and the breaking of the mirror. Humanity *is* the mirror; it is the illusion. The mirror must be broken! The soul has incarnated all these centuries into an illusion—a grand one. This is what the apocalypse is all about—the soul is waking up. You and your fellow souls are awakening from your own illusion. It is about pulling down the Veil that has hidden the soul from itself all these lifetimes.

"You can only see bits so far from where you are. Your species is still shrouded by that Veil. Even though it is thinning, it still constitutes the self-centered, form-identified nature of humanity. You have to have misgivings about what I'm telling you. I would urge you to *doubt* my words profoundly in fact. This profundity of doubt is another trigger for growth in your time. It is another mechanism for breaking the mirror. 'Experience it all,' I counsel. Yet do not be trapped by those experiences of doubt and fear. Slice through them with the sword of vigilance. *Use* your fears and *play* with them; always rebound into the awareness of who you really are."

"OK. And *who* would you say am I? I mean it. Really."

The café seems eerily silent for a moment. I echo the question in my thoughts. It's a question that never stops asking itself in my mind. I look seriously at you. You reply, "Here's what you are: You are the unknown. The Source. You cannot be named or placed within a thought that the mind can digest. You are formless and endless—an unspeakably vast principle of Life, ranging throughout the Cosmos, condensing down into windows—portals— of experience and identity, as individuals and groups and races. You inhabit planets and stars and galaxies. But what you really are is so far beyond these forms as to be incomprehensible in the language of your current conditioning. *What* you are far exceeds *who* you are!"

"Oh," I mumble, feeling the gravity of what you say.

You chuckle, pausing your oratory. "So don't be discouraged by 'false evidence appearing real'. Look through the chaos and tumult of the Great Storm, into the eye of greatness that you *are*, in your heart. That is vigilance! Your species is *dying* to reveal mine. It is laboring and wrestling within itself to the utmost right now. This is truly glorious. What a time to be alive! What a time to die!"

I set my glass down. I've been clutching it fiercely all the time you've been talking. I look up into your eyes and feel the earlier question returning. "So, what about this 'break' I need? And the distance I've been feeling from my work?"

You reach over and touch the back of my hand with your long, slim fingers. I think, *Uh-oh!* But nothing happens. You say softly, "You know, you don't *have* to do this." The energy in your touch is icy, stopping my blood.

I squint. "What do you mean? I don't have to do *what?*"

"Write this book."

"Come again," I gasp, pulling my hand away quickly.

Suddenly there is a young woman being ushered to a seat next to us; the space is a cramped French bistro. Her attempt to squeeze into the tight passage causes an empty glass to fall off the table. It shatters on the hard tile floor, and makes an unwelcome noise. This is followed by embarrassed looks from around the room. The café takes a deep breath into silence. Seconds later, people turn back to their social business, and the blanket of chatter and anonymity gradually returns. The waiter, annoyed, brings out a broom and cleans up. The woman blushes and apologizes.

"Did *I* make that break?" I sputter, in a low voice, an intuition rising.

"Yes, of course. You're creating this whole subdimension. Relax. It's all part of your scene."

I turn my empty glass with my fingers, gazing at it thoughtfully before looking up at you. "My *scene?* What's that? And what do you *mean,* I don't *have to* write this book? I'm half the way through it already."

"Remember, I told you our mission was accomplished and done with the *first* book. If this letter writing is too stressful, we could switch over to another timeline if we wanted to. There we would only have *one* book. I'm sure Omis could arrange that for us."

"Wait. No. I *want* to write the book. I don't know what you're talking about. Do *you* want me to stop writing it?"

Now another commotion erupts. The waiter drops a small plate of *pommes frites* in exactly the same spot where the glass broke a few minutes before. It too shatters. I jerk around and look at you. You're smiling.

"OK, O. Please help. What do I need to do to I keep anything else from breaking?" I gulp. "Are we talking about me 'breaking' the books?"

"You needed a 'break', remember."

"O my god, O, you're sitting there *joking* about this?"

You look at me calmly as the waiter sweeps up again; this time, *he's* the one who's embarrassed. "It's all part of your scene. You *are* the scene here—you, plus the customers *and* the waiter—like in a dream. All of you are the poets and the playwrights."

I stop and center myself for a moment, feeling the wine's palliative effect. I look into your eyes, searching for some stability. You gaze back and send me an energy stream. *This is good.* I relax, smile and take a deep breath. I slowly survey the 'scene'; the place is calmer, quieter now. *I'm* calmer. There *does* seem to be a linkage with my sensibilities.

You begin again, "That's better. Now, about your scene: Surely, you must realize that your stay Paris is a *scenario* in your life."

I sigh, "Well, I sort of get that, but what do you mean by a 'scene'? This is also my *reality* right now."

"Yes—as much a reality as any dream can be. Of course, when you reread this incident five months from now, how real will it be? What I mean by a 'scene' is what Shakespeare and company meant: 'All the world's a stage. And all the men and women merely players; they have their exists and entrances.' And more than mere players; we are the playwrights too. Your *scene* is what your conscious being is drafting into it in the moment. The script is always generated as it is acted—by your soul, by *our* soul, my friend. Later then, it is transcribed into time and form. The real question here is *'when* do you exist? When do you exit?'"

"O, I'm sorry. This is all too bizarre. I don't understand why you're being so mysterious. *Must* I exit?"

"We all must exit and enter. Curious, don't you think, that Shakespeare placed the word 'exit' first? You are crafting your exit from this lifetime here, dear one. No. Don't be alarmed. It's not happening right away, and certainly not on this trip. But, you know—you're coming to know—just how short a lifetime is. Every one of these people sitting around us here, you and me included, are vapors in the breeze. We pass through swiftly and silently—out of one scene and into the next."

"So why did Shakespeare place 'exit' first?"

"Because as we exit we know our scene. Until then we are unknown."

I sigh and realize the depth of feeling your words convey to me. *Yes, this is all so poignant. We're all swiftly passing through, leaving no real traces in the end, except what we've written into our souls.* You hear my thoughts and nod.

"It is touching and sad." You pause to reflect. "You know, the French have a word I would prefer to use here. It is *tristesse.* It can mean simple 'sadness'. Yet it can also mean something more subtle and existential. There's a poetic line I recall in French: *'triste comme un bonnet de nuit'*—[sad like a bonnet of night.] We all write our scripts with a good measure of this emotion. Feel it, here, in the midst of conviviality and life."

I do feel it, perhaps even more because of the lively atmosphere. It's such a contrast of emotions. Together the two polarities round out the scene and wrap it in that sweet, dark 'bonnet'.

You whisper, just loud enough for me to hear, "This is what you're scripting. You're designing it all to be just the way it is—from deep levels of consciousness. You are making it mysterious, troublesome, uncertain, *triste*—and with breaking dishes." You wink lightly and I look away.

"All right. Suppose I *don't* quit writing this damned book, how do I get back on track, into alignment? I need inspiration here, not platitudes!"

"My friend, inspiration can come in platitudes or in breaking dishes. Look for it in whatever form it is served."

I put my hands flat on the table and try to understand what you're saying. *Read between the lines.* Sudden laughter erupts from a far corner; it interrupts my thoughts. *There's inspiration everywhere, even in breaking dishes, even in the laugher of strangers.*

"No one's a stranger," I pronounce aloud, to my surprise. "Everyone here is a player on the stage, doing their parts, our parts—my script, their script. We don't really know it's a play most of the time. But I *do know* right now somehow! Each person is writing his or her own script, just like I am. Somehow we manage to synchronize all our different scripts—except when we don't. Maybe that's when things break?"

You answer, "No. That's when things *really* synchronize. Breaking a glass in a crowded room is a point of focus and synchronicity for everyone. Each person, for that moment, is totally alert and present."

I reply, "Yes. I see. So, what am I supposed to do about it? What's next? I'm not going to stop writing the letters—unless you order me to."

"Don't worry. I don't give orders. Somehow, I didn't think you'd want to stop. I just wanted to make the offer." You smile mischievously. "So, shall we order our dinner?"

Letter Sixty-Three
Three Last Suggestions

We finish our meal in pleasant banter, enjoying the rare opportunity to be together alone, relaxing. No more dishes have been broken. I pay the bill since you are not carrying any money. *Is this a vigilan setup, or what?* I smile, knowing you're probably catching my thought. We stroll out into the peaceful evening. It's neither warm nor cold—a temperature typical of Paris, I've found. People pass us leisurely in the street, speaking in quiet voices, chuckling, wandering like we are.

You look to me as we walk, and say, "I'd like to revisit an old theme of ours, if you don't mind."

"Which old theme would that be? I can think of a dozen of them off the top of my head."

You smile, dipping your head forward for a moment. "The three suggestions."

"Ah, yes," I react. "You have more to say on that subject? I'm always amazed at how you can keep expanding those. Who would have thought you could find so much in something so simple."

You accidentally brush my hand with yours. I feel a subtle touch of electricity. You say, "Simplicity is the origin of depth. The deeper we go, the simpler we get. Truth is ultimate, pristine simplicity at its core."

I look at you. "I feel what you're saying must be true, but I can't really get my mind around it. Maybe I never will understand."

"Not with the 'little mind'; no," you say. "That mind craves complexity. But as we have mentioned before, there is another level in your nature, a greater mind—*manas*. It is the model for the narrow mentality you know and love. *Manas* is the *essence* of intelligence; little mind is intellect. You will feel its presence and think *its* thoughts gradually more and more as you step into awakening. In this mind, you *will* understand."

"Will I ever actually wake up, O? I have my doubts. That notion still seems like just a dream."

You laugh, "Hah. Awakening seems like a *dream?* That's a good one. Remember what the avatar said: 'In those dreams we're truly awake.'"

I whine, "From the human perspective, awakening seems so unlikely. Our egos are so embedded, so woven into our minds, our sense of self."

"Indeed," you reply. "That's why we advise getting out of your minds and out of your 'self'. Your true awareness isn't trapped there. It's only visiting, sleeping in this dream of who your mind *thinks* you are. It has everything upside, believing *it* is awake and your true consciousness is a dream. The mind is hopelessly threaded into the fabric of ego. It's true. This form of mind is passing out of your existence now. That is the species' death we have spoken of. As you pass through that, you will soon be able to put your attention in the 'other' awareness, beyond the mind as you know it.

"Listen, I do understand what you're going through." You take my hand intentionally this time. Sparks fly across my eyes. I feel a sudden rush of clarity in my head; my mind seems to be opening out into a space much greater and clearer—not encumbered by my ego. Understanding of what you're saying arrives into me as a flood.

My awareness flows down with it into the mind, interwoven with ego veins and psychic cobwebs. It follows them, reversing their polarity and infiltrating the whole with a cleansing wash of brilliance. It feels like I'm thinking and sensing simultaneously, but in a way very different from either. It's all inside out from the way I normally think. It's a resonance with the roots of the universe, not just the surface. It fills me with sacred satisfaction. I know suddenly that the depths are pure and empty of any clutter from above, from where my thoughts normally reside. This is the simple essence of understanding!

I look up, sighing, and sigh again, "Thanks for that, O. I know I can't hold onto this awareness right now. Will I ever feel it again?"

"Yes, of course. Your awakening will accelerate considerably once we finish this '*damned* book' of yours."

"You know I didn't really mean that." I blush.

"Well, why not express your emotions? Feel what you feel, dear human. We need you to continue *being* human for this period. It's the only way we can make our linkage across time. Without your humanity and your ego, this entire project would have been impossible; and besides, there would have been no need for it. The collective, collapsing human ego is the driving force within a vast awakening for both our species. I suspect, from what Omis has said, that it's vital for the angelans as well."

We turn a corner and find some steps leading up, steeply, onto the butte of Montmartre. You're obviously ready to resume the topic of the three suggestions. "I will proceed in a different order this time. That seems to fit our conversation better. First suggestion: *Feel your authenticity like never before.* Feel it as the purity and simplicity that it is, as a way of knowing the depths of your be-ing. Those depths lie rooted in the immeasurable, unknown Source that we all are. It is immense and simple. It is wholeness and Oneness.

"Know, thus, the *unknown.* Let this paradox come alive in you. It will be opening the channels of Life itself. All is one in this realization. Come forth from here into all your world, into all you do. Bring the sacred into living. This is what you've been missing, every one of you. The doors can come open wide when you find the place of authenticity within.

"To find this place is to meet the Source halfway. You reach in, and it reaches out in one act. It empowers your reach as it comes forth. Yet you, the individual spark, must play your part. To play is to write your *scene.* Feel the script in your hands as you act out your dramas of life; look behind the scene to the forces at play within you, creating your actions and dimensions at all times. You must believe it is *you* who is seeking and making the approach.

We have climbed the long stairway, near the top of the butte. I'm panting. You, however, are speaking without strain. I don't bother to wonder about this anymore. This is, after all, like a dream of awakening. Your words are carrying me into a very detached state.

You glance back down the way we've come, appreciating the view, and continue, "I know this may sound contrary to what I've said before, but listen through, and do not judge. From this state of *belief* and *seeking,* you make your start. Take the first step *out of unconsciousness.* You make your choices and set your intention to bring the Oneness into the outer form. Every action you take from here on is an action based upon Oneness. Every form that you ever man-ifest or encounter, is filled with the formlessness of your true being.

"This is the sacred. This is what it means to be *authentic,* and to be the true author of your script. You—each and all—crave the sacred in your lives. You know deeply that it has been missing for ages. Yes, many of you have had pas-sages in the light, flashes of inspiration and revelation. These are all good. But they are only the bait, drawing you in like a fish that wants to be caught.

"Once you taste this bait, this sharp hook in your mouth, you are pierced with sudden knowing. This knowing strips away the belief systems and the endless seeking. You have made the second step; the first one—belief—is abandoned. You have discovered the 'straight and narrow path', spoken of in scriptures—the needle and its point. You have allowed pure, straight simplicity to inject itself into your troubled blood.

"Every action, in reality, is authentic and sacred, as is every moment. If you would find the sacred, *accept* the sacred. Only the misperception that it is *not* holy brings in your distress. Learn to look at life as blessed; turn it to Life. You may use the mind for this part. It can understand the elementary layers of sacredness. Let it *learn*. This will be an opening. Let that opening work within you—deeper than thought and learning. The *thought* of sacredness is not false; it is only limited. But it taps into truer depth.

"Accept it. Dream about it, as I know you have. Taste its sweetness and salt, its bitter, sour and pungent. Let this dream not escape into blandness. Sit still with your authentic, sacred being. It is how you come into the world. It is your continuous, endless *birth*. The *eternal beginning* is your sacred Source. This is the Now. It never stops being born—as you yourself even, never stop entering into your life. With each breath, you come to the world anew— reconstructed, revitalized. And so, formless being creates all forms. This is your authentic mission."

You look over at the curving streets and then out at the delicately glistening city that we have brought into view. Together we take a deep breath of the clear air. You continue, "The five senses define our creations in form. But this is not limited to mere seeing, hearing and touching. It is rooted in basic, universal *sensation,* underlying all form expression; it connects directly from Source.

"*Sensation* is Oneness feeling itself into our senses. Some have called this the sixth sense or the root portal. Through this portal, we admit Source to live and breathe in us. Why do this?" You pause for effect. "Because if we are not bringing forth Source into our lives, we are admitting *resistance:* In the absence of Source there is *only* resistance.

"So, Source awareness reaches the planes of incarnation through sensation and sense—through the mystical 'one' and 'five'."

"Thank you," I answer. "I've wondered about those numbers. I see now that you're saying 'five' is the number of our senses; and 'one' connotes our primary *sensation*."

"That is so; it is a two-way path—into and out of duality. Source expresses outwardly into complexity. In the other direction, complexity evolves back into the simplicity of Source through the same portal. The vast cosmic process is identical with the individual, local one: Source—the One—expresses itself into each of us through this means. Source is the Prime Individual."

"I think I understand. But I have a small question: You've told me to allow and accept the moment as it is. Is this what you mean by 'admitting' Source into ourselves? But then you say, '*don't* admit resistance'. This is probably just a semantic thing."

You reply casually to my question, "I have advised you to admit 'what is' into your awareness; if resistance is what you're feeling, allow it. But be not *persuaded* by it; do not act according to its dictates. Retain your authenticity, the authority of your presence."

The view of the city is soft and dark, spread on a wide, soft canvas. Lights twinkle everywhere below; the red taillights of cars weave in strings along the fissures between buildings. *Have I created this? Is it part of my script? I guess so, in some mysterious way. My brain creates the images my eyes see, composing them out of nerve impulses and electrochemicals. This, at least, I create.*

"Originally, the word 'admit' it meant 'to put into'. When you *admit* a thing, you play an active role; you invest your presence. When I advise you to *not* admit resistance, I'm saying don't invest your energy into resistance. What you *put in,* you will experience. Resistance is contrary to authenticity, contrary to Source. Paradoxically, however, I would advise you to put your authenticity into any resistance you feel."

"Paradox indeed." I frown. "What could you possibly mean by 'putting authenticity into resistance'?"

"Coming to resistance from the direction of authenticity, it looks different. Your approach is different. Truthfully, there is no letting in or sending out. This is illusion. We project, but do not send forth spirit into creation. The heart is the lodging place of our presence. Energy in all the Cosmos is the same, one identity—divine heart and Source; it neither comes nor goes. Forms come and go, not spirit, not energy. Formlessness remains unchanging, lying at the motivating center of all change. The moment is pure stillness and yet it is the engine of all momentum and motion.

"'How can this be?' I ask, thinking of the electricity in the lights below. "Aren't we always sending out energy into the world?"

"What is sent forth is the projection, the *project.* Remember? Information, not energy, moves the Cosmos. Energy is ever-present, everywhere at one with Source. Information is what changes and moves out into the array of space, finding its opportunity to manifest form according to destiny, according to the projection of Source. The secret of manifestation is to realize that energy is always everywhere—at one; only the information, the intention, moves and transforms, in the presence of spirit.

"This is the crux of your illusion and your resistance, my friend. Energy remains forever pure and simple, otherwise it would lose its power to inspire manifestation. Your authentic being remains always at the center, the calm point within the *storm of form.* From here, it empowers all your life and events. It cannot depart from its place. What appears as energy in the physical world, we call 'force'. From this fabrication, the *forces* of duality come into being—

dark and light, yin and yang, future and past. From this formation also comes the illusion of *control*.

"Thus is resistance an interface with form. From the perspective of the center, it appears as a cloak, seeking to be worn. It seeks to reverse the flow of creation and to smother the flame in the hearth. It does this, of course, with divine injunction and initiative. Resistance, too, is an agent of the manifesting forces. It is playing its role on the stage of duality. Until you awaken, it will continue to participate with you, for the purposes of friction—movement forward and back, for and against, shifting between shadow and bright.

"I suggest that you appreciate this form—resistance—as it is, as the dancer in the masquerade ball. It is there for your amusement and edification. But once knowing opens to you, the learning is transcended. The mind will have completed its lessons and the teacher must depart. Listen now to the moment, for your elevation and direction.

"I have earlier advised that you not identify with resistance. That is to say, do not put on this cloak as part of your wardrobe. It offers its 'gift' of separation to you and long have you accepted it without question. It would have you—the formless being—identify with the world of form, and remain held fast in its illusion. But now you can easily detect and decipher its designs. You can see there is no cloak—the king has no clothes. The mask you wear—the persona—has eyeholes."

I finally ask you to pause, still gazing down at Paris from the mountaintop; I try to pick out familiar structures; there is the *Gare du Nord* and there, the *Pantheon,* and of course the Eiffel Tower. "All right, O. I see what you're saying. But I'm still at the stage where I feel resistance popping up all the time, all around me, especially in simple ways. Like right now: I feel a chilly breeze on my neck and I want it to stop. It irritates me, and I detect a mood shift because of it. How can we deal with such ordinary annoyances that always seem to creep in? How can we stop resistance from slipping in under the radar?"

You smile at me like an older sister, waiting for me to catch up with a simple lesson. "This too shall pass. You are in the process of gradually increasing your appreciation and presence. You are looking at what is all around you—the mask and cloak. Know that each resistance you recognize is aiding you to better reveal your true being. Accept its gifts to you, *until* they are no longer useful. Soon they will pass away, unneeded. They will not slip in unnoticed because you will be seeing through the eyeholes of the moment itself.

"Once this level is gained, you may reverse the flow. Doing this will reveal resistance to itself. It is not simply a matter that *you* awaken; it is that you become a channel of awakening for all *matter,* all creation. Be aware that you are not allowing resistance to take over your presence. Rather, you are infusing your presence into the *form* that is resistance, and sending forth a fresh new, awakened form."

I pull my collar and scarf closer around my neck and continue, "OK. I see this little resistance as an opportunity to feel the warmth of the new French scarf I bought. So what of the third suggestion? I'm assuming it will be about *noticing?*"

"Ah, you're such an intuitive fellow," you tease. "Indeed it does. And now, continuing to look out from authenticity, through resistance, we will examine observation itself from a new direction."

I nod, trying—with minimal success—to apply my attention in some new, inside-out way. You look at me, amused, and carry on, "From the center of your being, from the *sacred* you, your vision is the 'eye within the eye', the 'jewel in the heart of the lotus'. Your noticing, from this angle, is similar to resistance in a way."

"Really?" I wonder.

"It is a cloak, just like resistance, worn in the physical world, by your deeper awareness; but it's just the opposite of resistance. 'Noticing' carries out the mission of awakening directly and positively, not by opposition. It is a force of facilitation not friction. It aids the flow of mystery and appreciation into your experience. Observation is inborn within the mechanics of projection.

"We say, 'look out upon your world with the inner eye, the single eye— unified from Oneness, at Source.' In contrast, look into the heart of profundity within you. The Void is bringing itself into your presence. Have you ever wondered what's *really* going on? What you're missing? Have you ever been in that space of wonder at all the details and complexities that appear to manifest randomly around you? Observe. This complexity is hiding something—the ultimate simplicity of the Void itself. Your persona, of course, will a-*void* this at all costs. To avoid is to attempt an escape from emptiness.

"Cloaked in resistance and separation, ego wants only to look at the surface of events and how you need to be *protected* from them—nothing deeper. The 'deep' alarms it; the Void terrifies ego. Ego would say to you, 'You don't want to go there. You *can't* go there.' It would tell you that the mysteries of your being are impenetrable and frightening, something to escape from. Look from below the ego at its way of keeping you on the surface. Look from the depths of your being; it will be easy to spot. Look at that irritation you mentioned before—notice the *superficiality* of it. See your ego's resistance to depth.

"Hear this: Look upward from purity and simplicity, and indeed from the heart of the vast emptiness itself. Dissolve the cloaks of separation and denial. Power forth into and through the form, *any* form. As humble as the 'noticing' is, it is to that degree empowering. No form can withstand the gaze of the Void. Look with the eye of Oneness. You are the pupil at its center. The Emptiness is your new teacher—without words or thoughts. This great master does not wait for your little mind to learn. It demands that you *know*—from your own presence, from the Void itself.

"Let me say this about Oneness: There is nothing abstract or vague about it; it's not a platitude. This is the center of your being; it is totally *present* and real in you—and in all the world. Without knowing it as your center of being—all being—you don't know it at all; you *know* nothing. Oneness is the bridge between formlessness and form, at the very core of vitality, empowerment and Life. I'm suggesting that you *use* it to awaken!"

I stop you. "Yes. It's the 'vehicle of awakening', you said once. O, this is heavy stuff, and a little disturbing to me. Let me scribble down some notes and ponder it for a minute before you go on. I don't know if I'm getting it—translating—correctly, but I'm trying."

"You're doing fine, my dear brother. Don't worry about the details right now. The needed adjustments will be provided later as you review the material. This is a good opportunity to make a note for you about our method: When you write your words for these letters, you are actually *remembering* experiences that have already taken place in an imaginal dimension we have created. This derives out of the transposition effect. Your transcription seems to you like you're making up the story and the experience freshly, but it is truly a matter of recalling and translating."

"Well, isn't that interesting! I will give that further thought later."

"Now, when your 'empty' awareness looks out through the *pupil*—the eye—of your manifested form, it is creating a scene. Your act of noticing, taken from this newness and beginning, coupled with imagination, is what writes the script. Stay with your energy Source. As much as it appears to you as emptiness, it is where your fullness comes from. Shakespeare wrote about it in *A Midsummer Night's Dream:*

> *And as imagination bodies forth*
> *The forms of things unknown, the poet's pen*
> *Turns them to shapes and gives to airy nothing*
> *A local habitation and a name.*

"OK, a beautiful quote that I love. But I don't see how we can live in both worlds—of form and formlessness—at the same time, the unknown *and* the local 'habitation'?"

"But you *do* live in both worlds. The dance between reality and illusion lights up the entire spectrum. We are incarnate to perform this dance of destiny. It is the creative act that reveals Oneness to itself. There is nothing wrong in the illusion, nor in interacting with it; but awareness is what counts. *Consciousness is formless. Formlessness is power!* Relate to your form world, with its events and actions, mysteries, as each situation demands. Do not withdraw your presence or engagement. But also do not be *fooled.* You are creating the scene, writing it, as the presence within you is writing your own outer form.

"Let resistance be met with simple noticing. Resistance will continue to demand that you be unconscious to presence. Turn the tables. You have the power of noticing. Use your formlessness, your power, to offer awareness into the resistance; this is your ultimate gift to the illusion. At each turn, by simple observation, you pour forth the elixir of evolution into the would-be negation and stagnation.

"Here is where opposites unite. *Noticing* trumps unconsciousness. It is simple and modest, grounded in true being. Resistance is complex and arrogant, distracted by the glitter of density, grounded in friction and denial of being. Assert your simple being and you will prevail."

Standing here, looking out upon the premier city of France, I ask, "So, what about the French Resistance? What about *that* resistance?"

You raise your arm and point out into the city. "There is a natural and sacred form of resistance that I described in the second letter: It is the refusal to embrace what is untrue and inauthentic. It does not deny truth.

"The French Resistance brought a measure of awakening into the nation. Yes, it used a theme of *negation.* However, in this case, it served to undermined the oppressive forces that would deny evolution. It turned inside-out, the force being imposed from without. Natural resistance kept authenticity alive in the darkest and most unconscious of times. In essence, it was a testimony to purity, vision and simple witnessing—from the secret, 'underground' places of the heart."

You pause and then sigh, "Yes. Paris is a good place to be; I'm glad you brought me to this destiny. Now, look out there in the distance. You will see a space of nothingness."

I raise my eyebrows and pull my head back. "Come again—a space of *nothingness?* What could you possibly mean?"

"I mean the Bastille! You know it was a great fortress and prison before the Revolution. It was torn down in 1789 and its memory became a living symbol. It remains to your day, a great shrine in the psyche of this nation and the world. When it stood in stone and mortar, it signified repression. Once the form was destroyed, the *formless* was brought forth and claimed the space, symbolizing freedom. The Bastille is a psychic monument to the formless."

"I get it. There's no building, nothing where it once stood. There's only a solitary column in the center of a great circle, the *Place de la Bastille*. At the top of it, there's a statue, called *le Génie de la Liberté*, [the Spirit of Freedom]."

"Indeed. With that theme in mind, let me summarize my points. First, I'm suggesting an inside-out approach, looking out from the center of authentic being; it is the soul of reality behind the mask of persona. Look out from your infinite emptiness. This is the *real* you! Soul's gift to you is consciousness and power. You, the witness in the world, give back to it your 'awareness'. *When consciousness and awareness truly meet, you awaken!*

"The destiny of *authentic being* is to empower the expansion of awareness. The destiny of *noticing* is to apply this awareness in the presence of consciousness—the 'I am'. The destiny of *resistance* is to goad the awareness into expansion. It supplies the friction for movement—an opposing force; that is to say, the 'equal and opposite reaction'. At the same time, 'noticing' offers the means to profit from the opposition; it opens the way for consciousness to enter. Grand dualities are at play.

"Both *opposition* to knowing and *facilitation* of knowing are brought together in this formula. Control and force come first; they are followed by freedom and power. Resistance-observation merges into an equation, an 'equality'. The French used it in their famous motto: *Liberté, Egalité, Fraternité*. Together they dance, until the dualities are conjoined and the authentic spirit is made free. 'The truth shall make you free.' Oneness is thus born through humanity upon the Earth. I encourage you to consider the liberty afforded by viewing the world from the depths of your being. I offer these suggestions to you as a breath for your lungs of spirit. Breathe deeply, authentically, and enjoy the dance of freedom upon the stage of form."

Letter Sixty-Four
Playground

You reach around my shoulder and turn me gently away from the view. "Come with me now. There's something I want to show you." We step back from the ledge. The air is chilly; I pull my collar tight again.

Suddenly, with no warning, the whole scene changes. It's a sunny, warm day; I'm still clutching my scarf. I'm so startled, I almost trip. Confusion spins my head. After a moment of reeling, I turn on you, annoyed. "O, please don't *do* that!"

You giggle like a child, "Ah, let me have some fun surprising you."

"You're *constantly* surprising me. You don't have to make any special effort for that." I finally calm myself and laugh. "All right. Play your games with me. I'm the guinea pig human," I feign a pout.

"Come on," you urge. "It's not that bad. We play *together*, don't we?"

I retort, "But I don't have the power to surprise you like that. It's not a fair game."

"Oh, but you do surprise me, my friend. You humans are all a great wonder to us. I wouldn't have it any other way."

I relent. "Yes we do play together. And I do enjoy it, I admit. OK, here we are in fine, warm weather suddenly." I see flowers on the trees and shake my head. It seems to be spring. "And where might we be going on this fine Parisian *winter night?* What is it you want to show me?"

You do not respond except to point uphill, along a narrow, cobblestone street. A motor scooter whines past and disappears. "You'll see." I decide not to ask further. We slip into friendly banter at last, happy to be strolling together over the top of the butte, past the basilica of Sacré Cœur. I look up for a moment at the statue of Archangel Michael mounted on the roof. *I know you!* I whisper in my mind. Then we head down beside the *Musée* de Montmartre and its vineyard. A curved lane descends to the south and then rises up again as it turns west. You direct me expertly at every turn.

"How is it that you know Paris so well, O?"

"Remember, I've lived every life that you have, and then some. And I have the privilege of drawing back past memories at will."

"You do? I didn't know that."

"It's one of the advantages of dropping the Veil of Illusion. My mind has much more access to the full database of experiences. That would be the *Akasha,* of course.

"Does this access include future lives as well?"

"Yes, it does. And future experiences in the current life. However, we are rarely interested in such details. If we knew everything that was going to happen to us, we would lose the great joy of living on Earth—in the moment—and embracing the unknown."

We stop on a corner. I ask, "And what about past lives? How much do you normally remember?"

You look around in several directions, seeming to listen to something. Finally, I wonder, *Could you be a little lost?* Without losing a beat, you answer, "Only a little. Past memories are much the same—like right now. I've been asking my memories for direction. We like the mystery to exist everywhere possible. Most of our past lives remain unknown to us, unless there's a strong reason to bring them back.

"All experience is in the moment, of course. The distinction of past, present and future is part of the illusion of form. And, this may come as a surprise to you, but it is the unknown that *keeps* us in the present moment, embraced by the Now. The sense of simultaneous anticipation and appreciation is a wonderful stimulus to alertness. From the soul's perspective, all time is now. It is for this reason that awakening is nothing more than becoming *as the soul is*—yet still incarnate."

"That sounds like a contradiction. How can you become *like the soul* and yet be in a body?"

"Your question is well taken. There *is* a difference between the soul and the incarnation. It would not serve to have its full presence here; there would be no reason for lifetimes or evolution at all. I suppose it's all about the soul—or indeed Source—*fooling* itself into experiencing novelty in the universe. It must enter a partial amnesia in order to feel the joy of discovery and evolution. Our souls follow suit, as they put forth our lifetimes here.

"Humans, in their time, had no choice but to forget. Vigilans have the choice *not* to forget, but we choose to play the game, in our way. Thus we can approach the unknown with joy. Our freedom from incessant thought is a big help. Seeing as the soul sees, while being incarnate, *is* a paradox, nevertheless. Remember, paradox signals the approach to truth. Awakening is exactly that. The truth lies in the awakened heart; awakened mind comes next. No amount of mental forgetfulness will dislodge truth from the heart."

Here on the little plateau, we've stopped, away from the busy streets, surrounded by five-story houses and apartment buildings. To the side is a garden with fruit trees. Small birds make chipping sounds. Beside the garden there is a playground for children. It's empty.

But there is again a sudden change. As we walk, the air forms a barely visible bubble around us. In a flash I see the vesica shape; then it disappears. We have been transported somewhere—through a portal. But the garden and the playground are still here. The trees are different now. The grounds are cleaner and arranged in an oval, and a low wall skirts the outer edge. In the air there's a feeling of clarity; it tastes sweeter, fresher. And there are children in the playground. A few adults sit on benches. You direct us to sit on one.

I glance around and notice the people are wearing unfamiliar clothing. "What now, O? Where are we?" *The better question would be 'when' are we?.*

"These are vigilan children, in a vigilan world. We are still in Paris, some years in your future," you reply.

"Remarkable. That's the difference I felt. The whole atmosphere is easier, calmer now. I like this feeling."

"Yes, you do indeed."

We sit in silence. After a few minutes, a ball rolls across the fine, white gravel, up to our feet. A little girl, with long blond hair, chases after it. She's perhaps seven years old. She is wearing a kind of jumpsuit in lavender. Instinctively, I pick up the ball and start to toss it back to her. Lightning flashes inside my head; and then it goes much deeper than that. I drop the ball, feeling dizzy and displaced. The girl and I stare at each other. I sense she is just as startled as I am. But she's not afraid. I sense, inwardly, she's *never* been afraid—at least not in the way *I* am right now.

The child keeps walking, very slowly, toward me. Her gaze is calm and direct, unwavering. I see you watching, out of the corner of my eye. *What is this?* An elastic presence begins to flow between the child and me. It's like we've met before, like we may even be *related* somehow.

She stops several feet away and stares straight into my eyes, saying, *"Bienvenue, monsieur. Etes-vous perdu?*—[Welcome, sir. Are you lost?]"

I look quickly away from that piercing gaze, and find my eyes hitting yours. You look at me impassively and nod.

The child continues, "Will you throw me the ball, monsieur? Please."

I reach down, pick up the ball again and toss it to her. She smiles and runs away. *Simple. Nothing out of the ordinary—and yet...* She is playing with several of her friends in the center of the open space. I watch, amused at their excitement and freshness; they're so full of enthusiasm. Finally, I look to you.

"So, O. This is very nice, but would you mind telling me why we're here?"

"Just be patient. I'm sure events will begin to unfold very soon."

Sure enough, the ball rolls up to my feet again, and the girl chases it. This time, however, *she* picks it up and tosses it back to her friends. Then she asks if she can sit down with us. We both smile and invite her to sit between us.

She then introduces herself. *"Bonjour.* My name is Phileina. You're strangers here, I think. You have a funny way of speaking, monsieur" Then she repeats her original question to me. "Are you lost? I think my mother can help you if you are. Would you like to meet *maman?"*

Her sweet gaze is mesmerizing. Her eyes twinkle, looking up at mine. I answer, unsure of myself, "Well, certainly. Why do you think she can help us?"

Phileina cocks her head to one side and squints into my eyes, as though the answer is quite obvious. "Because she is the best person at finding things, and finding people too. I'll bet she knows just where you want to go. Wait here. I'll get her."

She jumps down and skips across the square. I shake my head and ask you, "What's going on, O? Who *is* this girl and who is her mother? Do we know her?"

"This little girl is *you,* in your next lifetime—me in a previous one," you say simply.

My jaw drops, and I begin to stutter, "What? I, uh… me? A little girl? How?"

"Do you remember what Black told you?"

I stop and stare at you, trying to get my senses around this. "That little girl is *me?* And her—my—mother is *Black,* here in this life? How am I supposed to relate to this? You've shown me some pretty bizarre things, O, but this takes the cake. This one is affecting me inside in a very personal way. Why are you showing me this?"

"I'm not showing it to you; *I'm* just the vehicle that you are using to show it to yourself. This is your destiny, your *script.* You are writing this—from deep within. That's why it feels so personal. This is the real moment of Life for you!"

"What year are we in?" I ask, whispering.

"It's probably about 200 years in your future, I would say."

Now Phileina comes back across the playground, pulling a woman— apparently her mother. The woman is very tall, with long blond hair, wearing a flowing white dress. I stand up as she approaches. The girl spontaneously grabs my hand and puts it into the woman's hand. We stare at each other for a long time. You too are staring silently. There's a blooming recognition amongst us all. This is definitely Black! She knows there is a strong connection, but I'm not sure if she has realized all the details yet.

I finally break the silence. "Black, is it you? Do you remember us?"

"My name is Breanne. I *do* remember you two—from a long *time* distance. 'Black' might be another name for me. Yes," the woman answers slowly, also in French. Then she throws back her head and long hair back, as if to laugh. But she only says, *"Très étrange!*—[Very strange!]—I am remembering you from the *future. C'est ça, n'est pas?*—[That's it, isn't it?]*"

You reach forward and touch Breanne's hand. There is obviously a trans- mission between the two of you, a deep recognition. You say, "We are here as part of the unfolding awareness, to ask for your insights. Thank you for your hospitality."

Breanne smiles and looks at her daughter then at me, "Curious, is it not? The connection is electric. Do you feel it, monsieur?"

I sigh and start, "Well, of course. I've been told that your daughter is my future incarnation. Is that true?"

She hesitates. "It would appear so. And you, madam, are of the same soul as well. This is indeed a strange thing for us all."

You repeat her words, "Yes, for us all."

Breanne looks a little puzzled. "But what precisely brought you here? This is a sub-dimension, correct? And how did you create it?"

I shake my head, staring at Breanne. "Wait. That's supposed to be *my* line. You mean *you* don't know either? I would like very much to know why I am here." I turn and look at you more sternly.

You sigh, "All right. What I understand of this is that we have been guided here by angelans, to participate in some ritual of inner growth, some kind of initiation. I assume this has to do with your daughter."

Breanne has closed her eyes while you were speaking. Now she nods, re- ceiving more information out of the ethers. "You said 'angelans'?"

"Well, yes. I'm not sure how much you know about them in your time. We're still discovering much about them in mine."

Breanne's eyes brighten. "This makes sense to me. You see, I am of the Source-gazer *métier*. We are scientists who study the Void and the Source to evaluate its influence upon our world. Ah, but you know this, I'm sure."

You nod affirmation.

"I am preparing my daughter to follow this calling. What interests me about the 'angelans' you mentioned is that we have found evidence of their elusive race, *homo angelicus,* living within or around the Void. But we have only made fleeting contact with them. Their presence seems strongest in the place of the Akasha.*"*

I interrupt, "Outstanding. This is like circles within circles rewinding in my mind. I've heard all this before from several different directions. So, we're all learning about them together—*whatever* time it is."

She continues, questioning, "Yes. But are these beings are more open to you in the future? And have they brought you here?"

You answer, "They brought us here, but they are still a mystery to us. The timeframe for our understanding seems to be *no time* at all."

You look over to me and detect my impatience. "Now, please back to *why* we're here…"

Breanne has her own idea now. Looking at me she says, "I'm sensing an explanation: Phileina is about to begin a new level of study. And I feel that you too are about to take a major step in your awakening. If you do this, you will help my daughter and me as well. Consciousness is flowing profoundly within this encounter—for all of us."

You nod in appreciation, glancing quickly at me. The little girl turns a circle playfully beside us then looks up at her mother. "*Maman*, may I ask a question?"

"Certainly, *chérie*."

Phileina pushes her hair back from her forehead and looks up. "Monsieur, will you join our family? Will you become my brother?"

Then she stops and ponders, quizzically. "You will be my older-younger brother, I think. Isn't that curious!"

I say, smiling back and bending down to her level, "Yes. Isn't that curious. I don't really understand it either. I am from a younger time, but I'm older than you."

She grabs her mother's hand and leans in toward her shyly, still looking at me. Her brow wrinkles as she gathers in her young intuition. Finally, she is ready to speak. "You will give me a *present,* I think. You are here to give me a present. Older brothers give gifts to their young sisters. Isn't that right?"

I respond, "I would be happy to give you a gift. What will it be? Uh, what would you like?" I look up at Breanne, then you, hoping to get a clue. There is suddenly a connection between our eyes—all of us at once, including the child. In some bizarre way, we are all staring into each other's eyes at the same time. My mind tries feebly to understand. *It's the 'single' eye in each of us that is connecting.*

You move close in to this small circle, putting your arm around my shoulder and doing the same with Breanne. Breanne takes my hand and then the hand of her daughter. We stand motionless on the gravel, in the playground— in Paris, on Earth, in space. And the space enters us as though for the first time. It is reborn this moment. Our bodies and minds whirl around the space—at the center of being—in an ecstatic dance, like four dervishes turning as one. The world around us spins in synchrony. The whole universe is spinning with this tiny group.

We are each aware of the others' sensations and realizations, flowing in synchrony, like the breathing of one being. A timeless pulse beats in us. The pulse returns us to duality. Suddenly we are just two souls—Breanne and myself. Yet within my being, I am both you and the child as well: I am three incarnations in one form. Standing before me is Black—my mother, my elder, my mentor. Electric light streams from her heart into mine; her eyes into mine; and now from her mind into mine.

She whispers in a voice that I can only accept as my 'teacher'—for long ages in my wheel of life on Earth. I hear her words like each is an encyclopedia of information, entering and forming the structure of my self. "You are here to open the way for the child. This is her first initiation of this life. You bring a talent of depth from many lives lived in pursuit of this moment. Your talent will soon take form in her presence. It is your gift to her, to yourself, and the beginning of *training* into Source, for both of you."

To my surprise, my own voice rises spontaneously. "I willingly give myself to this mission. It is a high joy to be here for this. Open me wide and further, into Oneness with destiny."

Black raises her arms to the sky in a receptive gesture, and as she does, we both rise up. Mile after mile, we ascend into a darkening space. Our ephemeral bodies enter a kind of heavenly arena, up into the embrace of a great, floating cathedral in space. There's no floor in this church; we have entered it from below. Its form is simple—several dozen vertical beams of light, arching together along the top of a huge colonnade. The beams are translucent, pastel rainbow hues.

The scene is dreamlike and magical. Peace and bliss saturate the air. The hallowed air swallows up the high excitement I would otherwise feel. I slowly turn my eyes around the space. This is a place of obvious sacredness. Now I realize there are other beings here, arranged in ranks around us. They are monitors of reverence and resonance—true peacekeepers.

I know intuitively these beings represent pure harmony. They are like candles floating inside this cathedral. Their heads are flames, flowing gently in a spiritual breeze. Otherwise they stand in perfect stillness, with no motion. I sense they possess extremely advanced consciousness. They instantly know me through and through.

As I bring my attention to them, these 'flame' beings radiate an aura of invitation. I feel it in my heart first; then I see it visibly between us. This aura is pearlescent, like the arches, cast of filmy light. It pulls me in like a fishnet. I will myself to float over to one of the beings. It—he or she, or both—is finely transparent, like everything here. I stand in awe. Never have I seen such an august presence. It translates an incalculable wisdom. I feel myself stretched up to match its height. In a moment I feel my body becoming transparent like it.

Next, I'm silently invited to move closer. I draw right into the flame itself, aligning my body with its body, my head with its head. I am superimposed entirely within this profound creature. Without a murmur, there is sudden communion; I feel myself *becoming* a message. "This is communication through *identification,*" it proclaims. "This is how we shall be together, how we shall speak together. Know that this is the way you are to commune with your future incarnation. Now, let us commence to describe to you, what 'identification' really is."

Letter Sixty-Five
Spirit into Matter

I am completely inside this being of quiet flame. I understand *identification* without having it explained. The experience demonstrates what it is—a molecular sharing of space, an infusion. *Like tea,* I think. The underlying Oneness is clear, yet I still sense a subtle differentiation—there is water and there is tea. And this 'identification' requires more than one participant—hence duality. Now I realize the presence of you and Phileina in the same way; there are so many mergers within me right now, it feels like a confluence of wandering rivers.

Auras from all the flame creatures—a dozen or so—overlap and interweave amongst themselves. Subtly, another level of consciousness reveals itself; it is a greater being that is composed of all the individualities of the flames. To them it is the 'fire' to their flames; it is the cathedral above. Everything is glowingly alive, we visitors too. We are now living parts of the experience. I look around for Black. She is nearby, superimposed within another of the flames.

For now, the communication is amongst us all. We are all 'identified' in one message. Words begin to form in my mind. It is some kind of timeless, telepathic download that I will here attempt to reflect as a conversation. The flames whisper, "You are in place with us as a differentiation within non-differentiation. You, to us, are a pulsation—in and out of our space. You will feel it in your skin and internal organs as a flux of merger and release."

I respond with a memory from the tiny depths of my own form. "At the bottom of the River Niger, I experienced this same phenomenon—sliding in and out of existence. It was there that I first encountered the vesica piscis."

"Exactly. It is the same in principle. You are existing and *not,* in pulsation. This is the *pulse of creation.* A more accurate way is to say that you do not exist and then you dream that you do. The dream of existence is what creation is. It is dreamt out of the state of non-existence. We—the flames—live continuously in this flux; we are the flux of your pulse. We are guardians of the peace, in one sense. We *are* the peace in another."

"Why would peace need guardians?" I ask.

"Only in the dream does peace need guardians. There are forces and forms in the duality worlds that would take peace for themselves and turn it into a duality—war and peace, for example. This is a distortion of the power we represent. It is our destiny to uphold the *purity of peace* as it expresses into duality worlds, and not let it be claimed by pretenders to peace—those who would make a mockery of it. Peace is the essence of power. No force is as strong as this power. Therefore, we are not protecting it from harm; there is no need for that. We only guard the presentation of this peace into your world."

I bow and acknowledge. "Well, thank you for welcoming us here, especially in this intimate way. I've never felt closer to another being than this—this 'identification'."

As I consider what I've just said, my whole body seems to glow like a cool fire, up through my torso and into my head. I feel light as I say, "Please continue, and tell me what identification is."

"Of course. This is indeed what you are experiencing right now. Words to describe it will only take you away from this state. However, for your letters, words are required, we understand. Identification is the placement of one soul *within* another for the purposes of recognition, reverence and resonance. You could call it 'communion' or 'relationship'. Thoughts, feelings and sensations are shared; presence is joined among two or more individuated forms. It is the most direct means of interweaving destinies.

"Our thoughts and words are your thoughts and words. Identification is itself a high principle of evolving awareness. It is the form of being that your angelans will assume when their evolution progresses and merges with that of the high angels. Identification is a state of threshold into yet finer, subtler stages of Oneness.

"There is no end to the progressions of subtlety and fineness. We are threshold beings ourselves, in the heart of your precious Threshold. We are guardians of all portals into your Cosmos. We are embodiments the vesica piscis, the vital flame of being-ness at the mouth of the Void."

I feel your mind urging me to consider the derivation of the word 'identification'. You explain, "The word comes from Latin, meaning 'the same'; before that, from Sanskrit meaning, even more simply, 'this'."

The presence of the flame speaks in its way, *"This* is the *same.* There is no difference between each of us—except for perspective. Your presence here introduces the sense of dislocation and 'being between'. We recognize no 'between-ness', except that which comes as we identify into your state of mind. There is no distance in us. The distance is in *you.* And this is only a function of your perceptive apparatus. It creates the illusion of separation. In reality, we *are* you. As we place ourselves within your being, we are the *same.* We all are *this.*

"Identification is also a vehicle for education and imparting information. In this state, time is suspended. Hence, large volumes of teaching can be shared and infused instantly. Such is the manner of your infusion at this moment. These words that you write are an approximation, a 'download' of the instantaneous presentation you are receiving. Identification is, therefore, the principle behind the 'seed-links' you are already familiar with."

"And what about your own identification with the greater 'cathedral' being, of which you're a part?"

"Yes. It is the same principle. 'As above, so below' is an expression of this phenomenon. Truly, the entire dream, the universe of existence and form that you know as your current home, is founded here. Source identifies with Void. The Cosmos of souls identifies with Source; you and your lives identify with souls. We identify with the progenitor of our destiny—the 'cathedral', as you call it. It is the 'seat' of our soul." *I hear your voice informing me that the word 'cathedral' comes from Greek, meaning 'seat' or 'throne'.*

"How is it that both your lesser and the greater beings are together in one place and time."

The flames respond, "It is all identification: We are guardians of the peace; and we are the peace itself. Thus we are lesser and greater, simultaneously. It is our nature to identify in these two directions—yet without duality. It is your nature to do the same, only in a different form. Your form is the 'time' form. Through what you call 'evolution' you are lesser and greater over a span of time. Your personal self gradually becomes your soul self. But, in reality, outside of time, you are just as identified with the greater as are we; you are at one with your soul.

"Now, this teaching is intended to remind you that all beings are held within One Being. This is our shared identity. It is for this reason that to practice identification in a lower sense, as in identification with form takes you away from true being. It takes you into illusion and ego. It is a *sin*—a thwarting of evolution and true consciousness. We mean 'sin' in the Greek sense of the word, as in 'an arrow falling short of its mark'."

I feel you smiling affirmation at this word link. I respond, "I'm a little surprised to hear you use the word 'sin'. In my culture, this concept is associated with judgment and religious condemnation."

"We understand that usage. It is for precisely this reason that we call your attention to it. There is truly only *one* 'sin': It is failing to honor your destiny. Within each destiny, is inscribed your soul's mission on Earth. It is always a direct expression from Source into Life. What is sin, then, is the identification with form and is not Source.

"It is no sin to fall short of the expectations and dictates of a religious leader or a moral system, except in the context of identification with form. The typical 'sins' within religious doctrine are offenses against *form*, not against formlessness, which is to say Source. Thus, usage of the word 'sin' has become a sin itself; it has promoted the identification with form.

"Resistance to formless Source is the fundamental *sin* of your world. It is the basis of all other failings. Resistance is a misrepresentation of your inner nature. It causes you to 'miss the mark' of your destiny again and again in your lives on Earth. Of course, we know this is all according to design within the dream you have chosen—the Veil of Illusion. And then, paradoxically, it *is* your destiny to 'live in sin'. Regardless of this, it is now time to lift that Veil and end the dream—to 'go and sin no more'. It is time for *awakening*. Therefore, we say, look at your resistance, humans. See it for what it is. See through it to that which it would deny and negate the formless Source. That is, of course, your own true being."

"I think I get the message—from you and from my own teacher, O, certainly. But she has taught me about 'natural' resistance. What about that? I've been told that's OK."

"This 'resistance' is a word only. It is actually the opposite of *human* resistance. It is rather 'nature': Nature is the reverse of identification with form. Natural resistance uses the *identical* word and concept to release the denial. It is a play-on-words that wisdom will divine for you. Look *within*, always, to find the wisdom hidden in words and thoughts. Do not stop on the surface—in the human mind—when determining your understanding."

I am caught by a phrase here: "Nature is the opposite of identification with form? I've never heard that before. Would you please explain?"

"Nature means continual, never-ceasing renewal and rebirth. It is represented in the religious insistence on being 'born again', in order to be 'saved from sin'. The deep truth inside this distortion is that Source is always renewing itself in and through you; the sin is to not recognize and identify with it. Nature is total, pure identification with Source."

Immediately, I receive a message from your mind: *"The root of the word 'nature' is 'nascence', 'birth' in Latin—that from which you are born and gives birth to you—and your beginning."* I look within the flames and see that this thought has registered with them.

"Great. I like that one. Really. It seems so *natural,*" I mumble. Then I remember what led us into this conversation in the first place. "So, what is happening here with me and my future incarnations? What is it about 'identification' and your presence that will assist in this communion?"

The flame voice grows more solemn, if that's possible. "You are here as an initiation of consciousness. You are participating in the rebirth of your own being. Nature has led you to this destiny. Phileina, Orange and you are, of course, one soul. Together you are converging into a time point, so that each will know your three-fold manifestation of Source. We are here to draw out Source into your soul, to reveal the three-as-one in you that you may move inwardly into your mission. We appreciate that you are a *natural* Source-gazer, dear child."

I respond, "I—we—are honored, I'm sure. Is there anything you need me to do? What's the next step?"

"You will engage your innate talent and destiny together, yet in three distinct forms: For your human form, this will be an opening of prescience; for Phileina it will be the commencement of direct training; for Orange it will be a remembrance and reactivation of skills that have been masked up to this point in her lifetime."

The voice drops into silence. The silence grows and surrounds us with an imponderable sense of peace. It's like an infinite tunnel, living in the center of my heart, reaching forever into the Void. I feel a foreshadowing of events to come. The peace then whispers out from that center. It gathers into a voice again, one last time, "Having spoken thus—through your tongue and mind— we now return you, blessed and renewed, to your mother and mentor, Breanne."

Abruptly, the flame beings move away from us. The disengagement is wrenching, like vital organs are being sucked out of me. I reel for a moment. I feel you and Phileina shift uneasily as well. Breanne swiftly moves to my side and places her hand on the small of my back. As energy flows into me, I am calm and balanced, intact again. *Thank you, mother.*

The flame creatures take up a new formation within the cathedral space; it is an oval circle—a vesica—facing us all around. They begin to glow brighter. Then there is a white flash, and the whole scene shape-shifts into a large transparent lens; we are at its center. In an instant, it all shrinks down and closes to a point, right between Breanne and me, at the level of our hearts. It vanishes into nothing.

Suddenly we're back, standing together on the playground, as four individuals. We're all a little out of breath—*from the climb?* I wonder. Silently, we stand very still, looking at each other and appreciating the situation. Still quite tuned in, I sense what each of you is thinking. I allow your feelings to absorb into mine. The peace and reverence of the flame beings remains all around.

For your part, O, I see you are delighted to realize that *you, too, are a Source-gazer.* You are now inhaling deeply of your own presence and re-born memories. Phileina, for her part, is excited, flushed with exuberant anticipation of a new adventure in growing up. Her eager freshness is most endearing, childlike and inspiring. She is full of innocence and openness. Breanne, on the other hand, is absorbing the field of emotion and the mantel of responsibility that has just been placed upon her shoulders. She is pondering the nature of her maturity as it relates to us. She is reaching back into the unknown to find relevant past life memories. As for me, I am simply waiting gratefully to be given the next message.

I ask, "What now?"

Sensing a need of the moment, you take Phileina by the hand. She has begun to squirm, as children always do when grown-ups are too serious. I watch calmly, waiting. You lead her out to the open square, pick up the ball and toss it to her. Several other children join in a spontaneous game with you both.

Breanne, watching as well, sighs and looks up to the sky, then back to me. "I suppose this is where we begin. Let me start with a little memory of a past life when you knew me as your dear friend. It was a time when I fully explored the 'mother' principle, in all its facets. I was not *your* mother then, of course." She looks me in the eye with a demure smile.

"But I was tending the farm, a family, animals and many friends. I was opening to the strength of the feminine principle and learning to teach by example, by embrace. I was immersed in land stewardship, wholesome food and cooking, deep caring for nature and for my community. This was the commencement of my career as a mentor for many younger souls. You and I first met in that context so we would know each other intimately and open our souls and destinies to each other."

I interrupt, remembering clearly our first meeting and all the adventures we pursued thereafter, "I am still living through that time, even as I write this letter. Don't tell me the ending."

Breanne laughs, releasing some of her tension. "Have no fear. There is no ending to our relationship—as you can see here. The letters you write now—in your time—are one of the vehicles for cementing our ongoing creation. You, the explorer, the independent wanderer and voyager, gazing into space, needed to encounter my incarnation—the stable, grounded maternal force, holding the space of Earth. I was exploring, too, the inner dimensions, and manifesting them onto the planet. Together, we teamed up to put your books into form; this you well know.

"Together, we took your inspiration and my *grounding,* and shaped an integrated expression of practical idealism. It was, and is, an expression of the *formless in form.* This is what you and I share as a mission and destiny. I have passed through a number of lives, in various timeframes, between that one and this—

several more than you and Orange. I have been preparing for the task at hand—to be your mentor."

She takes a long, deep breath, reflecting on more than I can imagine. "We defined it once as 'magic'—bringing spirit into matter. At the beginning of our lives together, we were young and naïve, in a soul sense. This is as it was designed to be, of course—as we *scripted* it. We were starting out on a long road toward the very 'center of being' itself.

After another pause and deep breath, she sighs, "Ah, it is a pleasure to recall the early days."

I answer in kind, "It is for me as well, especially since I'm still living those days. Is there advice you would give me and my friend—that is to say, *your* earlier self?"

"Only to live your experience to the full level of appreciation your souls demand. There are many opportunities and distractions in any lifetime. Be alert to the deep measure of your presence within each other. You are irrepressibly bonded and blessed. This will be the best advice you can have."

"We used to wonder if we were twin souls. Can you comment on that?"

"Yes, I can. And no, we are not. That is, not in the sense I think you mean. Twin souls have many forms, of course. Some are on the surface of experience, others in the depths, over many lifetimes. In that sense, you and I share the sensibilities of twinship. As you know, the so-called 'twin-soul' phenomenon is the expression of a single soul dividing into two parts. This is for the purpose of living in what is called 'parallax appreciation'—that is, to know the duality world from two angles simultaneously, and making them *one*. This is not precisely our course. However, all souls are 'one soul' in the end, and in reality. Therefore, when two individuals meet in the outer world and join destinies, there is the reflection of Oneness in their duality. This gives rise to the sense of twinship for sure."

"Very interesting," I comment. "So how long does it continue, our close relationship? Can you see that in both our futures?"

"I can indeed. And as I said, there is no ending."

"Ah," I smirk. "But I've learned enough about duality to know that what has a beginning *must* have an end!"

Breanne touches my hand gently. "We begin in duality, yes; and he duality must have an end. But *we,* and our relationship, do *not* end. We have now entered into Oneness. And there is no end."

She then grips my hand more firmly and brings her other hand to the top of my head. An electric current surges between her hands. The bottom drops out. We are once again taking that familiar plunge—straight into the Void.

Letter Sixty-Six
Place of Knowing

Breanne has turned into the presence I know as Black. Her dark and crimson robes are flowing. They whip fiercely as we fall toward the silent darkness. She is clutching my hand and spinning me around, like a flag in the wind.

Gradually, I find my voice. *I thought I wouldn't be able to speak.* "B, why does entering the Void always feel like *falling?*" She doesn't answer immediately, so I take stock of what I see in the space. Images are passing swiftly; there are sights and sounds—even smells—from what seems to be every epoch in history, the future and other worlds as well.

Black finally speaks. "You feel the falling because it is *below* your normal awareness. It is the depth of emptiness beneath your stability; it takes you *down*, below your mind. We say, 'fall into the moment,' as an expression of acceptance."

"You know, I've always had a fear of falling."

"Of that I am aware." Her bright white hair is swirling around her face. "Of course you have this fear. Why would a human being in his right mind not fear the Void? What we are doing takes courage."

"I thought I wasn't supposed to fear."

"There is nothing that you are 'supposed to do or not do'. All is as it is. You are free; this is nature. Fear is be useful in stimulating courage and freedom, just as shadow stimulates appreciation of the light. You cannot have courage unless you first have know fear.

"Esoterically, your species fears falling because you *have* fallen—from grace. The flame beings put it in the language of *sin:* 'falling short of the mark'. Your species has tumbled right out of heaven in order to participate in the world of illusion. The Veil of Forgetfulness is the 'curtain that has fallen'. But all is as you designed it to be; and as you are scripting it in the continuing drama of evolution."

"So, we humans are born with a fear of falling," I repeat the simple idea to plant it in my mind. "Because of the illusion that we are abandoned, that our higher selves *may not* exist, because we innately feel this drop from the heights of awareness."

Black nods and shifts the subject. "This is nature—from the beginning. Recall, the original meaning of 'nature' is *birth*. You have heard us say many times 'begin again' in the spirit of 'newness'. Do you know why that is?"

As we fall, our bizarre conversation continues. I grit my teeth and reply, "Well, I assume it's because every moment is a new creation around us. Every moment is fresh, like the rush of this wind."

"Yes. And there's something else in it, something simpler, more profound."

"Ah, yes." Suddenly I get it. "The 'beginning' is *Source*. They are one and the same."

"Exactly. Source is the essence of newness. This is its only *quality!* Know this and you know Source. All other attributes ascribed to it, such as the Unknown or the Creator, Life or God, the Alpha and Omega, are founded in this quality. In 'newness' lies all passion."

Our descent at last slows to a gradual slide. It gives me an opportunity to catch my breath and look at the passing images in more detail. There are vast landscapes, receding into the distance; they seem to be creating themselves as they spread. Cities of great splendor shine in the sun, while others are horrible, full of squalor and shadows. There are close-up faces of people with all manner or emotion and expression, coursing through events and actions. I ask, "B, what are all these images about?"

"Ah, you noticed," she jests with an inviting smile, still gripping my hand. "They link with the *newness* we were just talking about. They are all scenes of some form of *beginning*, somewhere in the Cosmos. This is because we are within the Threshold. It is the place of all seeded forms. It is here that we will commence our new project; I will explain that in a moment. It is here that we will bring Phileina for her initiation, and bring O for her remembrance. The Threshold is the expression of endless beginning."

"Why are you and I coming here without them?"

"You and I are at the center of the new project. It is our role to prepare the way—in essence. You and I were born into our current lives with the talent in place, relative to our incarnations, of course. Phileina is developing the skill within herself fresh. She needs our help. O will subsequently be drawn into remembrance through the actions of we three."

"Why is Phileina just beginning if I already have the talent?" I wonder.

"Because you are a precursor, a premonition, if you will."

"OK. So, did you have this 'premonition' in your former persona, in my time?"

"Yes," she replies. "Both of the friends who are collaborating with you in O's project have demonstrated this ability innately. It is precisely for this reason that they resonate with you and with the project. Now they will align with *my* project as well."

Our gossamer forms are hovering in stillness, no longer descending. The images have all evaporated and we're surrounded by the façade of the Void. I feel the usual sensation of floating above the surface of a great, invisible planet. The vibration in my bones is beginning to resonate throughout my body. I feel that familiar interconnection with the Cosmos, like a scintillating web, reaching into me deeply, from far away. *It's primordial, fundamental electricity.*

"What is this new project of yours then? Is it like O's transposition of time project?"

"It has its own unique essence; yet all essence is one, and thus the two are related."

I decide to react to her confusing language. "The one is two, the two are one and essence is the twain shall ever meet. Is that what you mean?"

She chuckles and continues, "Like the transposition project, this new one will also have import for your time. We shall call it simply the 'Life of Source'. It is based upon our *métier* of Source gazing."

"Hmm." I pause with reflection. "B, to be honest, I'm not sure I have room in me for another project like that."

"Nonsense, my son, you have infinite 'room' in you. You *are* infinity itself. Do not worry; there's nothing you have to 'buy' to redeem this coupon, to say it like a human. Your decision can wait. I only want to introduce the idea of it now. And besides, this project will not require you to write another book— unless, of course, you decide to create it yourself."

She winks; then she looks at me with deep patience and, indeed, reverence. I don't quite know what to make of this. Her words are taking me by surprise. *So, what's new about that! What is she saying though? I'm resisting.* At last I have an idea: *I'll treat it like a seed-link and explore it later.* I push it off into the ethers and recall what the flame people said. Seed-links are an expression of *identification;* they are a linkage with Source. I can look at B's 'new project' that way. I'll come to terms with it later—in *that* moment. *Source, help us all!*

Black resumes, "This project involves all of your closest future friends—O and Omis, Phileina and me, and another person besides. I'll explain that when the timing is right. How could you want to be left out of it?"

"Wait. I'm still just a human, with an ego. And I'm tired—worn out in fact. You others have shed that inhibition. I would be at a distinct disadvantage."

"On the contrary, you—and your two dear human friends—would have the greatest advantage of all. You would be the ones amongst us to receive the richest, deepest blessing, the grandest opening. Your awareness of Source would be boosted immeasurably, which is to say the awareness of yourselves and your world. Think of it: It is the promise of greater closeness to Source and to the very Life of all. So, I will describe the details of my new project later in this manuscript."

"Do you want me to make a decision right now?"

"No, definitely not; it would be premature and I know your mind would refuse. Right now we are here to lay the groundwork for Phileina's initiation. I believe she might have mentioned a *gift* you would bring to her. Yes?"

"She did. Can you help me with that? What can I bring her? What do I have that she would want? I'd be happy to give her anything in my power to give, but I don't know what."

Black looks into me, against the shining emptiness below. Her face takes on the look of Breanne. She says, "Give her your heart and soul. Give her your living essence. *Give her your Life!* This is the only thing you have to give. She is young and impressionable. This is the time for her soul to open within her in a vibrant new way. But it requires a deep, living union with her past."

I am taken aback. "B, I'm not sure what you're getting at. Give her my *life?* Really? That's a tall order. Nevertheless, I'll do my best to be open and hear you out."

"You will be participating in an ancient, mystical tradition that has always existed in some form. I'm sure you've heard of the process whereby future forms of one's soul return into the past to *assist* in a given lifetime, as spirit or angel guidance. O, of course, is that for you. There is a yet more profound expression of this. What is not so well known is the practice of *past* lives influencing and assisting *future* lives—and bestowing upon them *gifts*. Through the agency of their soul's presence, they can offer up themselves to higher fulfillment. It is all *in the family,* so to speak. These offerings require intense commitment and transcendence—soul bridging. They require intense presence, and hence ceremonial ritual.

"It has become customary among certain schools of vigilans to have visits from their former incarnations at the time of initiation. There is a profound reciprocal effect in this interchange; the previous selves benefit as much as the immediate ones. Humans, from *their* perspective, normally do not remember these experiences, except as dreams. But I must tell you these are no ordinary dreams! Some humans realized what was happening and found ways within themselves to honor the dreams and to visit their future incarnations intentionally. Those individuals, while unaware of the full extent of the benefit, were blazing trails into the awakening of their entire race. Every bridge you build, every portal you open, aids the whole race."

Just now the Threshold is gleaming around us, inviting us to be absorbed into its mystery. I think of my gift to Phileina and of dying; I remember my brushes with death. *It's not so bad, you know.*

Black reads my thinking and says, "I'm not asking you to *die;* not in the physical sense. I'm only suggesting that you give up your Life, surrender your portal into Source to your future self."

I chuckle, "That sounds like the same thing to me."

"Not at all. Dying is *leaving* the world. What you would give to Phileina is an act of *joining* the world, the new world of *her* making. You and she will make it together."

"Being here now, B, in this magical, near-death space, I am willing to give up my Life, or anything else I have, to Phileina. I'm fine with it. But it certainly sounds like *dying* to me. Nevertheless, I'm ready. Please tell me what this would be like. Wait." Suddenly I'm flushed with the presence of my own soul. You, O, are with me. *I'm not being asked to make this decision alone!*

With a joint voice I now speak, "I do not need to hear words tell me about this gift. I now realize that the gift must be made from the *heart*—before the *head* knows the explanation. I freely commit to this gift, whatever it means. I *feel* that with all my heart and soul. I invest my whole Life into the initiation of that little girl, who is my very soul flesh and soul blood. I surrender."

Breanne answers solemnly through B's voice and through a greater voice as well, "We hear your soul speak, dear presence. We are grateful beyond measure for this 'gift beyond price'. You are giving us the 'pearl' of your essence. Be assured, persona, there will be no loss to you, at all. Only gain. You will see."

With that, Breanne's image dissolves and Black returns. She reaches down, taking both my hands, and declares, "Let us now enter the ceremony."

I can only wonder. We begin to move in a way I've never experienced before. We seem to be entering the Void, but we're remaining still. The feeling is like being sucked into myself, an implosion into a central vortex inside. We are irresistibly moving and yet standing immovable, perfectly still. *I emphasize the word 'perfectly'.* It is yet another encounter with paradox.

My consciousness is turned inside out. I feel light shining from every pore. I'm radiant beyond light and darkness. The whole Cosmos is inside me, and yet it is all so simple. The near Oneness makes it so. I sense the Threshold everywhere, woven into the awareness of this state.

From this simple, infinite self I can wrap into and around the Void. The presence of true power grows out of this simplicity. My soul crumbles and reveals behind it, the raw supremacy of Emptiness. I know Source as *Self*. My words are phantoms as they attempt to describe what I sense, slipping and sliding on the frictionless terrain. A declaration from Meister Eckhart stirs to my memory: "The eye with which I see God is the same eye with which God sees me."

I am held in suspension between heaven and Earth, between Oneness and duality. Slowly, Black announces with great reverence, "Now you know what Source gazing *really* is. You have seen God; you *are* God! The mind cannot match the understanding that you now have gained. Let it rest within your deeper sensibilities without placing words on it; not yet. Later you may fabricate explanations, as you will."

Words must be used here, at least in part. I trust to the presence behind them to communicate an essence to the reader. *Trust the 'identification' of the flame beings,* I hear echoed in my mind. I fall to my knees now and bow. It is the only action that seems to fit my circumstance. Here is the ceremony: I am bowing to the center of being. I am releasing all resistance, all falling short of grace. Source is now intimate within me—the 'I am' identity. It is who and what I am, yet it is also who I serve. To serve the essence of the Self is the most sacred of honors. It is a sacredness that reaches out to every corner of the universe. *I am that. We are that!*

Even in the farthest, most profane generations, there is this bloom of the sacred, beginning to open. As seen from here, the bud and the flower are one. Time is irrelevant, useful only as a gardener's tool to shape and prune the one, eternal plant. The profane is the mud from which the lotus springs. It is all one; it is all good. These, again, are only words. Good is not the opposite of evil. It has no opposite when time is removed, was never born.

We two float for a long while, as I contemplate. There is a passage of some sort, measured in growth, if not in time. I am growing and fulfilling some immediate destiny. Black watches—observing, noticing and sensing. I watch back. This is the essence of appreciation. Within the two of us, worlds are transforming, preparing for their expression. And yet, *nothing is happening here.* It is perfect stillness. I can see the stillness visually, stretching out like a beautiful desert, opening a grand space for the creation and growth of all forms.

"Black, what is this 'ceremony'? It seems that nothing is happening. I can tell *something* is happening here, but I don't know what it is."

"Once again, you are 'Mr. Jones', eh? You're the one who sees something happening, but doesn't know what it is? Know that this is a vital role you play: It is good to realize you do not know. There is no need for explanation, no need for reasons. You know the answers—all of them—in the *place of knowing*. This is where it is; you are 'where it's at'. There's no other place that matters.

"Nevertheless, for the letters, I will explain. This 'ceremony' is the space of sacred realization and connection with destiny. It is a transformation—as you have already sensed—of your form, in order that you may deliver your gift appropriately to your future incarnation. It likewise is much more than that: You are transforming your human life in preparation for awakening—you and millions like you on the Earth of your time. Now hear this: *You are awakening!*

"We are putting words on paper in these letters to assist in the stimulation of *waking dreams*, lucid and vibrant in your so-called 'waking' life. Your species believes, of course, it is already awake in habits and routines, its 'news media' and its political dramas. But in reality it is still fast asleep—with the emphasis on 'fast'. The pace of information is increasing, accelerating to a frenzy. Soon it will reach escape velocity—the speed of light.

"Your race is dreaming of what it fears. Fear, alas, must still guide the current collective vision. We, the appointed guides of your race for this epoch, would instill another kind of dream now, prior to your true wakefulness—a dream of fearlessness. You know, of course, these things must progress in *stages* in the world of form and time. So, at this stage we would instill a lucid dream of transformation and revelation into your current slumber. From this dream you can gradually, finally, come *awake*. It is an easing of your path, a letting go of resistance."

I sigh. "I think I understand. It's not so easy to wake up directly from the dark dreams of fear and doomsday we currently have; they are nightmares. Most humans see a world of looming economic crisis, wars, espionage and government control; they see unavoidable environmental catastrophe and ravaging diseases. I fall victim to these influences often myself. But you are proposing to put a lighter, more hopeful dream into the mix. I really like that. With this dream, we have a better platform to use for fuller consciousness when it comes."

Black answers, "Exactly so. This is the series of letters you are writing. These are for you as an individual, and for all others who would resonate with them. The letters, I must say of course, are not the only portals for your species' new dreams. There are many weaving themselves, as we speak and write, into the awareness and dreams of humanity. But, make no mistake: These letters are playing their seminal part in the preparation of the Earth. They bring with them a lessening and lightening; it is up to you, the readers and appreciators, to then generate the *lightning*.

"Into your waking dream, this ceremony is inserting the presence of peace, and the identification with newness. It is a rebirth of your etheric form. From this form, you will now commence to offer your gift to Phileina. Let it now be so: 'Bloom' in place of doom."

Letter Sixty-Seven
Hole in the Heart

With a grand and stunning flourish, Omis appears out of the Void, his huge wings spread wide above us, unfurling an awesome display of majesty. He stands at least five times taller than before. He allows his angelan aura to pervade the field for a long moment. There is no mistaking his authority here. He is obviously backed by many ranks of compatriots from his new incarnational race. This is our 'master of ceremonies' indeed!

Gradually, slowly, with due reverence, his colossal figure shrinks down to the form of Old Man, our old familiar OM. The wings disappear in stages, and in their place are Breanne and Phileina on one side, you, O, and another figure on the other. I can't make out the person beside you at first—a mystery. The space is still electrified with the energy of Omis' appearance. Each of our forms is outlined in glowing light. An overwhelming sense of peace centers upon us. *But it's a different face of peace than I felt in the flame cathedral; this is more acute and substantial.*

As the etheric dust settles into silence, I realize who the fifth person is. *It's Invm! Why on Earth is* he *here?* My mind is given a sliver of opportunity. There is much to *not* understand in what's going on. *What have I gotten myself into?* In spite of the peace that has arrived with Omis, I personally have a sense of apprehension.

Omis looks all around and beyond us, as if seeing a gathered throng of people in the emptiness. Perhaps he *does* see them. *I don't.* But even as I think this, I gradually *do* see them. Slowly, the veil is lifted and there are many hundreds of individuals around us in the background. They are arrayed in ranks in a great oval space. It takes several seconds before I realize I'm looking at the *congress* back in Paris. We are apparently in the center of the amphitheater above the Seine. The assembled participants are apparently here to bear witness to this ceremony. *More cause for my growing apprehension.*

You float over and take me by the arm. It feels good to have you close. I'm a bit overwhelmed. I glance around at the mass of people in our audience. Somehow my eyes fall upon Green. He is sitting rapt, in awe perhaps of his future incarnation. *I should think so!*

Omis speaks, and his voice is strong, "We are gathered here together to bless and inaugurate the passage out of childhood for our young friend, Phileina of Montmartre." His arm sweeps over the little girl, who is timidly hugging the side of her mother, looking up at Omis, like a grandfather god.

This is a bewildering event for her, obviously. I have no idea what preparations have been provided before this. But I can sense that no matter what they were, it could not have delivered the impact she's now feeling.

Once again, I know viscerally what Phileina is feeling and thinking; my future self is filtering into my awareness. I sense her vigilan awe and fearlessness in face of the unknown. She is eager to move ahead. And yet there is a hesitation. She still deeply appreciates her status as a child—the world she has known up until now. She wants to retain that aspect of herself. This, however, is a ceremony for parting of the ways. And she knows it.

Phileina looks over to me and realizes I'm feeling her feelings. She looks deep into my eyes with the kindest look I've ever seen. She lifts her hand and wipes a tear from her cheek. Then she extends that hand out in my direction. I see the tear glistening on her finger.

I'm with you, girl, I radiate a thought as I reach out and touch the tear.

Omis continues, gesturing out to the watching congress, "The way is opening for us in the presence of this event. We are all elevated as this child lifts up her being into the new expression. We each participate in her passage. It is for this that we are called together—to witness and to engage our own growth and destiny."

In silence, the angelan slowly moves his arms and causes our group to be rearranged. Now Breanne and Black are flanking Omis. Invm is moved directly behind him, into a position of shadow and mystery. Standing—floating—in front, in the light, is Phileina, with you on her right, me on her left. Our group has formed a semi-circle, with Omis at the center, facing the young girl.

Suddenly it dawns on me. *This is my own awakening! This child is* me *in my next life. This is when I become* truly *vigilan!* The thought of it crushes me. I fold down before Omis in a deep bow. In the same moment, I am transported into the body of the child. Not just feeling her feelings, I *am* her now, looking out through her eyes, feeling her apprehension and eagerness, entering the fulfillment of my ages of incarnations as human. I feel my hands gripping to the left and right. You are looking down at me in utter compassion from your fully vigilan womanhood. I am the young initiate, about to be brought into understanding and newness. I look to my left and see my old form, bowed in submission and release. I, as Phileina, pass your compassion onto him through my being.

Then I'm back in my human body. I am bent and anxious, not knowing, not trusting the unknown enough yet to let go. By comparison, my fear is enormous; this little one has *no* fear. *I have it all!* But she is transmitting such profound compassion—directed from you—that I finally start to relax. In a flash observation, I realize I'm a living embodiment of the duality that says peace *has* an opposite. I fluctuate continuously through that polarity. The peace I felt in the presence of the flames, the fearlessness in Phileina are the real thing, the *real* identity. Here now I'm buffeted like a tiny boat on the stormy ocean of peace and agitation.

When, at last, I regain some composure and look up, I realize everyone is *waiting* for me. I'm the holdout in this ceremony. *I'm supposed to be offering my gift to Phileina.* Yet all I can do is focus on my own struggle. Embarrassed, I look around. You and Omis and the others stare intently, compassionately at me. The crowd in the amphitheater looks on, as patient as ever. Then I realize there's another whole layer of observers, ones characterized by great compassion. Behind the transparency of the amphitheater, there are hosts of angels or angelans—*I can't really tell the difference*—also watching. *They're all waiting for me to do something. What?* I stand up straight finally, hoping that I will realize what is required of me.

Now Omis speaks, "My son, you have made your realization. You have seen your place and your scenario. That is all that is required—that and your willingness to give. And you have already demonstrated it by just being here. Your soul is ready. Open now your heart!"

With that, the angelan thrusts his right hand out. It seems to project from his body across the distance between us—right into me. *This is no illusion. It's really happening!* His hand has entered my chest and is pulling out again—holding my beating heart! I stare, frozen, but strangely, *not* with fear. I've somehow been anesthetized to that. I'm frozen in amazement. *How can this be happening?* I feel like an Aztec sacrifice!

In a flash I am slung back to a past life memory, when I actually *was* sacrificed on the altar, high atop a Mexican pyramid. I relive that predicament in my mind. In an incarnation long ago, I had been well prepared and indoctrinated before hand. I was sacrificing myself willingly. I had taken a drug to block the pain, so it was not as horrifying as one might imagine. I actually *wanted* to do this. It was a great honor to serve my people and my gods in this way. I was a willing martyr.

As the priest struck the blade into my chest and pulled out the organ, dripping and pumping with red, dark liquid, I watched. It seemed like an eternity; time slowed to a crawl. The gathered crowd below was stirring and chanting in response to the priest's invocations. Once my brain had died, I continued to watch from the etheric body, floating above.

The chants of the priest gradually transformed in my ears into a foretelling of destiny for my people and my land. At this point I had lost any attachment to my old form. I was simply looking at the unfolding event with wonder and fresh wisdom. At last I rose away toward the realm of my gods; the words that echoed in my aura were, "Mother of God, *Madre de Mexico!*" The Aztec priest's face had transformed into that of the Virgin Mary, holding my heart against her own.

Omis holds my heart—*not* dripping blood, thankfully—pulsing with light, and stares forcefully into my eyes. In my shared awareness with Phileina, I know he is simultaneously staring also into *her* eyes. He moves to stand before her and, in a motion as swift as before, thrusts my heart inside *her* chest. I gasp. *Again I'm not afraid.* Fear has been banished. I am simply struck by the power of the gesture.

I am an empty being. My heart has been removed. *But I'm still alive somehow.* It occurs to me, with no small humility, that my heart has been added to the list of martyrs who preceded me on Montmartre—the mountain of martyrs. Now, the truly amazing thing happens. I can feel my heart beating inside Phileina's body. She now has two hearts! And I have none. *Is this how I die, then?* I wonder. *Is this my final death as a human? Is Phileina's beginning my end?* No, I'm still alive. I look to you for some answer, some indication that this can truly be happening.

You bow your head reverently, but do not approach me. Instead you bend and embrace the little girl. I feel that embrace. There is something of me *alive* in her. I laugh inside myself, *Duh, of course there is!* You look up at me at last and project a thought, *"You'll be all right. This is going to take some adjustment though."* I realize you had no idea this would happen either. You're 'adjusting' just as I am. *But you're better at it than me!*

I swivel my head, looking at each person in the small circle. Then I turn my vision beyond and begin finding the eyes in the audience. In a matter of minutes, it seems I have looked thousands of people directly in the eyes; energy returns to me from each individual. Now I follow this action out into the hosts of angels and angelans. There beyond also, are Mihelo and Gavrea. Each one gives me energy through the eyes. That energy is transferring into my body, running down my aura, into the chakras. All the chakras in my body are spinning in perfect harmony, merging, fusing into one chakra—the *heart* chakra.

Now there is truly only one energy center in my aura. It begins to pour forth a liquid light into my physical form, into the center of my chest, where there is an empty hole. I am told, by some deep and wise voice from the assembly, that this is an ancient tradition—creating the 'hole in the heart'. Under the proper conditions and guidance, the entire universe can then reside in this hole—whole. The vitality continues to pour into my chest from the heart opening. It is assembling some strange form there—*like* a heart, yet with a hole in its center. It opens out into the stars! *I have many questions to ask when this over.*

All attention now turns away from me to Phileina. She is standing still as crystal in a shaft of silver light. The light is coming right out of the Void itself. The girl's silver-gold hair gleams brightly. She has her hands cupped over her chest and her eyes closed, a beatific smile on her face. Never have I seen a lovelier child. I realize in this moment, she is dearer to me than my own life, my own body and heart. I am glad to give her my heart. It is as though I have known her since creation. The mental comprehension that she is my own incarnation is one thing. The feeling and joy that goes with this encounter is something else completely.

Omis whispers down inaudible words that take magical forms in the air. We can see them. The words have become fairy-like creatures dancing in the silver beam; they light upon Phileina's shoulders. Gradually they absorb into her skin. The angelan continues this 'word play' for a while and then abruptly stops. He announces audibly to all, "We shall now enter the Void. Phileina, are you ready?"

The little girl breathes deeply and straightens to her full stature. Her voice, however, quavers as she answers, *"Oui, monsieur."*

"Come with me, then, dear one. You will enjoy this. It is simply your introduction to a new part of life. This is the beginning. Thus will you know directly, the Source. It is your very *own* Source."

The giant angelic figure reaches out his hands and lifts up Phileina against his mighty breast, wrapping her in his wings. She is tiny by comparison. As we all watch, the two forms enter the silver shaft and are drawn down, melting into the light. They disappear into emptiness. Stillness. Wonder.

The surface of the deep is quivering and rippling out into the atmosphere. Opalescent colors cascade around us all. One of the ripples catches me by the scruff of my neck. I am suddenly jerked up into the silvery beam and then, unceremoniously, down—straight into the Void. I feel myself melt in, just as Omis and Phileina did.

I'm now rushing headlong into the Great Abyss at a raging speed. In seconds I catch up with Omis and the girl. Omis reaches around me with one great arm as we descend, deeper and deeper; I'm held firmly next to Phileina. We're in the Void, for sure, but somehow we're retaining our forms. Every other time I've come here, my memory has blanked out and I have dissolved into nothing. This time we seem to be in a bubble descending into the formless.

Omis answers my thought, "We are indeed in a protective aura. We are bringing a bit of the Threshold with us. You might say we're *projecting* into the projector. I realize neither of you have been properly introduced to the Void." He looks at me. "That is why you're here in a supporting role."

I look at Phileina. Her eyes are wide open, her mouth as well. She's never seen anything like this. She looks at me and asks, "Brother *monsieur*, do you know where we're going?"

"Not really, Phileina. And it isn't necessary to call me 'monsieur'. Do you know who I am?"

She shakes her head, but something is beginning to register, "I thought you were my new brother, but now I see something else. You come from an older time—many, many years older."

"Yes, I do, about 200 years. *Effectivement, je suis la personne que* tu *étais à l'epoque*. ['Actually', I am the person *you* used to be in that time.] Do you know about re-incarnation?"

She nods slowly as if uncertain, but then answers, "It's only natural to have come from before, I guess. Others have always been there in the past, inside us. How have you come here then? Why are you not still in the past?"

I laugh out loud as I ponder that question. She looks at me, wondering. Finally I say simply, "That's a long story. I'm not sure I have a good answer for you. I am here as a kind of projection, just like we are projecting down into the Void with Uncle Omis. May we call you 'Uncle Omis'?" I look up into the angelan's impassive face, trying to get him to smile.

Now the Void is changing color. Its silver darkness is turning to a golden one. There is still no form, except for our bubble. *What can we hope to see in this endless emptiness?* I wonder.

Omis answers, "I don't mind the 'uncle'. You humans do have a peculiar sense of humor; I know from my own memories. I accept. I know you mean no disrespect. Regarding what we can hope to see: We will not see anything with our 'eyes' in here. Our forms in this projection are but illusions. Our minds will translate the sensations into some sort of vision. But we will only know, in our hearts, what is really happening. And we do have *hearts*, do we not?" I swear I can see a slight smile on his lips.

Letter Sixty-Eight
Essence of Eternity

Omis continues, "Let me remind you both. This is the Void, *Evam*—the Great Emptiness. It is the bottom of the deepest abyss in creation, before creation. It is the formless foundation of all forms. Out of its non-substance arise all substances in the phenomenal worlds. Here is reality; *there* is what reality has projected."

I see nothing. The blackness has closed in on our little bubble thoroughly; yet there is no pressure, nothing to press. In my heart I know presence is here nonetheless. This is the original essence from which we generate all experience, including the Now. My vision is at a loss.

Intuition tells me I must *see* with my heart. *But, alas, where is that heart? It now beats within this young girl beside me.* Wherever my heart is, I must teach it to see. The hole in my own chest must now pulse and take on the part of vision in these reaches.

Omis bends down and peers into the eyes of Phileina. She is remarkably open and accepting of these bizarre events. But as the angelan faces her directly now, I sense a bit of apprehension; she's thinking of her mother and how far away Breanne seems.

He performs more of his magic; Omis suddenly shrinks down. He first assumes the form of OM; then he swiftly shrinks even further, into a new shape—a teddy bear. In this fuzzy, endearing form he jumps up onto Phileina's shoulder. She smiles instinctively and, for a long moment, just waits. Finally with a laugh, she reaches and pulls him down into her arms, cuddling him like a toy doll. He smiles up into her eyes. *Très bizarre!*

He looks at her with large, button eyes and begins to sing a French lullaby. She knows the words and smiles again, beginning to sing quietly along with him. This has the instant effect of calming and restoring her to full, vigilan presence. *So quickly back into centered appreciation.* The little Omis bear jumps out of her arms and back onto her shoulder; he leans toward her ear and begins to tell her a story.

"Once, a very long time ago, right here where we are now, there were no people and no things. There was not even *space* here. There was no *time* either."

Phileina reacts, "So, it wasn't even a long *time* ago, Uncle. You're not making sense!"

Omis stands up on her shoulder and says, "Ah, but *sense* had not been invented yet either. Nothing made any *sense* at all yet. You were just waking up then. It was just the beginning of you."

"Of me?" she asks. "I was here then? I don't remember it."

"I know. But that's why we've come back—to remember. That's why I want to tell you this story. You see, you were the first one here."

"Me? Why was *I* the first?"

"Because each of us sees it that way—from our own eyes. There was only *one*. We were all together in just one soul—you, me, everyone. We were *all* first; and we still *are*. In the Source, there is only one point of view; and time never existed. Even now. We have returned to the place of *beginning*."

She nods her head and urges. "Uncle Omis, please tell the story."

The little animal sits down next to Phileina's ear and continues, "Yes, I will continue. Now, in the beginning you were making up *sense*."

"Uncle, this is very confusing. Are you confusing me on purpose?"

"Hmm," he replies. "Yes, I suppose I am. That's the way we angelans do. It's kind of like telling *riddles*. We like for you to find the answers for yourself. Therefore, we tell you riddles."

She straightens herself up and responds, "In that case, it's OK. I like riddles. I'm good at answering them. In fact I think I already know the answer to yours."

"You do?" The teddy bear looks surprised. "What is it then?"

"I was making up sense. And that means *senses* too."

"Exactly. When you started making sense, *all* the senses started. For example, you decided that *hearing* would be a good idea, so you could *listen* to things."

"But, monsieur, you said there was nothing to listen to."

"Yes," he says, acting a little vexed. "So then you had to create *things* to listen to—birds and volcanoes and oceans and people. But you couldn't see any of them yet."

She exclaims, "So I invented *seeing*. I get it. Then I invented touch and taste and smell."

The angelan bear smiles. "Indeed—*all* those senses. Today there are only five of them usually, but in the beginning there were many more. And then you had to create all the things to see and hear and touch with those senses. You started making a *lot* of sense! And that's where things began getting complicated, and confusing."

He pauses for a breath. "I'm getting ahead of myself. Before you could *see* anything with the sense of sight, you had to find the *light.*"

"The light?" she asks. "You mean it was lost?"

"Sort of. It was hiding in the darkness."

"The light was hiding? Why?" She interrupts again. *I'm beginning to think this child is a bit precocious.*

"Because that is light's nature. It waits in the darkness until it is found."

"I don't understand," she declaims. *Neither do I. My mind is muddled.*

"Light waits for us to be *ready* for it. If it comes out of hiding too soon, we miss the point and the *spark* of it. If we don't have eyes to see it, or consciousness to appreciate it, it stays hidden. It waits for us to make up our minds and our senses. Until we can make sense of the light, it stays down in the darkness."

"So then, Uncle, how did I find the light?"

"You got *ready:* After you made up all those senses, you made up time. And the light knew it was *time* to be found! It opened a little window and peaked out." Omis, the bear, puts his paws over his face and gestures, peaking through them.

"I looked into the window? And I saw the light inside?"

"That's it! You looked in and you saw, just like now. It was just in time! That's why we're here again in the dark. Our bubble is the same window, and we're all looking through it with you."

She frowns. "But I don't see the light now. Where is it?"

"It's still hiding because you haven't invented one last thing."

She takes the little bear off her shoulder and holds him out in front, studying his features closely. "What?"

"Do you remember me saying we can't use ordinary eyes in here? Well, there's another kind of eye we need for seeing."

She stands quietly for a moment. Then, Phileina's intuition lights up. "Another riddle!"

She doesn't say anything else, but looks around, as if anticipating something. Then a deep voice rises up, as if composing itself out of the very stillness. It sends shivers through the air. It chants the words, "What stirs the darkness of the deep? What lights the vision that we seek?"

Phileina listens silently for a moment. Then she exclaims excitedly, "It's the heart. The *eyes* of the heart!"

I shake my head, not understanding. I ask, "Phileina, what do you mean by that?"

"I can *see* with my heart. We all can," she states, as if it is plain as day. "But there's only *one* eye in the heart, not two. It looks out from Source, from where Oneness is."

I feel like I'm way out of my league listening to this little girl. She understands things instantly that have taken me ages to even wonder about.

Phileina continues, "And I know something else: That's where the first *sense* came from—it's only one sense at first. The eye in the heart started it all; it started all the other senses too."

She puts the animated toy bear down and looks over at me. "I never knew that before. Did you?"

"No, not at all," I shrug, acknowledging that her intuition is outstripping mine. "But I guess that's why I'm here with you."

"That's right," says Omis. He suddenly expands to the size and shape of OM again and continues, looking at me. "The heart is the progenitor of the senses, the underlying sensation—vibration—you have felt many times during your incubations."

He turns back to the girl. "Can you see the *beginning* I was telling you about? It's still here. It has never stopped being here."

"Yes, I know it's here. It's inside me. It never goes away or changes."

I notice now, that there has indeed been a major change in the girl's demeanor. She is maturing before my eyes, coming into wisdom beyond her years. I look at Omis and see that, out of his heart, he is pouring a fine strain of light; it is streaming directly into *her* heart—the heart that is *my* heart and hers together—into our *twin* hearts.

It finally occurs to me to ask, "Omis, why does Phileina need two hearts? What's *that* about?"

He turns to me, looking down at my chest. "You have given her this gift for two reasons: There are always two reasons in the duality worlds. The first is that she is taking the 'heart initiation' and requires two kinds of sensibility for this. It is to start the pulse—duality, forth and back, the cycling out and in. She needs to bring *your* experience into her being at this transition—your own maturity and wisdom, *such as it is."* He smiles. "She is another aspect of your twin soul. This is the foundation she needs to start the process within her.

"The second reason is that you, my friend and son, have needed to give up your heart for some time now. You have sought it in your outer world, in your search for loves and lovers. But here you have found the true avenue within, toward center. You have given your true love *to* your true love—your own soul, reborn and renewed in Phileina. It is thus that true love, true heart, comes to those who long to be at one. It has indeed left you with the hole in the center of your being. This hole is an *eye*, a vesica or portal, if you will. Through that eye your vision will pass—through the Void—to the other side."

I gasp, "Are you saying there's another side to the Void?"

Omis laughs, "Isn't Life full of surprises! Yes. It is, for you, a great mystery and paradox. I will explain, for your mind, in a moment." He looks back to Phileina.

She says, "I know about paradoxes. I just learned it from my hearts—both of them. They are talking to each other. I can hear them speaking inside me. They are *teaching* each other."

She stops for a moment, "But there's still only *one eye* between them. It's like they need *two* to make *one*."

Instantly, we are flooded with light, gleaming in iridescence. I shield my eyes, but the brightness penetrates me nevertheless. I cannot blind it out here—not now that Phileina has used my own heart to discover its light. I decide to watch, since I have no choice. The luminance is like a rapidly moving tunnel, passing around us—and through us—erupting continuously from a deep, indescribable center. *Either it's passing us, or we're falling into it—perhaps both.*

"Perhaps neither," Omis answers my thought. "Motion is merely a symbol for it. It is the way of this light to appear always as a passage—it is the *ultimate portal*. It is the essence of *newness* itself. In this light you can see the *beginning* of all things, never ending. If you've ever had the impulse to 'begin again', this light was the origin of that desire. Here, we have the *zero point* of creation. Tell me, friend, what do you make of it?"

I'm baffled, overwhelmed. *What can he mean?* For some reason, I can't answer. My mind is blocking a response. I wrestle with myself. *Stop! I'm in the Void, bubble or not. I can reach into this 'essence of eternity' for any answer to any question.* In this moment, I see that I've been harboring a subtle resistance. I've been denying inspiration to myself—through feeling inferior to my future incarnation. I brought my own resistance with me into the Void—inside this projected bubble. *What a sacrilege,* I chastise myself. Then, of course, I see that *that,* too, is resistance.

With the help of the Void in me, I take a deeper look at my mind and its thoughts of limitation. It is just a simple mechanical part of my greater being. It's like a little *clicking toy.* I will myself to reach out into the greater being—of light and dark—around us. My resistance whimpers and quivers for a moment; then it dissolves into a mist, swirling before the single 'eye'. That misplaced energy hovers briefly before me, searching for a place to go. Then it sweeps in a rush back into my energy body and is absorbed.

I know the answer to Omis' question. I stare directly into the fierce light of many colors. Appreciation wells up and tears flow. "What I make of this light, old friend, is that the Source—the *very* Source—is actually *visible* to us. It is the 'other side of the Void'. Here, through the eye of the heart, we can see God! God is the light and love of Source."

"Bravo!" he smiles and puts a large hand on my shoulder; the other he places on Phileina's little shoulder. She is teary with joy and smiling too, having already intuited all this long ago.

Letter Sixty-Nine
Source Gazing

Omis takes our hands in his. Together we gaze into the rushing Source. *Can this truly be the origin of everything in the Cosmos?* My heart says, "Yes!" Yet there are no words that can carry this back to the mind.

The light is ever-changing—rising and dissolving, turning and swirling. It is the ultimate, original *whirling dervish.* It is a transcendental, multi-dimensional kaleidoscope. The more I look, the more dazzling and mesmerizing it is, and the more I'm drawn in. *My eyes are not really seeing this; something else is sensing—it is the 'other' awareness.* There are occasional explosions and implosions, jets and spouts, tornadoes and vortices—simultaneous eruption and collapse.

The images are like what I've seen of the sun's surface, and yet a thousand times *more*—more colorful, more astounding, more intoxicating. And, true to Omis' story, it stimulates *all* the senses, not just the visual. Sounds and smells, even tastes ripple through me. The *touch* of this river of light is delightful to our skin. Powerful, awe-stirring emotions flow out as well; lofty ideas, philosophies and words spread out upon the breath of God. Beautiful poetry and music sing in this wind tunnel. There is no end to the language that could be applied to this sight. And after all the words and languages that ever existed, there would still be insufficient verses to describe this *uni*verse.

So, this *is Source gazing!* I swallow. Now I hear B's voice in my head. *"This is just the first level, darling. There are uncountable levels beyond this."*

I'm swamped suddenly with a feeling of smallness at the thought of being here. A dark wedge of resistance tries to flicker up in me, as it often does. It challenges, 'who are *you* to be here, witnessing *this?* Who do you think you *are?* You don't have the *right* to be here!'

Without a further thought, however, I turn away and laugh at this final attempt of my ego. The answer to my doubts comes swiftly and firmly from the 'I am' presence in me, '*I am God. I have the right!*'

Now I realize what is being communicated. It's all about *identification* again. The flame people were teaching this. Ego is asking me to identify back with *it* and with its patterns of resistance; ego would have me identify with doubt and separation. 'Who are you?' it asks. 'What is your *identity?'* Now, in this place, I can easily see that even the ego is giving me clues to transcendent answers: *I choose my* true *identity—Source! I choose reality.* My identity is Oneness. My singular vision—through the eye of heart—is testimony to that Oneness. There is no real *observer* in the eye, separated from its *object* of observation. Reality is an all-seeing, sensing-being Oneness.

There can be no real separation from Source. Source is always within and around us; it is through us entirely, in every atom and speck of existence. In every space we fill, it fills *us*. Source is so close it allows us to pretend not to see it. We can pretend its not there, or that it's separate from us for a time. We can choose to resist it. But even these actions, when viewed from Source, are linkages to the truth. Even resistance—the ego's question of identity—is a bridge between the dream and the reality. True identity will not be denied. Doubt and fear are links to their opposite polarities—love and faith.

The flames of Source continue to whip through us; it is unceasing, relentless creation and destruction. We three beings, and our bubble, dissolve into the fiery explosion; we are swallowed up fully, lost into its midst. And yet, no, we are *not* lost at all; we are *found!* And in this, Phileina has found her light. This foundation is our essence. *From here, we—as Source—do initiate and embrace it all; and we extinguish it in the end!*

Omis decrees, "This is the most profound experience you or any other creature can ever have. Yes, this is Source gazing! And it goes on endlessly, beyond forever. Phileina, this is your inheritance. This is the true gift our friend from the past has given you this day. This is your initiation! You stand now on the threshold of all your destinies. Do you accept it?"

She looks very small, standing between us. *But she is great of heart, great of character.* Tears are streaming down her face now. *They* are the answer to the angelan's question. She needs say nothing more. She nods assent, nevertheless, to complete the ritual.

Together, we begin withdrawing from the Void. Our heart eye dims and rests back below its beating pulse. We are ecstatic as we push out of the Void and back into the Threshold, to meet our friends.

I expect to emerge onto the playground in Paris. But no—we have returned to the veranda, in the mountains of the Sun. You and I, B and Invm and Omis are seated around the low table, just as before. Phileina and Breanne are nowhere to be seen. I jerk around inside, feeling a piercing loss. I implore of Omis, "Where have they gone?"

"They haven't gone anywhere. They remain in their world, in their time, just where you found them."

"But, but…" I stammer.

You place your hand on my arm and whisper, "I too found myself very attracted to Phileina and Breanne. There will be other opportunities to see them, however. I assure you. Don't be upset. Try to use their departure as a means of release. Let go of the form and feel the formless space they have left for us."

"I'm sorry. I just got really attached to that little girl." By voice breaks as tears flow. "Oh my god…" I clasp my hands to my chest, feeling frantically for my heartbeat. "Does she really have my heart? Did you really take my heart and put it in her, Omis?"

"What's done is done. You know for yourself what happened. Be not dismayed. The hole you have opened in your *new* heart space is worth a great price in the world of awakening. You have paid that price and given that bequest to your future self. It is a noble and sacred act."

I stand up and pace around the veranda, not knowing how to feel or what to do. I'm still rubbing my chest and feeling for my pulse. There is a new tightness and shuddering there. *I can't believe this.*

Black joins me and puts her arm around my shoulder. Motherly energy flows into me from her. I look her in the eye gratefully. She places her hand on my chest and then lifts my hand to hers. "Heart to heart, we are one, my brother, my son, my daughter to be. Link with me now, here, that we may never depart from our souls' path. That hole in your heart, as disturbing as it may seem, will be very useful to you in the coming years. Accept that from me as a prophecy."

I find a semblance of my calm center again and return with B to the table. More minutes pass. Having exhausted my self-pity, I look around at you and the others. My still weeping eyes catch Invm's eyes. Something within me insists on asking another question. The four of you look at me as though waiting for me to ask it.

I stutter, "B, where, uh, did Omis take you and Invm?"

Black and Invm look at each other, knowingly. Omis smiles; perhaps he's wanting to divert attention. He nods to them. "Yes. What of that? I will let Black begin this story."

You look at B with intense curiosity. I've never seen that expression on your face before. B straightens and glances briefly at the Sirian before she begins, slowly at first. "Omis took us to Paris as well. But it was slightly earlier than your visit there. It was at the time of my first meeting of Phileina's father."

I now must have an expression similar to yours. B continues, "I was young, attending a conference near the *Champs de Mars* and the Eiffel Tower. The conference had brought together students from various countries. I, of course, was French. I met a young man from New Zealand. We began talking and found we had a lot in common; there were many synchronicities in our lives. He decided to stay in Paris for a few days after the conference. During that time, we fell in love. It all unfolded so smoothly; it was clearly an time of destiny. The young man was Invm."

I look at the Sirian with astonishment. It dawns on me, *He will be my father in the next life?* He smiles and graciously bows his large, slender head. He says, "I had no remembrance of this until Omis showed us. B had sensed it from the beginning, however, as soon as we met on Mars. It seems that the soul keeps its secrets well—until the time comes for revelation."

Black says, "We were destined to cross the universe to be together in that life it turns out. There was a deeper need for rejoining our two races—at a soul level—to produce the child Phileina. Very soon after she was born, Invm exited that incarnation and returned to his soul's homeland of Sirius. He lived only 35 years on Earth."

Invm breaks in with a high-pitched cough, "That was quite long enough, thank you. I mean no disrespect, but it can be very difficult to make such a shift out of an accustomed incarnational culture. I was uncomfortable for that whole, short lifetime. It seemed as though I was continuously adjusting to new surroundings. Indeed, I *was.*"

Black continues, "It was difficult for Phileina to lose her father so young. She was four years old when he died. This is extremely unusual in vigilan culture, where death does not normally come so early. It left psychological effects that demanded all my intuitive skills to mitigate. Of course, behind the scenes, it was all by design. My skills needed honing in this way. And for Phileina, the loss opened her appreciative centers and general sensitivity more rapidly."

I look back and forth between the two friends. "And so, what did Omis show you?"

B looks appreciatively at Invm. "We relived our whole time together in Paris—the romance, the love, the sharing. What a wonderful city for that. The time of his passing was particularly emotional." She brushes a tear from her eye and blinks rapidly. "I, for my part, am still emotional about it."

Invm interjects, "Having lived as a human for thirty five Earth years, I am able to recall the emotions as well. We Sirians generally do not have such expressive feelings in our own bodies. It was cleansing to relive my encounters and departures on Earth—cathartic, as you would say. Omis provided us both with a great service in reconnecting and re-evaluating our respective positions. We realized that our roles, too, were instrumental in his unfolding project, destined for several hundred years later. And importantly, Phileina's life is a key component in the development of Orange's destiny. It generated important linkages to the work we do now on Mars and throughout your solar system. Phileina, during her adult life, made significant discoveries in the inner dimensions. She discovered many new techniques for Source gazing. These have aided our scientists ever since, including those monitors you have encountered at Ostraness."

You acknowledge his comment. "I'm feeling the presence of that little French girl in me more and more. I know, for example, that her explorations of Source enabled me to be born with the confidence to embark on my own career. The unfolding mystery is a wonder to behold. The way all of us here are interrelated is a magnificent scenario, clearly designed by the oversoul spanning many individual lifetimes."

Invm adds, "Omis is to be credited for navigating us into this understanding." He pauses with a sudden realization. "And in fact in orchestrating the entire *script.*"

The Old Man, has remained characteristically silent and observing; he stares at us impassively. After a minute of silent appreciation, he starts. "From my perspective, now in the angelan race, I have been made privy to those deeper levels of the oversoul. I can testify that it is even grander and more interwoven than you suspect. As we continue our journey together—in alignment with the production of our friend's book—I will expose you to some of the wonders yet to be unfolded. The 'project', dear colleagues, continues to reveal itself as ever more profound. I see it now embracing the entire Earth experience."

After some more, meditative silence, I begin to look around. I stand and walk over to the balustrade. There far below I see the golden slopes, layering off into the far distance. It may be a frozen sunscape, yet in it I sense raw power and vitality. I also feel the underlying inferno—so near, so fierce, so unassailable. It is a reminder of the Source, deeply etched in my recent memory.

Returning to my seat, I ask, "Omis, does the fact that your home is here have anything to do with the Source and the Void?"

"Of course it does. Each star in the Cosmos is one tiny face of the Source, just as dark space embodies the Void. The radiations in and out of these star openings, including the grand family of interstellar forms—black holes, galaxy streams and threads of dark matter. All these are prime interfaces between the inner and outer worlds on the macrocosmic scale. In the microcosm, our bodies and chakras follow suit; so too do molecules and atoms, subatomic particles, and the like. All creation and space is one vast, cosmic portal—Source. *And Source is the portal into the Void.*" He waves his arms above his head, then down toward the vista. "We are here, in this dimension of my home, as a function of our work in the Threshold. I draw much inspiration and vitalization from it. And so shall you as well."

The four of us sit silently again, allowing the sensation of radiance to sweep up through us. The more I ponder, the more I sense the emptiness again. At last I break the silence. "Omis, speak to me again of the Void. What is it truly? I know there's something I'm missing."

The three of you look at me strangely for a moment; then in unison, begin to laugh. Omis surprises me with a broad smile on his face. "Something you're missing? Well, where do I start? All right, forgive us; we've had a little amusement at your expense. Thank you for that. Within the Void there is indeed an infinity you are missing. But we are *all* missing it. You're not alone. That is the essence of it all. *The Void is precisely what is* missing *in all existence!*

"There is so much in that emptiness yet to be revealed; it is beyond any capacity for measurement. This is why your profession of Source gazing is so enchanting. The revelations are continuous and endless. These are the fount of all discovery and knowledge in the world. The Cosmos, in every moment of all time, is waiting breathlessly for this elixir of creation to pour forth. As we have repeated many times, it is the Source of unending beginnings."

I'm a little ashamed of my empty-headedness in the presence of you all, but I allow that to pass quickly. *I'm just human, after all.* "Well, about that idea of endless beginnings—if stars represent the Source, how is it that they die? That's an *ending."*

You reply, "The physical stars are within the *duality* world, yes. They come and go; they're born and they die, over serenely long time spans. Nevertheless, they also embrace within themselves the depth of Oneness; and they never do actually depart from it. In addition, Source is the stimulus of 'beginning' behind both birth *and* death. Behind each side of duality expression is the impetus to *newness.* In death there is newness from Source, just as in birth."

Omis takes up again, "To address your first question, you humans are always trying to *fill in* the Void, no matter how you may feel it in your lives. Your minds and egos like to dwell on the surface. You, rightly, fear what lies below. It is not your *human* identity. It is *alien* to that persona. Below you the Void does lie, nonetheless, quietly, persistently waiting for those lone moments when your surficial distractions run out. Then it rises—*almost* to the surface, yet not quite there.

"The Void does not truly come to the surface. Not fully. The surface is a façade, an illusory form. The Void is *reality.* You will never find it in superficiality. It beckons you always—from within. Reality—authenticity—is always there within you speaking to you in the still, small voice. No matter how you try, you cannot hide from reality."

I interrupt, "Is *that* the ultimate reality then? Nothing? Everything is just *nothing*, total emptiness and meaninglessness?"

Omis squints, "Have you not heard what I said? That 'nothingness' is the fount of all your 'things', of all creation. As for 'meaning', that *must* come out of the emptiness, out of the vast formless being. There is nowhere else it can come from. The Void is hardly devoid of meaning. It is the formless raw material out of which meaning grows.

"Meaning cannot derive from itself—that is, not from the form it takes on in your world; this cannot be a *first cause*. That would be *truly* meaningless. As an example, red cannot derive from red; to say so would be without informational value. Red must have a source that is not its own form. Red derives from the prismatic splitting or pure white light; it comes from incarnate visual perception. In the same way, meaning comes from the prismatic splitting of the emptiness, projected into the sensibilities of creatures such as you and me. Source, though never *separate,* must always be perceived as 'other' than that which is derived from it. Otherwise derivation itself is meaningless.

"I know that O would agree with me." He looks to you for a moment. "She loves to point out secret meanings of words, hidden in their roots. This is the point I would make: Every thing must derive from *no thing* by some path. Meaning must derive from a state that precedes meaning. Thus the Void is by no means meaning*less.*

"But humanity, obsessed with wanting *more* of everything, and feeling acute scarcity all around it, does denigrate the nothingness of the Void and tries to relegate it to inconsequential. Your species wants to make it irrelevant. Your fear dictates your psychology; that fear, however, actually conceals an innate *knowing* within you. If the Void were truly irrelevant, there would be no need to fear it. By your fear, you acknowledge the power lying at its core.

"By attempting to *fill* the Void within you, you turn to all manner of delusions, distractions and addictions. You turn your backs on the Now, filling it up with form-bound and time-bound reactions. You identify with these things in a vain attempt to displace power from its true foundation and put it into the ego and mind. This cannot work, as you well know. The surface has no power except as derived from below. Thus does your ego fear real power and mask it over with its version of power—control. All your fears are, in fact, reactions against the depths within your own being; they take form at the interface with the Void. For many this is the threshold of fear.

"We advise that you accept the Void as your ultimate reality; you would thus address your fears face-on. There could be no greater 'reality show'. For the evolution of your species to proceed, you must pass through that threshold of fear, doubt and abandonment in order to find peace. But be assured, the Void is the Source of the only peace and power there truly is."

I finally relax; I drop my arms and lean my head back. With your help, with Omis and B and Invm around me, I let go into that peace and presence. *I know what he says is true.* I now sit, squarely in the moment, and look out onto the still surface of the sun—the center for our solar system—at intensely close range. I could not have a finer view. The energy enters me and swells. The sun is my center and soul, my *logos* and solar angle; it has given me everything. Suddenly I'm overcome with an urge to return to Paris, and to see Phileina once more.

Letter Seventy
Cœur Sacral

I'm standing in the playground again. Breanne and Phileina are with me. *You, Orange, are not.* It's just we three. The little girl looks up at me, so pretty and fresh, so full of enthusiasm for life. "We are now a family, are we not, monsieur?"

I smile, "Yes, indeed we are. I'm so happy to be here again. I went somewhere else on the way back. Did you come directly here?"

"Yes," Breanne answers. "Where did you go?"

"O and I went back with Omis. He has a grand mansion—on the surface of the sun, if you can believe it."

She laughs softly, "I can believe anything you tell me about Omis. His presence is a true marvel."

Phileina grabs my hand and looks up. "I've been to his house on the sun, you know."

I look down surprised. "You have? When was that?"

"I don't know, monsieur. But I remember it. Maybe I'm remembering *your* memory. Maybe a dream."

I ponder the small child's face for a moment. "Anything is possible, Phileina. I wouldn't be surprised if you *were* remembering my memories. We have a very close connection, you know."

"I know," she sighs, as though she's suddenly feeling the weight of maturity in her young mind. "I'm growing up very fast—all at once it seems. I feel strange. I *know* things now I didn't have to *learn*. Do you know what I mean, monsieur?"

"Yes, quite." I look her in the eye. "Please call me *frère*, 'brother'. 'Monsieur' sounds so formal. OK?"

"I like that, *mon frère. Grand frère.*"

"So, what do you remember about Omis' house?"

"It is beautiful and very old, in a very old place—the oldest place in our solar system. I know it's where the Earth and all the other planets came from. It's where all our things here, including people, came from. Uncle Omis has his home in the place where everything comes from."

Breanne looks on serenely, but is listening closely. Phileina ponders for a moment before continuing. "But I think, more important, it's where *God* comes from. I do *know* God now. Not like before though, *grand frère?* Do you understand?"

"I do understand. You mean Source."

"Yes, but *God—Dieu—*too. 'God' is the name we can use for Source if we want to. It's more friendly, I think."

She stops, wrinkling her little brow, then points at the sun. "I can see God in the sky. Look there. It's so bright. But isn't it funny; every night it disappears into the dark. It goes down into night."

"Yeah, maybe it's what Source does; it goes back to the Void," I answer. "Isn't that interesting. What do you think it does when it goes back into the dark?"

"Well," she replies thoughtfully, but as a child. "Everybody needs to sleep. Right?"

Breanne and I laugh. She says, "Just so. We all need a good night's sleep. And there's no better place than the Void for that."

Then the girl adds an explanation, "God and Source are really the same, I know. But I still like 'Dieu'. It makes me feel better. "

"Hmm. I've got no problem with that, Phileina. But in my time, many people used the name 'God' to *separate* themselves from others. They missed the point of God. They thought *their* God was different from other people's God. Christians, Muslims, Hindus and Buddhists had God all locked up inside their beliefs. Religions had become so complicated."

She looks up brightly, still holding my hand. "I think it's much simpler now."

"I think so too. It's good to be alive in this time—even if I'm only here for a visit."

"You're welcome to visit us anytime, brother. I'm sure you will come back again."

I reflect, a bit sadly, "I sure would like to think that, *petite sœur.*"

Clouds have come over the sun above us. I feel the gray air and shiver, when I think I might never return again. *Why am I back here at all? Why was I drawn to Phileina again? I want to be here, but why?*

Breanne is suddenly stirred with an intuition, as if in answer to my thought. She looks up into the sky and then at each of us.

Phileina announces, "I should like to take a, *maman.* walk would do us all good. May we?"

That feels right. We both agree, nodding, and set off. Phileina says a few words to her friends on the playground, and then comes along. I pause for a moment, watching the small girl and the tall woman going before.

The street turns steeply upward when we leave the playground. In silence we climb. *I wonder what they're thinking.* I sense my companions aren't using thought at all right now. Rather, they're appreciating this moment directly. Their minds are clear, their senses crisp and alert. Using them as inspiration, I ease myself, step by step up the path; I begin to emulate their style of awareness. My thoughts, too, gradually wisp away.

As we ascend, the weather continues to change. A cloud has wrapped itself around the butte, and a thin fog drifts down. The air is chilly. I wonder, but it doesn't bother me. I accept, just as my companions do. Falling in with them, my senses sharpen with each step. I feel the uneven stones underfoot in a new way. My shoes seem transparent; each surface takes on a touch and a presence. There are small plants—weeds, to my human mind—between some of the cobbles. They smell sweet and radiate a gentle light into the foggy air. I can even smell them.

Phileina senses my observation and picks one of the tiny flowers, handing it to me. It seems to melt into the palm of my hand. *It is identifying with me, communicating the same way the flame people did.* It's melting into my form, with a message: It tells me of the permanence of Life—and the *impermanence* of form; all forms pass quickly, but peace, presence and abundance remain. I can taste the flower's essence through the molecules of my hand. I thank it and put it gently into my shirt pocket.

Buildings slide past us in the gray mist. As I turn attention on them, they begin to tell me *their* silent stories. I sense into ancient decades and centuries. Briefly, in a filmy vision I see the people who lived here long ago. I realize my mind is not interpreting these stories. If so, they would turn into a tangle of data. In my expanded state it is all clear and simple, well ordered.

Over there is a gate where, a century ago, two friends entered and only one came out. One died inside; it was a *beginning.* His death was peaceful and destined to be. On the other side of the street is a window where a lover watched her husband disappear down the street, 300 hundred years ago. He did not return for a very long time, after many voyages at sea. By then, many things had changed. The street itself speaks to me as well. It tells of footprints from a thousand years of artists and travelers, fighters and monks, moving through the day and night. I marvel at the intimacy and detail of these stories. They would continue forever, if I allowed them.

At last, we're atop the Butte of Montmartre. The basilica of Sacré Cœur stands white and tall, imposingly above us, its spires cloaked in the closeness of the clouds. Breanne stops us here, again in silence. I look at Phileina. She shrugs and smiles, indicating her sympathies with my curiosity. There are a few people on the street, but not many by the standards of my day. The throngs of tourists I've always associated with this place are not to be seen. There is one small group of admirers staring down the slope into the city, almost invisible in the haze.

Breanne pulls us aside and begins, somewhat solemnly, "This site has a long history—long before a church was here. The history is told in the name, *Sacré Cœur:* This means 'coronated' or 'crowned' heart. Today the name has changed to *Cœur Sacral,* or 'heart made sacred'. I will explain the reason for this change in a moment.

"This butte has long been the creative heart of Paris, indeed, even before the city existed. History has swept around its ramparts. Druids settled here on the high ground, escaping the swamps down by the river. The Romans built a temple to Mars here when they conquered the land. They gave it the name *Lutetia Parisiorum.* Gypsum mines were eventually tunneled deeply into the butte over the centuries. The subterranean openings left behind are a key element in the heart of Paris. They represent the 'hole in the heart' of this city.

"Over the centuries, many people were killed here and became martyrs. The name of Montmartre is a linguistic coincidence of the words, 'Mars' and 'martyr'. In one symbolic event in your third century, Roman conquerors beheaded the first bishop of Paris, Denis, near this spot. Legend recounts that the saint picked up his head and walked away with it. In the late 1800s, many anarchist rebels of the *Commune de Paris* were entombed in the mines during a violent period of insurrection. The national government was intent on reclaiming this suburb of Paris for itself.

"At that time, this basilica was built amidst great religious and secular turmoil. Its placement was a symbol of religious dominance in Paris—hence the 'crowned heart'. For nearly two centuries feelings, directed toward this symbol, were divided and hostile. Time passed, however, and evolution healed the old wounds—just as Mars was once conceived to be solely a symbol of masculine, military might. Appreciation does evolve."

I interrupt, "May I ask about that? The Martian connection to Paris keeps coming up. Do you know what that's about?"

"Yes. I know that we view Mars quite differently from the way humanity did. But it is all a matter of evolving sensibilities. The Greek forerunner of Mars was Ares; he was believed to be purely an aggressive, intimidating force. In Roman times, Mars was still the war god, but he was also the bringer of peace, the tamer of wilderness; he was the provider of agriculture and general nourishment. This was the start of bringing in more feminine attributes. The Romans finally conceived of his marriage with Venus; this foreshadowed our modern understanding.

"In the vigilan world, particularly in Paris, we connect with the Martian archetype because of our city's historic intercourse with war, love and creativity. It is here that we recognize the value of transmutation in these forces. Mars, once a symbol of might, is now a symbol of transformation and of coming into maturity—balancing male and female. Father Mars is merged with Mother Wisdom, Sophia—a symbol of Oneness."

"And now, what does Mars have to do the with the sacred heart of the city that we find here on Montmartre?" I ask. "Clearly there must be a linkage since the basilica sits on a former temple to Mars."

"Yes. The heart is the place for merging of all members of the one body. It is the center, both in people and in cities alike. Mars was placed atop the Druid heart and thus generated a pattern of martyrdom here. Bishop Denis was decapitated, placing the 'head' symbolism back into prominence. Then, amidst turmoil and battle, the symbol of the heart returned, but only in a 'crowned' form. The head of the church, a male-dominated institution, established dominion over the heart. As you can observe, the form of the basilica is a very male, construction, thrusting up in five phallic spires from below.

"The true sacred heart lies *within* the mountain, not on top of it. As you stand before the basilica and gaze out over the City of Light, you can feel it beneath your feet. You can feel the masculine and feminine aspects of your nature come into an embrace. Mars enters the sacred depths of your heart. For humans, I understand, this was not always a comfortable experience." She pauses, and then says, "Let us go in and discover."

At first I assume she means it metaphorically. But now Breanne points to a stairway on the side of the imposing marble structure. There's a small doorway down a mote-like passage on the side. She beckons us to follow her. I nod, and we descend. Inside, Breanne speaks to an old woman who sits near the door.

The woman nods solemnly and begins searching drawers in her desk. Finally she produces several large, ancient keys made of iron. Looking carefully at them and then at Breanne she hands them over. With the keys, we enter the crypt beneath *Cœur Sacral*. Suddenly I feel a rush. *Now, we're getting somewhere.* Silently, we walk around the dark, inner circumference. The space is filled with statuary, but we do not stop to study it. Rather, Breanne leads us into a central chapel, down a flight of stone steps.

We cross the floor and circle around the altar. Behind it, she pulls back a heavy rug to reveal an old wooden trapdoor. I take a deep breath. *Just what I suspected.* Breanne inserts one of the old keys into the lock. A series of loud clicks announce the movement of tumblers. Then, at her prompting, I help hoist open the slab. Hinges creek with age and disuse. I suspect no one has been through this door in a long time. Below is blackness.

"Are we going down there, *maman?*" Phileina asks timidly.

"Yes. There's nothing to be concerned about. It's dark, but we have a light—and we have permission. Be careful on the stairs; they're steep. Follow me." The woman steps cautiously over the edge, then down into the hole. As she does so, she turns on a kind of flashlight—a globe of light that hovers in the air. It follows her down. I help Phileina onto the steps. She grips my hand tightly, and I feel her trust of me growing.

We climb down the dusty planks. Large, ancient blocks form the walls. Soon the passageway slopes away and winds to our right. The light orb is just enough to help us avoid occasional objects stacked along the tunnel. Its luminance ends a few feet away. Otherwise there is only dark and stillness. We're descending a slow spiral into the mountain. Silence blankets our steps, absorbing their echoes. A sense of reverence grows stronger, the deeper we go.

At last the passage ends. We stand in a long, wide cave that looks like a wine cellar. Great pillars hold up the stone ceiling. The dusty white is from gypsum ore, I assume. Breanne looks around curiously, trying to get her bearings. She's been here before, obviously, but not in a long time. Off to the sides of the cave, I can make out alcoves where things have been placed in storage. There are small statues and other mysterious shapes.

Now, Breanne says in a hushed voice, as though not wanting to wake the dead, "I haven't been here since my own initiation, decades ago. It's all coming back to me though. There's another door somewhere down here. Come along, I think it's this way."

Letter Seventy-One
Scryer's Pool

Our footfalls disturb a silence that has prevailed for centuries. Our feet mark the carpet of dust as we pass, three huddled figures following a dim light into the shadowy unknown. I see vague footprints from long ago, now dusted over white. I feel no anxiety; with these two far and future friends, I am totally at ease. There is a true sense of shared presence. We are family.

The *unknown* is walking with us too. I feel it as though it is another form, stepping lightly beside and around us, in us. It's exactly the way I felt when I encountered Faith, as a real person next to me, years ago on a night bus in the mountains of Mexico. But this is the first time I've sensed the presence of 'mystery' in this way. This presence is just as alive as faith was that night. A realization sends chills up my spine: The presence of *faith* and the presence of the *unknown* are identical. In its character I feel courage, adventurousness, an eager, welcoming embrace, a pure curiosity. But nothing to fear. At the same time there is great *apprehension*.

This apprehension is inspiring, like a yet-to-be-uttered desire for appreciation. I think of what you would say right now. *'Apprehend' comes from the Latin— 'to learn, to acquire knowledge'.* The appreciation grows inside me, along with the sense of venturing. This is a wonderful feeling—on the brink of discovery and revelation. In this vigilan time, I'm adapting to the sensibilities around me. I realize I'm actually joyous to be in this dark, strange, claustrophobic world— with my two beloved sisters.

At the far end of the cavern there looms a large metal door, black with age. We walk up to the portal and stare. The door is twice as high as I am. I study its ornate decorations of animal shapes—wolves, dogs, woodpeckers and vultures. *Strange.*

Breanne answers my thought in kind: *"These are the animals associated with Mars. I will explain later."* She then produces another key and turns it in the lock. This time the sound is much heavier, more solid. On the final turn, as the latch releases, the door springs out from the frame. Phileina jumps back involuntarily and grabs the edge of my coat.

Breanne swings the heavy door open half a meter, just enough for us to pass through. The globe-light goes in first; we peer after it. There is another cavernous space and a long, straight stairway, disappearing down into more blackness. The stairs are steep and dustier even than the passage behind us. We all clasp hands for support as we descend yet again. It doesn't take long to reach the bottom, but it feels like an eternity. We have entered yet another timeless zone.

A flat, circular floor lies at the bottom of the stairs. Rough-hewn walls rise all around and arch into a dome, barely visible above. In the center of the floor, under the dome, is a large round table. It looks like an altar, about waist high, two meters across. As we cautiously approach, I see the top is perfectly flat. When the light-globe moves over it, I'm stunned. The whole surface is a wide, round mirror, lying flat. Incomprehensibly, it has no dust on it. It is a deep black, but shines with perfect, clear luminance.

I stand back, waiting for Breanne's next instructions. Phileina, however, walks right up and peers over the edge, just below her chin. She is suddenly frozen. She sees something in the mirror that has riveted her attention. *It's not just her reflection?* Breanne motions me to wait. Her daughter is utterly motionless.

Breanne whispers, "Phileina has entered the portal. She is safe in the embrace of the emptiness. This emptiness is the 'hole' in the Sacred Heart. For anyone who looks upon it, the world changes. However, beware. Gazing upon this without preparation can be fatal. The Heart will suck you into itself and extinguish your form. I am confident, however, that your visits to the Void have prepared you sufficiently for this."

I gulp and take a deep breath of inspiration. *Life and death are so close here.* I muse.

You reply in my mind, *"And they are actually close at each moment of our lives—if you only knew."*

"What you will see in the Sacred Heart is your own soul, joined with the soul of the universe," she advises calmly, yet with a piercing edge.

"The soul of the universe?" I question feebly. "I've never thought of such a thing. Wouldn't that just be the Source?"

"There is no depth without soul," she continues. "Even Source needs a soul to bridge into our world. The soul has a very specific function in this regard. It is our portal into Oneness and it is the avenue that Source uses to enter duality. There is but one soul, yet paradoxically there are many. The soul is a great mirror, reflecting the world of spirit upon itself, and the unformed into the world of form. Reality is revealed into the Grand Illusion by means of the soul.

She notices my concern as I look at the child in front of us, frozen at the edge of the mirror. She says, "Phileina has entered upon that bridge now. She is transported into a space that you will soon enter. Do not be concerned. She is in the hands of her own soul—*your* soul!

"There are no words to describe the true depths of essence. Many words and thoughts, nevertheless have been used over time to etch the silhouette of our deep nature. Many have thought that they knew what the soul was. Some have made definitive pronouncements about it. Poets, thinkers, philosophers, songwriters, and teachers have tried to portray what they have felt and what they thought they knew. They have *all* failed. *And* they have all succeeded."

I react, "How could they do both?"

"Their *failure* lies in the human persona itself. It is a necessary, but flawed pillar of the metamorphic bridge. It must, in fact, *fail* in order to enable the spirit to enter across that pass. The failure lies in the ego—it must first fail before spirit truly comes. But to fail in this task is to succeed in another. The *success* lies in the act of triggering a response from the other side. Spirit has accepted the invitation to open the portal. Your artists and seekers of all ages, one by one, have lifted the Veil, a small glimpse at a time. Their success is that they wondered and watched and wanted. They opened the way.

"You see, the soul is nothing more nor less than the intimate portal of Life. All forms have Life, and all forms have soul. The soul brings formlessness and form together—and at the same point, holds them apart. This portal is the means for transmission and transmutation, the ebb and flow of creation and procreation. It is also the door of dissolution and death: *Know death and you will know your soul.* It is both personal and impersonal. In our depth being we are joined at the heart with the world of opposites and contrasts, shadow and light, density and destiny.

"My ultimate point here is that the soul is *undefinable*. It is the carrier of mystery, the face of the unknown. You have just felt the persona of that 'unknown' as a living being, I know. It can indeed take on such ephemeral forms. Yet too, it is the prime instrument of elusiveness. From of its fount springs forth the original flood of illusion and the final return out of it. This is the *prodigal* soul! By virtue of its ineffable nature, its presence is allowed to expand eternally. Its depth continues always to grow more profound and its height soars ever higher. And let me add, what I've told you here, is only scratching the surface. It is only the beginning."

At this, Breanne winks at me with a smile. *She obviously sees more in this than I do.* Now she motions confidently with a sweep of her arm out toward the mirror. She signals me to look into the surface, as Phileina has done. I hesitate, taking stock of my situation—my readiness and the apparent risk associated with it. Slowly, I step up behind Phileina and timidly peer over the top of her head. *Am I trying to use her as a shield?* But there is no longer any time for wondering.

What I see in the mirror is like nothing I've ever beheld before. I'm frozen into the flow. What I see is a tube or shaft whirling into infinite depth, going into the screen—the scryer's pool. At the same time it is coming *out* infinitely, up and into me, swallowing me whole. Without a thought, I know this is the universe. It is not like the stars and galaxies I have always known in black space. This is profoundly different: It is the inside-out Cosmos. I am viewing it through the eyes of dark matter.

I can only say these words about it: *I have just* swallowed *the whole universe.* This vast domain sits uncomfortably in my throat, expanding incessantly, threatening to *explode* me. Then it seems to pass down and up my body, my chakras, touching each one, assessing each one. I am under a microscope—from the inside. The universe is assessing my humble, little form, associating itself with me, universally and in particular.

In a great ripping gesture, I am split inside out. My infinite depth is now all outside me. And the universe has become nothing more than a tiny dot in the center of this new presence. Preposterously, it begins to speak to me from that tiny point. Vibrations ripple out upon my senses. "I am the soul of you—the heart and soul of everything you will ever be. Retain these words forever in your sensate core: *I am!* Return them never to unconsciousness. We may now speak to each other, as though we were in the space of time and form."

"I can speak to you," I say, in a way just to test out the offer.

"Yes. Of course, you've done this many times before, in many ways. This is not the first; nor is it the last. And yet it *is* the first *and* the last: Alpha and Omega. And let us not exclude your other form—here is our dear little Phileina."

At that moment, I see the girl before me. She radiates immaculate light and smiles at me with intensity far beyond her years. Then I see *you* in her, behind her eyes. We three are now here together—in soul. You and Phileina open your arms to me and I'm drawn in, irresistibly into the love that only the soul-self can deliver. *What a relief!* I think. The feeling is that of a homecoming beyond imagining. I have returned into what I truly am. *I am!*

Suddenly I'm much more—a whole host of other individuals. We stretch back into the far, dark dust of history and incarnation, and out into the misty distant future. These are all of me—of you and Phileina. We are all these creatures, lived and yet-to-live on Earth and elsewhere, some only in dreams, some only in aspirations; others exist in vastly advanced states of being, almost beyond form. We are all properties of this one soul. *What a panoply!* We incarnations are standing in truth and love before the essence-presence; and each one feels as I do. Now is the fulfillment of the vision I first had on the vesica bridge in Seattle, at Lake Union. This is the reality of it all, as known by my—our—own soul.

"What is the meaning of this?" our voice cries out in a thousand echoes, as each incarnation asks the simultaneous, same question.

The soul answers, "It is you. *You* are the meaning. I have given you, each of you, this assignment as I pushed you out into the worlds. Go forth and make meaning! 'What *would* you mean?' I have asked. What would you make? What will you do with your *will?* Some of you have returned to us with 'meanness'—a poignant distortion. Hah! What a surprise to us all! But indeed it is all good and goodness, *especially* the distortions. They hone the sharp edges of meaning. Now, in this space you can each see and know what *I* mean."

Your mind, O, now comes forth for us. You say, "Of course, I'm inspired to make us look at this rich word: *Mean* originally meant 'mind'. It has subsequently passed through many forms, taking on the sense of 'motivation', 'midst' and 'middle'. In the negative, it came to connote 'meanness' and the 'lack of willingness to share'. In mathematics, the *mean* signifies 'equally far from two extremes'. This relates to the noble 'middle' path, not straying out to the far extremes, returning to the common center—as we do now, in this moment. This is *meaning.*"

The soul proclaims, "Well said. We are one soul, one body and yet many. I touch each of you in heart and mind and *meaning* in this moment. Take my breath into your lungs and hold it there eternally. Walk out into your lives and be refreshed. Be reborn in confidence and authenticity of being. See clearly now, each one of you, in your own way, in your own circumstance."

I look around at the thousands of life forms our soul has produced. There are ancient beings in all walks of life; there are future evolutions into vastly enlightened circumstances. You and Phileina and I seem to be relatively in the middle—at the 'mean' point. Perhaps the screen is filled out to the same extremes for each of the incarnations; I don't know. Perhaps our soul's forms extend infinitely in all directions.

I decide to ask. "How do you recommend that I—we—relate to you? How do I address you? I am at a loss, at this moment, to know the whole of who you are. How far out do you—we—extend?"

The soul answers intimately, directly into my heart, "You do not have to look at me as outside, as 'other' than your own consciousness. I am *you.* You are *me.* I am your divine *self.* We can speak from two sides of a voice in the duality worlds, but in reality there is no separation, not even one of perspective.

With a simple twist of being you can see the whole scheme from my eye. Twist now. Give it a try."

I don't really understanding what the soul means. Nevertheless, I stop my questioning. I fold my mind over upon itself and let go. *No understanding is necessary!* I am simply the one and only being here. I have a thousand different eyes. I have only one eye. What I see is a galaxy of facets of this self, spread across a grand tableau with forms and formless essences, continuously in flux. I am like a fluid diamond, turning, flowing, reflecting the self-generated light within the self-conceived darkness, within the self-born emptiness. I am God unto myself.

Then I remember. I have long spoken to the soul, using the name 'God-Self'—GS for short. Writing these letters, I put that conversation on hold. Now, in this magnificent moment, I know what it is to speak from 'both sides of the voice'. There is only one voice, one diamond floating in the center of nowhere and nothing. The Void and the Voice are one. That one is *I am.*

I am aware of the need for outer expression with this voice, out into the duality creation. The need is generated and fulfilled with the same timeless gesture. All the facets, the grand and simple jewel, spin like stars in the Cosmos. I watch with love and fascination—divine appreciation.

The sparkling star facets of *I am* turn in endless splendor. Each sparkle is a lifetime, flashing in and out of the Void. But it does not truly begin or end. Each is timeless, lasting for this moment, which is eternal. Each is continuously creating itself, beginning again forever—constant *newness.* I create beginnings and endings out this newness. I am the great experimenter, explorer, designer, diviner.

Snap. I'm back as an incarnate self. I choose this for the delight of it. I bring delight back to the soul as my gift. I'm taking the impetus into myself and with it; I'm generating the experiment, the exploration and the *meaning. We're back to that!* I'm delivering meaning back to the soul. *This is my ultimate gift.* I am pleased. *But what does it all mean?* Only what I experience and interpret with presence, in the Now, is what it means.

Letter Seventy-Two
Soul Talk

Suddenly I'm alone. Not where I was. These switchbacks are startling, but I'm getting used to them. I think I even anticipated this one by a split second. I'm now sitting in a comfortable room with a desk and bookshelves all around—a study. A small window looks out on a wooded, natural setting. There's a lit fireplace in the corner giving off a warm glow. I'm in a comfortable armchair next to the desk. An empty chair is on the other side of the desk, in front. I turn around slowly and survey the space. A few photographs and line drawings are framed on the walls between the books. An old rug covers a hardwood floor. I seem to be noticing everything. I also notice I'm giving *meaning* to all this. The room is a pleasant and peaceful space, perfectly suited to my senses.

A soft voice, neither male nor female—or rather *both*—comes from the direction of the empty chair. "Welcome to my world, son. I know this setting will make you comfortable. I know, I could have chosen a sidewalk café in Paris, but there would have been too much distraction. You would have been noticing everything constantly, giving *meaning* to it. Correct?"

I smile, "Hey, you're my soul. How could you not be correct?"

"I am all things that you are, and all things you ever will be. *Incorrect* is one of those things."

"What? *You* can be incorrect?"

The voice seems to smile invisibly. "As *you,* I can be incorrect. I know what that is like, yes. But my question was rhetorical. It was meant to elicit a realization, not to enter a debate. In this instance, as in most, I *am* correct."

"Yes, you are. The café would have been distracting. And I'm glad to be with you again. You are my familiar GS—God Self—right?"

"I am that. I am."

"Wonderful. I haven't written to you in so long now, and *never* in the context of these letters. I've been missing you. I'm sorry. But you know I've been pretty busy."

"I understand completely. I *am* your understanding, after all."

"Well, GS, how have you been? This is good. Wait. I get it. I understand. You were putting the idea into me from the start—that I wanted to talk to you."

"Just an invitation," the disembodied voice in the chair answers. "My command is your wish—or something like that. But I'm teasing. We *both* wanted to get back in touch."

I lean forward in my chair, scanning the empty area in front of the desk. "Say, why can't I *see* you? I mean, since we're here in a physical room and all. I've never actually *seen* you, you know."

"But you *have* seen me. Just now. You've glimpsed all my forms. And I presume you've looked in a mirror at yourself. That's me."

I laugh. "Yeah, those are your *forms*. But why not make a form right now for me to see."

"Would that give this conversation more meaning for you?"

I stop and think. *Would it?* "Yes. I think so."

Suddenly a ball of light appears, hovering above the chair. Then it melts down into an old woman. She asks, "Will this do?" The woman has short gray hair, cut straight and simple. Her face is handsome, chiseled with wrinkles on coppery skin. She looks infinitely wise.

I answer, "Yeah, fine. But why did you take this particular form?"

"Why did *you* choose this form? *You* are the 'meaning maker' here. I am only following *your* desire."

"Well, I guess this is the kind of person I would imagine you to be, *if* you had a form."

"Actually, this woman's form is a true composite—a 'mean', if you will—of all my Earth incarnations respecting gender, race and age."

I nod. "I see. That gives me something to think about. OK, GS. Why are we here? What's this all about? Why did we go into the crypt of Sacré Cœur? What is this meeting with Phileina all about? Where is this story heading in my book?"

The woman responds, "You haven't changed a bit, have you? You always have *so* many questions—and all at once. All right, this is good. Questions are good. But for my part, I prefer to answer them one at a time. That is, if you don't mind."

I grin. "Certainly."

"You and I are here to have a simple conversation. Everyone needs to talk to his soul from time to time. Everyone has her own way of doing it. Some write down their conversations like you. That's a fine way to do it."

I interrupt. "You know, I've tried to tell people about this method I call 'soul journaling'. I've even tried to teach it a few times. But I don't think anyone has ever decided to follow my advice."

"You don't know that for sure. All individuals follow their own paths, in the appropriate time. Your advice has never fallen on deaf ears, not when it was offered sincerely, from the heart. No one's advice from the heart is ever rejected. It may be transformed into meaning the listener can better interpret. That's only natural. Do not attach expectations to your advice. Expectations only serve to undermine. They inject ego and result in separation and diminishment, not communion."

"GS, it's so good to hear from you again—even if I *am* at a disadvantage intellectually. I always am. I remember how we used to communicate nearly every day for years. Then these letters started, and I didn't have time any more. It never occurred to me we'd ever have a conversation *in the book*. But now you're *here*! And it *was* you, right, in the pool at *Sacré Coeur*? Pretty amazing. I tend to forget about who you really are when we're just having an ordinary conversation. Sorry."

The old woman answers softly, "Don't be sorry for that. I am both the vast and the intimate you. I am pleased to be 'ordinary' with you. I am pleased to be exalted before you as well. This is everything—*all* that I am. It is what *you* are, too, dear one."

"Hold it for a moment. How am I supposed to take that, GS? You keep reminding me that 'I am you'. But I don't *feel* like you. I don't experience your life and place—certainly not the *scope* of your world."

"The point is this: It is time for you to awaken. It is time for you all to embrace the 'more' that you are. Since we are writing this to be read by others, I want to add that what I say applies to them also. The soul in them speaks within my words. Of course, be sure to read between the lines. The soul speaks in the still, small voice in the heart of each incarnate person. How that voice appears in the outer life varies widely. Listen sincerely and you will hear. You all *do* have ears to hear—inner ears!

"As for *feeling* like I feel. I beg to differ with you. You *do* feel like that. Go into your feelings, deeply, and there I am—always, eternally, in the moment. I am there, at the base of your sensations—as peace. Even in the midst of great physical or emotional distress, I, the peace, am there at the bottom of it all. When all suffering ends, peace remains. 'Rest in peace,' they say. It is a foundational truth. As for the breadth and depth of me, this can be embraced, as well, within your *imagination*.

"When you say you don't *experience* life as I do, this is a fact. We have different functions within the Life spectrum; but that is all. It is the only true distinction between us—*function*. Nevertheless, I continue to adjure you to know me and to know my Life. In this knowing and this shared sensation, you will elevate yourself into awakening. Remember me in your thoughts and feelings as often as you can. This is your path to becoming conscious.

"My function now, in your incarnation, is to be increasingly *present* for you, to remind you unceasingly that I exist, to overcome the doubts and denials of your ego world. There are many who try to convince you otherwise. Their mental reasoning has convinced them I do not exist. For them, *reason* has substituted itself for *meaning*. But their cause is unjust, untrue. Truth is ultimately all there is! The denials of truth will dissolve in direct proportion to your awakening, both in your own mind and in the forces around you."

I feel the words inside me as much as I hear them, perhaps more. I realize I've never been able to explain, even to myself, how this 'soul talk' works. *Am I actually* hearing *it in my mind? Am I making it up in my imagination? Or is my imagination a vehicle for communication? Is the transmission somehow contained within the written words themselves as I type or write? Is this 'channeling'? Some would call it that. I choose not to. Basically, I don't know. Maybe I'll never know exactly how this works.*

GS answers my unspoken thoughts. "You do already know the most important part of it all—that is, it *does* work! You have, countless times, gone back and reread the transmissions and found Life within them; it was too close to see as you were writing. If the reader would try this for him or herself, I would recommend the following: Record directly; then stop and rest. After an hour, go back and read the material over. You will know in your heart *what* is working, if not *how* it works.

"How it works is not readily apparent because this function is a *shared* one between us—the soul and its incarnate form; it is not fully in your dimension nor in mine. In this function, the formless grows beyond understanding with each word, thought and impression. Breanne explained it to you earlier at *Sacré Cœur:* Soul cannot be defined because soul is constantly expanding and transmuting into greater expressions of Source—beyond whatever definition you might choose. Neither soul nor Source nor God can be pinned down into a mental description. It is always *beginning* again in an endless exploration of consciousness. This is why it far surpasses understanding. That's why it is *peace."*

"OK, GS," I sigh. "That is good to hear and to know. And as *you* know, that part of *my* function is to keep on asking questions. What about Phileina? What good is it for me know about my next incarnation anyway? Why have you and O shown her to me?"

The old woman is silent for a while. Then she answers in a different tone, a different function. "Asking 'why' is not productive, because it takes you into the realm of mentality; it takes you away from experiential realization and sensation. 'What' is a better question; 'who' is even better. The answer, to 'what' and 'who', is always 'you'.

"The 'you' in this case is the particular incarnation called 'Phileina'. We all are focusing on her right now—all my incarnations; she is that important. She is performing a unique bridging function for us all. This small child is our *first* awakened 'incarnate'. More than that, the lifetime she is commencing is instrumental in building a foundation for Omis' project—the transposition of time. As you know, Black has yet another associated project in the offing—the 'Life of Source'.

"As for your other question, I will not tell you *where* this story is heading. That is for me to know and for you to find out, as they say. Trust the unknown. Celebrate it as your vigilan friends do. Let it invite you into the evolving history. I know you have misgivings about the mysterious manner of you're writing—knowing nothing about it. But don't worry. The story does continue. There are so many of us helping and offering guidance and input into this endeavor, you will never run out of ideas. *That* would in fact be quite unimaginable, my friend."

"That's good to hear," I reply weakly. "I'm concerned about never knowing what's next. What kind of writer writes this way, after all? It's crazy! But I hear what you're saying. And the evidence is there behind me at least, in what I've written. Still, it can be disturbing. I'm just not as comfortable with the unknown as you and the vigilans are."

"This is true. But your assignment from me is to *become* more comfortable with it. How difficult can it be to have such an assignment? Think about it. I'm just asking you to *be comfortable!* Really. It's easy. Accept the unknown as your partner, as a *presence*. Make friends with it. Go out into it, just as you are about to go out into your day in Paris right now. Yes, I'm saying this in real time. Have fun, my friend. It's all a matter of choice. Choose from the heart. Go out now. Return with a story. I extend my blessings."

I follow GS's advice and go out. I walk the streets and ride the métros for several hours. All along the way, I'm taking photographs and observing Parisians. Many miles later, I'm back at the keyboard.

"So, GS, I followed your advice. It *was* fun, on a beautiful spring day. Paris is a beautiful city, filled with beautiful souls—working to experience and bring meaning into their lives, it would seem. I was marveling that there are so many different directions to people's lives out there; it's a very busy 'world city'. Is that what you wanted me to see, by the way?"

"Exactly. All experience is an opportunity for the creation of meaning. Tell me about the meaning of your adventure. What *sense* did you make of it?"

I ponder, not knowing what to say. Then a memory rears up. "Well, on one of the métro trains, I remember a young woman. She stood up in front of the car full of people and announced, in a strong and confident voice, that she was homeless and single, without a job. At first, I didn't look at her; she was behind me in the car. I just listened. I understood her French clearly. Her voice was educated and articulate. When I finally saw her, I was surprised. She was in her early twenties, fairly well dressed, with a friendly smile. She also had a handsome dog with her.

"She explained to everyone that she had run out of public assistance, after looking for work for several years. She said she had nowhere else to turn, and didn't know what else to do. She asked for people to give her whatever coins they could spare so she could buy food for a meal tonight. I have seen many homeless people in Paris and even heard some give speeches on trains before. But there was something different about this one. I was very moved. In fact, it's even bringing tears to my eyes right now as I think about it. When she finished speaking and walked through the car, she had a confident smile on her face. Many people gave her money, including me."

GS responds, "Yes. I was moved as well. This young woman is experiencing a profound transformation in her life. It is her soul's way of awakening her. The confidence you observed in her is the soul presence being evoked. That is an awesome adventure you had, my son."

"Well, that was only a momentary thing. I did other things and went other places."

"I know. But this is the thing you remember most. This is the *meaning* you created."

I sit silently for several minutes, pondering the young woman and even praying for her. "Life can be so difficult for many people—maybe for all people, at times. The times I'm living in now are especially difficult—2012 and all. I myself am blessed with opportunities, prosperity, health, friends, and family. And yet I often end up feeling sorry for myself and inadequate, in spite of it. I know it's the ego causing that. But there are many people who are in so much greater need in this world than me. GS, is this the soul's doing? Do *their* souls set them up for these lives?"

"Yes and no. The soul pushes out the incarnate forms and urges them to experience *meaning* in life. Some of these are tough situations from the beginning—designed to produce rapid growth of awareness, to balance out weaknesses or mistakes from previous lives. But the form has free will. An individual persona can choose paths different from what the soul intends. Of course, for humans all this happens under the Veil of Forgetfulness. So, the individual can stray far from the original vision of any given incarnation, far from destiny. Thus you have the parable of the prodigal son. In that wonderful story, the son eventually returns, humbled and awakened, to his father's house. It is actually one of the most profound allegories—the *prodigal soul*. It is about a veteran persona returning to its soul and Source with renewed awareness.

"I recommend that you take a look at that ancient story, recounted in certain traditional writings. There are many clues to personal awakening in it. Allow me to explain a little: It describes a son who has departed his father's house and gone out into the world, living recklessly and unconsciously, without regard to consequences. He squanders his father's gift. In humiliation, misery and desperation, the son finally 'comes to himself'. He repents and returns humbly to his father, asking forgiveness.

"The father ignores his son's request to be taken back as one of the household servants. Instead, he rejoices and celebrates the return by preparing a grand feast. As I said, the father represents the soul, his son the persona. The father clothes his wayward son in his best robe and places a valuable gold ring on his finger. It is a kind of marriage ceremony between the persona and the soul. The ring could also symbolize coming 'full circle'—out of forgetfulness, into awareness.

"Each incarnation entering the world of illusion begins with a desire for freedom. It is the freedom to experience the *will*, to manifest and explore—to be independent. The price of this independence, however, is forgetfulness of one's origins, forgetfulness of Source and consciousness itself. After many lives of struggle and ignorance, the individual gradually begins to remember who he is and where he came from. In the end he comes to *himself*—and awakens in the presence of his maker."

I sit quietly again, staring at the form my soul has projected. The ancient woman has a slight, inscrutable smile. I return the smile. "Thank you for that insight, GS. I remember the prodigal son story. You're saying the soul isn't always responsible for the situations we end up in; we 'incarnates' do it to ourselves. The soul accepts whatever 'meaning' we gather from our experiences."

"Yes. That's it."

My mind begins to stir with this opportunity to ask questions. "I guess I'd like to get your perspective on these letters I've been writing. I never thought of asking you directly about them until now. Maybe I've been afraid to. But I will go ahead now. For instance, what about the 'hole in the heart' story and the tunnels under the crypt? What about the 'scrying' mirror? Why does

Phileina need my heart? What's your perspective on Mihelo and Omis—and on Orange, for that matter? I assume O's not here, so we can speak privately."

GS laughs again. "No, no, not at all. I am not keeping her away so we can speak privately *about* her. I have brought you here to be clear and focused, to be at ease. She is *you*, remember; she is me. We are one being. In essence, she *is* here right now—in me.

"So many questions!" She winks. "Let me say that your involvement in this whole project was in part my idea. In my function, I view the workings of the incarnate world in a *timeless* way, through many dimensions and systems of consciousness. I also work with other souls directly. We see available outcomes and options, the web of possibilities, well before any incarnation takes place. We know the comings and goings of all the players. We know the *souls*. And then, ultimately, all souls are one soul.

"I saw—to use your time-based logic—that our growth over these several lifetimes would be accelerated by association with Omis, Black, Invm and others. To make it happen, I needed to put you in touch with two of your 'future' incarnations—Phileina and Orange—in the course of *time*. This resulted in Omis' transposition project, directed at the three of you.

"Though Omis is now an angelan, he is not omniscient. Angelans do not function as souls on the planes of incarnation. His own soul still guides and supports him just I do you. There are many levels of creation and manifesting involved in producing lives on the physical planes. We souls look out and manage the intricacies, as per our role and function.

"However, no matter what the soul may envision, free will of the personas makes matters volatile. Change is constant. The correspondence between the soul realm and the incarnate world is continuously changing; adjustments to original ideas and schemes are needed constantly, even moment-by-moment. Therefore, the unknown is a powerful component in all our lives, and the great Life itself—Source! Don't you just love it?"

Letter Seventy-Three
Un-Formation

The room seems to spin for a second. It dissolves and recomposes like a three-dimensional video screen. Now all is calm again, as it was before. I react, "GS, what was that? I thought I saw things decomposing for a moment."

"Yes, you did. I was just distracted by one of your incarnations, facing a life-altering event. It's good to let you see what happens, even to a soul sometimes in the face of these *rascally* incarnate forms. This happened because we are using an Earth, time-based form for our communication. Don't worry, the persona in question has made a good choice and he will survive to finish that lifetime as intended. Now, where were we?"

I shrug. "This is fascinating. I'm getting more insight into how you operate than ever. I guess it's because of the situation we're in here—I mean, I'm in the middle of writing this book, and suddenly you and I are taking a 'time-out' to assess the whole substructure of how it came about, and what's going on behind the scenes. Am I correct?"

GS laughs, "Yes, even *you* can be correct! I'm introducing you to a level of the inner workings that will assist in your current assignment—that is, to generate more meaning for us along your path to awakening. Got it?"

"Yes."

"Now, I believe I was about to answer one of your questions. Let's take on the 'hole in the heart', shall we?"

"By all means. I found that very disturbing. Is it really true?"

"'Really' is a relative term. First, we're not talking about your dense physical heart. It's your etheric-physical heart that has changed—literally transplanted, yes, and fused with the heart of Phileina. But at that level, sharing of organs is not so unusual. It has been done before in cases where one needs the added push—or pulse—to reach a particular objective in incarnation. It happens when two or three lifetimes are very closely associated. Such is the case here.

"This process does not leave you without a heartbeat or a means to maintain your physical life, to be sure. Your etheric body continues to draw its energy and nourishment from Phileina now, that's all. The center of you has been displaced. And do not forget, it bestows upon you an added benefit. It has left you with an open portal in the center of your being. This has multiple meanings, of course, as anything esoteric does."

"I'm sure," I mumble, a little disrespectfully.

GS continues undeterred, "The ancient ceremony entailed a master, etherically 'operating' on his or her disciple. The heart of the disciple would be symbolically *broken* open and the Void introduced. The term 'broken heart' derives from this. To be 'heart-broken', as you know, means to feel the *emptiness* of someone's parting.

"Rumi wrote to God of such longing in the verse, 'Break my heart, Lord. Break it again and again, that I may be drawn ever closer to your love.' Your disturbance at losing your heart to Phileina is in a similar vein. It has served to draw you closer to her, to me and to Source."

I realize what the old woman means. I add, "I am so attached to that little girl—beyond what I could understand before. But now I see. I'm actually attached to my own heart in her."

"Indeed you are. In Paris on your current *séjour*, you have had many friends and visitors, several staying a week or longer. When they left, you felt the emptiness, the vacuum left behind them; their *presence* had been removed. I'm aware that you have used this feeling of emptiness to sense into the Void, into Source. It is a good practice. What you were doing, unwittingly, was *breaking* your own heart. You were activating the *hole* in your heart.

"To play with the words—in a meaningful way—the 'hole' is not actually something *missing* from your heart. It is really the 'whole' that has been inserted, exposed within the opening. The *hole* is the *whole*. It is the fullness of the Void, surrounding you from the inside out. In poetical terms, it is the embrace of the unending, holy night. To your mind, this appears to be a deficiency, a lack. But to the deeper awareness, it is an over-arching abundance, the foundation of all creation. It is home to the sacred unknown. The greatest mystery of all lives here: the identity of Oneness and Nothingness."

I ask, "Oneness and Nothingness are *identical?*"

"Indeed. But what can we say about it, really? We could try analyzing it with the mind. We could say your modern 'digital' world is founded on 1's and 0's—that is, 'on' and '*not* on'. Take time to ponder on the letter 'n'. What do you suppose it is about the letter 'n' that appears in such other words as, 'now', 'no', 'never', 'negation', 'name', 'nature', 'native'—and the French word for Void, '*néant*'. This sound is powerful and raw.

"Just *feel* the linkage between negation, Oneness and now. There is no other place to be; everything must come from that 'no' thing. The affirmation of form must come in the context and embrace of *no* form. Recall what has been given you: Remember that Oneness does not manifest; it always remains *unformed*. And this is at the center of your heart, of all hearts and all forms."

Silence fills the room. It is as though we have invoked the emptiness. The aged woman sits motionless, staring at the softly glowing fire. Outside, leaves rustle in a breeze. An owl calls out from the woods. In spite of these sounds, silence prevails. Stillness.

"So, what do I do with this *hole* in my heart? What good is it?"

"Are you asking 'what good is Oneness? The hole is the Oneness, my good fellow. It is the ultimate *good*. Through this opening in your heart will come 'all the gifts that wise men bring'. Wholeness and emptiness are now activated in your heart, for you to observe and enter into. Once you truly realize their presence you will not ask such foolish questions."

"Sorry. I'm just a little testy right now. I've heard so many platitudes and spiritual abstractions, I'm just not thinking straight."

"Ah but your *thinking* is indeed 'straight', too straight. What I seek to do is to *warp* it a bit, poke holes in it, wiggle it around, open it up more to presence. Your problem right now is that you are *thinking* about the hole in your heart and not truly feeling it; you are not entering into it and passing through the portal."

I query, "And what happens if I pass through this hole inside me? What's on the other side? What can I do with any of this information?"

"I would rather have you look for *un-formation*. The hole is the pathway *out of* formation, not another form to be filled in. Rest in the emptiness it provides. That emptiness is the doorway to the unknown. Invite the divine mystery into your life. Make it a friend; make it family. With it comes the *authentic being* that O talks about. You will become your authentic essence in manifestation. You will be *me,* for Pete's sake, walking consciously on the Earth."

"But if Phileina is the first of your incarnations to awaken, that means *I* am not awakened, nor *will* I awaken in this lifetime. So, what's the point? No matter what, I will have to wait to be born as that little girl first."

"Who said you would not awaken in this lifetime? I said Phileina is our first awakened 'incarnate'. That means she is the first lifetime to be awakened *from birth*. It is obviously true that you are not yet awakened. However, you are very close, dear friend, in spite of yourself. I realize, as Orange has repeatedly told you, it's important to remain 'unawake' for the time being—that is, with a fully-functioning ego—for the completion of your writing. That condition grounds her transmissions more surely. It helps you ask all those challenging questions you ask. Opposites attract! You are performing the role of the negative end of the magnet right now.

"But the books are ending soon—with the completion of this one. At that time you will be free to let go of ego and move into living presence. You *will* do this if you so choose. On the other hand, if you persist in pitying your poor state of 'unenlightenment', you may delay everything and cause a disturbing ripple out into your future incarnations.

GS gleams at me through the eyes of the woman. "As I noted, you rascally incarnates can be unpredictable; you all have *free will*. I invite you to get over your recalcitrance and seize the day. Make yourself comfortable with the *unknown*. What you do with the rest of your life, in terms of consciousness, has a direct bearing on the wellbeing of your future incarnations! You have a great responsibility—the ability to respond. You have a great opportunity. Rejoice in both."

"All right. I hear you. It's not that I don't *want* to make progress. It's just that it seems so far off and unlikely to me—awakening, I mean. My ego is so entrenched."

The old woman sighs, "You are so very close. Many millions of you on Earth right now are only a hair's breadth away from disempowering ego. When you finally, collectively, relax and realize your identification with form is *in*authentic—that it's not reality—an avalanche will be triggered across the world. Once a mere one percent of the world's population crosses that threshold of consciousness, the rest will follow. They will be swept up in the avalanche. This is another kind of '99 percent' that you currently hear about in the politics of your day."

I quickly calculate the numbers. "One percent? That would be about seventy million *awakened* people. Perhaps there *is* hope. But why would it only take *one* percent? How could one percent be so influential?"

"Look at it from the point of view of economics. One percent of humanity controlling most of the wealth in the world certainly has powerful influence over the 99 percent. The same ratio is even more formidable in the realm of spiritual awakening. Spirit is where the *real* power lies. An awakened one percent of the Earth's population will make incalculable differences. Watch and see. I use these numbers to make a point—that awakening is on the way. However, I do not want to imply that separation between one portion of the population and another is desirable. No. We are all *one*. We are all the '*One* percent'. With awakening will come the visceral realization of that fact—true authenticity.

"In your world today, division and divisiveness rule. The rich are divided from the poor. The enfranchised keep separate from the disenfranchised. The political right is cut off from the political left. The educated remove themselves from the uneducated. There are endless examples of intense separation all around you. One that you may not be paying much attention to is the spiritual-ly-minded versus the worldly-minded. Nevertheless, it is another example of the disease of divisiveness.

"The awakening souls on Earth must come to realize they are not separate from the so-called 'unenlightened masses'. When the understanding of this is turned to authenticity in your hearts, you will truly know *awakening*—not before. Realization of the non-manifesting Oneness of humanity is the prerequisite for advancement in evolution. This is the core of what brings evolution to consciousness. It is what gives birth to *Conscious Evolution.*"

"Wow. I never thought of it that way. I'm so glad you said it. This seems crystal clear to me now: It's about seeing through form. You know, I *am* feeling the Oneness myself more and more all the time. I don't think I'm alone in this. It used to be very hard for me to understand how we could all literally be 'one'. But now the *feeling* has superseded my *understanding.* I look around at people in my own country and here in Paris, and I sense a stirring recognition. It's not quite on the surface yet, but it is simmering in people's hearts. I'm sure of it. And if it only takes one percent, then I suddenly see real hope."

GS replies, "You've got it right about the simmering heart. The recognition of Oneness does not begin in the mind. It cannot. The mind separates and does not synthesize. The heart is where synthesis happens. I speak of the etheric heart, the center of all the energy centers in the body. I would point out to you that this is why your relationship with Phileina is so special. The two of you are creating a synthesis of etheric hearts, beyond time. Without this merging and sharing, your other future incarnation, Orange, would not be able to come into being as she now is. You, linking with Phileina, cause the O you know to become a potentiality."

"Whoa! Now that is a huge responsibility! But wait. If O is already living and generating her project, returning to connect with me, then that means we *did* work it out. We have already fulfilled our responsibility."

"This is indeed so. Now you're looking at it like a soul does. But let me remind you, there is still the responsibility to *act* upon your intuition, upon your authentic realization. In the world of form, these realizations must be acted out into manifestation. I have confidence that you understand this, and accept the mission I am putting upon you. Your books are a perfect example of this. You do accept what is, I know. That is living in the Now."

I slowly nod and take a deep breath. I look around the room and out the window. "Say, GS, where *is* this place? It's beautiful, and so peaceful."

"It is in your imagination, which is *my* imagination. Let's just say we're creating it together. It is no *specific* place, just a composite of elements that you have found comfortable during your life. Between the two of us, it's the kind of office we would choose to work in. This body I have assumed is the same kind of composite."

I turn my eyes back to the aged woman as another question arises. "I know we've covered this before, in private—just you and me—but it might be helpful for others to hear you explain how you can call yourself 'me', and have a conversation like this at all, given the fact that you are *not* a form; given the fact that you are the limitless, undefinable, immaculate soul. How can you sit here and talk to me like we're old friends?"

GS smirks and begins answering, "We *are* old friends. I am the *oldest* friend you will ever have. The way I reach you is this: I create the context for communion out of raw consciousness itself. What you're asking is 'how can Oneness divide itself into you and me for this communication?' How not? Duality is the name of our game in incarnation. Oneness is the presence behind it all, yes. Oneness is what we *really* are. But duality is how we express it, how we know it and live it into manifestation.

"I speak to you in language that you can understand and accept, within the limitations of your current form—*my* current form, as a projected incarnation. Am I just sitting here talking to myself? Yes. The same is true for you. But magically we can split our perspectives and manifest an *in situ* conversation. It is one of the ways souls nourish and guide their personas. There are myriad other ways, to be sure. I have a vast array of tools and functions at my disposal, in my realm and yours. You likewise have other functions. But for here and now, we sit and talk. Call it crazy and incredible, if you must; call it a miracle perhaps. I for one, enjoy it all immensely. I call it magic!

Letter Seventy-Four
Return of Mars

I'm standing with Phileina again before the mirror. Only seconds have passed. Together we're watching our deeper being unfold and refold below us on the screen. We realize ourselves again as two forms, and there is a desire to express some kind of message to our world—in her time and mine. But what message? She looks up at me, and stares for a moment. We both know it is a seed-link for later.

Breanne's voice comes from behind. "It is time for us to leave this place. There are good reasons not to linger here too long."

The shadows around the circle seem to be darker and deeper now. I can no longer see the dome above. I agree, there is something in the air that is almost menacing. It's nothing personal, but we seem to be in a space reserved for deeper magic than our two humble souls trying to sort themselves out. This hall is a meeting place for discarnate entities of many types, moving to and from the underworld, on business I cannot imagine. I decide not to ask Breanne about it, feeling such a question would disturb the delicate balance we have just achieved here.

Without a word, we turn up the steps and slip through the door left ajar. Breanne pushes it closed, with a loud clank, and turns the key in the lock. Tumblers scrape into place; the sound reverberates in the dark cavern. Amidst the echoes I could swear I hear a scurrying sound. *We're not alone anymore. I sense others here.* Though I see nothing when I look around.

"This way. Keep walking steadily," she commands, pushing our light out in front.

I shiver. "Is something in here with us?"

Swiveling quickly, I catch a shape disappearing behind one of the enormous pillars. I gasp. *The* unknown *doesn't seem so friendly suddenly, but it certainly is present!*

"Breanne, what was that?"

Phileina looks back too. But she's not afraid. Then I'm flushed with a memory. No, I actually *hear* GS's voice saying, *'Make friends with the unknown.'* My mind is in no mood for this. But still something in me—my own presence—comes to life. I turn and, amazingly, start to walk back toward the large metal door we just locked. It's very dark, out of the field of our light. *A presence is calling me.*

To my astonishment, I hear myself say, "Please go on without me. There's something else here I'm being asked to do. I don't know what it is yet, but I must do this. Just go back up to the crypt and wait for me there." *I haven't the faintest idea what I'm doing, but I know it's right.*

Breanne looks bewildered, but senses that she must allow this. She calls back to me, "I will leave one of these lights here for you. We'll meet you above then. *Bon courage!* Come along, Phileina."

The light hovers where Breanne has left it. I creep into the darkest corner of the cavern, hoping to see better. Fear is my ready companion, yet something holds it at bay. There it is again—a furtive movement behind the pillar, then another, behind another pillar. My eyes are now adjusted to the lack of light. I decide to sit against the wall and simply watch. It occurs to me, now might be the right time to call on the 'unknown' to guide me through this. With all my power of intention, I send out that appeal.

Immediately, I feel a strong, confident presence by my side. Without looking around, I reach into it with my senses. I project acceptance and *friendship*—following GS's advice. In return I feel it: a sense of approval, coupled with an openness to adventure. Nothing else. I wait. An almost playful sensation comes next. The presence seems excited to be here with me. It welcomes me as a partner in this game of 'hide and seek'.

Shadows, barely visible in the dimness, slide across the dark walls on the other side of the cave. At last I catch a glimpse of one of them—a wolf! And then a large bird shadow flickers past. *The animals on the door!* But when I look in the direction of the light, there's nothing to cast the shadow. *Very strange!*

Something reminds me not to be afraid of mere shadows. Surely. But now there are more of them. One by one, wolves and dogs and various birds flit across the space. They're like ghosts, casting dark images on the walls—invisible, save for the light they impede. *Breanne said these are the animals associated with Mars.* The numbers are increasing. They're all heading in the same direction—toward the great black door. As I strain to see, I realize they're disappearing when they get to it. *They're going through it! Why are they here? What are they doing?*

The presence stirs beside me in reaction to my questions. Wonder and appreciation of the spectacle radiates into me from its direction. I'm starting to feel the same excitement. We, together, are witnesses to some event, a ceremony of the dark underworld. It is being generated at the edge of awareness and visibility, at the edge of the unknown. Now my new friend tells me—though with no words—that I should imagine what the story is. At first, I refuse to understand. *Tell a story? But why?* The impression grows stronger. The

Unknown wants me to guess what's happening. "This will enhance appreciation of the mystery."

I sit in silence, wondering about the request. Then an idea comes into my head. It's an imaginative one. I finally accept the urging of the presence. Slowly words begin to form in my mind to tell the story. "Let's see. These animals have been summoned to the chamber below, to the scrying mirror. They are ghosts of dead animals drawn here by the Void—no, not the Void. It's something else they're attracted to, something in the Void."

What's in the Void that could be attracting them? Just tell the story! I think it's a ritual. What kind of ritual? I pause and wonder; ideas keep coming. "They're hunting, these animals. They're looking for something that is lost in the bowels of this mountain. They want to revive it and bring it to the surface. Is it something dead? No. It is something that was never born. Therefore, it never dies."

"What is it?" asks the presence.

My mind starts interfering with the flow; I begin to doubt. *How can I know what's truly happening? This is absurd. I'm just running on with nonsensical thinking!* With that, I receive a disapproving jolt form my partner. It strongly suggests I continue the story. It is having fun and doesn't want me to stop. The presence seems almost childlike and innocent, full of keen anticipation, ready to be surprised. *It doesn't know what's about to happen.* I look out toward the floating globe at the other end of the cavern. It too seems to be urging me to continue. I feel like I'm in a dream.

I continue, "All right. I imagine the animal shadows are dancing down below. Drumming sounds are coming from the deep, building gradually in tempo and volume. The animal shapes move in time to the beat. They have formed a circle around the mirror altar where Phileina and I stood. The birds are hovering above; the wolves and dogs are weaving together like prowling leopards in a wide oval. Suddenly the mirror stirs to life. It becomes a pool of bubbling foam. Steam rises up like from a cauldron. Now out of the pool comes a mighty arm—the arm of a very strong man; then head and shoulders, torso and a whole body. He is wearing ancient Roman clothing, holding a long spear. *It's Mars himself! The hunt of these animal shadows has resulted in the unearthing of Mars, the god of war!*

I shake my head at this, but decide to keep on. *It's just my imagination, after all: Mars has been lost in the bowels of this mountain since the Romans left, twenty centuries ago. Has he been in the Void? The Threshold? Is it now his time to be rediscovered and reinvented? Will he transform his mission? OK. That's my story, and I'll stick to it.* "He climbs out of the pool and stands amidst the circle of animals. The ritual becomes more animated than ever. The drums beat louder. The shadows leap and dive, swirl and toss. Now, as Mars waves his spear over them, they begin to take on physical shapes. They too are coming to life. They sweep up around their god and climb over one another, trying to get closer to him.

"At last, Mars lowers his spear to the ground with a jerk. Everything halts. All the animals and birds stop where they are, and pull back to the sides. Mars moves slowly out of the circle, looking around the space, taking stock of his situation—his emergence from the underworld. He looks up and sees the dome; then over at the stairs. He sees the door at the top of the stairs. He makes a decision and starts walking deliberately toward the stairs—in great warrior strides. Now he begins climbing."

I stop, apprehensive, and stare at the dark door. *What if this isn't just my imagination?* Behind that door is a stairway leading down into the scrying chamber, into the Void and the underworld. *This I know. Could Mars himself be on the other side right now, actually climbing those stairs?* The wonder of it is overwhelming. The presence beside me courses with delight. Apparently, my imaginative story has met with approval.

The Unknown is virtually bursting with its own enthusiasm. But now, in the midst of this, I sense the presence is giving me a new message. Just as this palpable mystery is about to unfold—the Martian enigma—and just as it is about to become *knowable*, I'm being told to stop, and let go of it. I'm being instructed to let this story remain *unknown* for the time being. For the strange presence beside me, Life is all about mystery. To make it known is to stifle its freshness. *The presence wants to seek, but* not *to find.*

I gasp aloud, "What? Don't you want me to know what happens?"

When the sound of my echoing voice falls off, everything drops into stillness. There's nothing here now—no presence, no shadows, no Mars. I shake my head. *Am I to be left with just this? Is this what the* unknown *is really up to? Does it just keep creating these situations and then disappearing?* No answer comes. I sit in silence for several more minutes. *I don't know. My not knowing is still the* unknown. *Must I make this too my friend?* As a compromise with my curiosity, I submit the whole business to a seed-link, and save the mystery for later. *Knowing will come another time, from another presence.*

Finally, I look over to the light far down at the end of the hall. It seems to be saying 'it's time to go'. Relieved, I stand up and start walking. *I've made friends with the Unknown, at least in some way. It's a start. What a strange presence it is! Unpredictable. Mercurial. Volatile. Delightful. I guess that's appropriate.* I start up the spiral ramp.

When I enter the crypt, Breanne and Phileina are glad to see me safe and sound. They help lift me up the last few steps, pulling on my arms. I'm thankful to be back too. Now that I'm secure, out of the cavern, my latent fears sweep up over me suddenly. I realize how frightened I could have been down there, how frightened I normally *would* have been. I feel the intensity of it.

Breanne sees the anxiety on my face, and asks, "Are you all right? What happened?"

Phileina asks, "Did you see anything? Did you meet the animals?"

I look, letting go of my fear. "How did you know there were animals?"

She smiles demurely and replies, "I have your heart, remember. I have the eye! I know what you're feeling—at least sometimes, especially when it's something I enjoy, like animals." Phileina makes a cute face. "I only get impressions though, not details."

I look at her and her mother, not knowing how much of my experience to describe to them. *It would sound crazy.* In silence, we close the trapdoor and replace the old rug. Outside the crypt, I begin telling the story. "The place we were, down below, is used by other beings, for other purposes. I saw the shadows of animals, yes, but never the animals themselves. They were ghost animals of the god, Mars."

On the street, the sun is now shining, but it's low in the sky, nearing sunset. I feel, sadly, my time with these two friends may be nearing its end. Still, there's a bit more to say. Breanne turns to me. "You know, the story of Mars and Paris is not finished. There is yet a chapter to be written about it. I sense you may have gained some insight into that."

"Yes, but it was not *only* Mars. I had another experience with the Unknown—its *presence*. I felt it like a living being, with emotions and intentions and ideas. But there's still a lot I don't understand. For instance, I don't understand when the unknown becomes the *known*. What happens to it then? How does it transition? Does the unknown just disappear? Or does it change into the 'known'?"

To my surprise, Phileina answers, "It *changes*. I know that. Because when I *know* something new, *I* change! If I change, *it* must change too."

Breanne responds, "That makes perfect sense, *chérie*. And besides, you and the unknown being are really one and the same essence. The unknown lives right inside you—right in your heart, to be exact. When you are seeing with your heart, you are looking through the eye of the unknown—as it is about to change into the known."

I wonder aloud, "The presence seemed almost capricious to me. It left me in the middle of a story, just when I felt I was about to *know* something. Why would it do that?"

Breanne answers, "I would say it was telling you about *yourself*, that you are making up the story and the meaning of your life. Your story rises out of the unknown presence within you. As much as humans sought to 'know themselves'—perhaps following the oracle's injunction—that is not possible in the mind. We cannot truly *know* who we are, because we *are* the unknown. Our essence cannot be defined; it has no form. The presence you met below was as close to a form as the unknown will ever take. It was asking you to recognize your own presence in it."

Phileina asks, "Maman, just what is *presence?*"

We both look at her quizzically. *What indeed?*

"Well, Phileina, that's a very good question." Breanne reflects for a moment. "Here's a meditation I learned at just your age. It goes like this: 'stillness-space-emptiness-openness-oneness-wonder-presence'. Each one of these words is a pointer into the next, and into your own true Self. From this viewpoint, *presence* can be said to come out of *Oneness*.

"Presence is the energy of consciousness that we send out around ourselves—out of the one being—in all directions, all the time; it embraces the moment. Presence is now. You could also say it is like the soul: You cannot put a complete definition on it. It grows and changes constantly. To understand presence we must experience it and *feel* it in the moment—as you already do. Presence is the unknown that we feel and put into action within ourselves, as we get to *know* the unknowable."

"Why should we try to know the *unknowable*, for Pete's sake? That's impossible!" I challenge.

Breanne turns to me. "Exactly. But we must act according to our nature. It is the *explorer's* way. In the dimension of paradox all opposites are true. The unknown becomes the known; the known becomes unknown. This is because the two are *identical* in essence. Our part is to participate in their mutual revelation; our part is to explore and seek to know what is hidden. When we do this the unknown 'changes', as Phileina has said."

Phileina sighs, "Even when it changes, it's still the same. Its *presence* is the same. I want it to stay that way. It makes such a good game!"

We let those words of a child hold in our ears as we walk back down the butte. The three of us amble down narrow streets and stone stairs, passing old picturesque buildings. We come, finally, to the place where Breanne and Phileina live—a five-story apartment house near the playground.

"Please come up and have tea with us," Breanne offers.

"I'd love to, but I don't think I can." I'm feeling myself slipping away from this dimension, back toward my own time. *Everything's getting blurry.* I stare down at my beautiful young next incarnation with a smile. "I'm so, so happy to meet you, Phileina and *you* Breanne—my beloved friend, B."

The little girl smiles back innocently, opening to the adventures of a whole lifetime ahead of her, in a wonderful city, with an impeccable teacher; yet in her eyes I see the weight of destiny. She says, with words beyond her years, "Thank you for your gift, *mon cher frère.* I will take good care of your heart. We will never be apart because of this, I know. Your gift will help me grow up and do my job. *You* have shown me where I came from. *Source* has shown me where I am. And *my mother* will now show me where I'm going. Thank you, thank you, every one."

Phileina pulls me down to her level and puts her arms around my neck, kissing both my cheeks. In this moment, my eyes begin to tear. The light dims. The sun sets on my future life.

Darkness. Then in a flash, I'm flying above the city of Paris, near the butte of Montmartre. I'm in a dream—a lucid dream. *I haven't had one of these in a long time. I must be careful not to get too excited. I know that's what would pull me straight awake. I want to have this dream.* I look down on the houses and streets. Everything is crystal clear. I can tell it's early spring. Nature is ready to burst forth with life; trees and bushes are in bud; birds are restless; animals are alert and eager in the streets and courtyards.

Slowly, the image starts to ripple. The distortion increases, centering my vision on the basilica. I see an enormous arm rising slowly; it's coming up right out of the roof of *Sacré Cœur;* then comes the head of Mars and his shoulders, as from the scrying pool. Soon, the Roman god is standing, fifty meters tall, towering over the butte and basilica; he lifts his giant spear triumphantly. His form is ephemeral, not dense; he floats as much as he stands. Nevertheless the sight of him is imposing; he looks exactly like the images that have survived from ancient times.

The fierce, warrior god glares around, getting his bearings, breathing deeply of the open air; he has been buried a long time. The city below is unusually quiet—asleep in the night. Now he bends down and brushes aside the whole basilica with a sweep of his spear. It disintegrates instantly. In its place is a small Roman temple. It must be the original temple to Mars, erected here twenty-two centuries ago. Pleased with himself, he moves away a dozen meters in one step. He gazes back and laughs out loud.

Now he turns with a great rustling of armor and skirts. He moves over to the edge of the butte and begins down the slope toward the river. In my dream state, I follow his course, floating above. I'm eager to see what he's up to, while at the same time I want to keep a wary, safe distance. His strides are giant spans, each covering city blocks. Every time his foot lands on a street or square, luminance spreads around it briefly. Dogs are stirred to barking all around as he passes; flocks of birds begin to swirl from all directions.

In minutes, the giant figure arrives at the *Champs de Mars*, at the edge of the Seine. I'm startled to see something is *missing:* the Eiffel Tower! Where it should be, there is only an empty field at the end of the *Champs*. I float around the space at a safe altitude and watch the god step into the plain. He stands directly at the end, where the tower would be; then he looks up to the heavens. His voice roars into the sky, "Come, Jupiter! Come, Apollo!"

After a moment, thunder from the clouds answers his cry. Lightning rains down all around him striking the plain in many swift strokes. The clouds roil above and gather in great, tumbling knots. I decide to pull back and watch the spectacle from a safer distance. There are creatures coming down from the storm clouds, like angels. They *are* angels! And there is one archangel. I immediately recognize Mihelo. Surprisingly, I see another familiar form: It is Omisoristinabo-jesuvium, flying at his side.

The sky is a cauldron, fire erupting down at intervals around the flying figures, descending from the Void itself. Then a voice splits the night, louder than any thunder. "It is I, Jupiter Zeus, heeding your call, my son. I hear; I heed. This is the moment of your resurrection. It has finally drawn forth upon the plane of your name. I grant you my full attention."

With that, a huge explosion and blinding light throbs upon the air like waves on the sea. Energy streams in from the very substance of the city. It converges upon the plain next to Mars and congeals into a form of the same height and stature as Mars; it is the figure of a goddess. Instantly I know it is *Venus*. She stands bright and clear—as voluptuous and feminine as Mars is virile and manly. Together, these great archetypes shine down upon the field beside the river that is blood and bosom to Paris.

Letter Seventy-Five
Mars in Paris

A blast of light, thick with substance, rushes down upon the two gods. In a lustrous ring, it embraces them; and they turn to embrace each other. They are mated in this moment.

"Let this union be set, in the presence of gods and angels," Jupiter commands from above the clouds. "Let it be said, henceforth that these are but one god, one goddess. And her name shall be joined as *Pax*, the Peace that passes understanding!"

With that, the ring closes tightly around the giants, squeezing them, fusing them. In an instant of transformation, standing alone at the head of the Champs de Mars is one beautiful being—both Venus and Mars joined as a single, brilliant, androgynous form. I feel relaxed enough to descend into the center of the open field and land upon the grass. I gaze up in awe at this new god upon the Earth. The spear of Mars is still in her transformed hands.

In one last gesture of my dream—the clouds recoil and concentrate a final rush. A thousand lightning bolts shriek down from a hole in the storm. They strike the tip of the spear and channel swiftly along it to the god's clenched hands. There, the electricity turns and follows the arms into the already bright body.

Now both arms lift high and vertical. In a potent thrust, Pax brings the shaft straight to the sky with a fiery explosion! Dust and smoke billow mightily from below. The deity has suddenly vanished. In its place is a shining image in light. The old, familiar tower of Monsieur Eiffel has returned. Its filaments twinkle and pulse before the night. Electricity sizzles in the air.

The storm has passed. Peace is on the plain at last. I look over to the crest of Montmartre and see that *Sacré Cœur* has likewise been restored. But its looks have changed. The basilica's bud-shaped spires have opened up—blossomed—into giant, white roses, towering to the sky. The golden statue of Archangel Michael, behind, has grown larger. Soaking all this in for a moment, I relax and study the landscape. Later, I will contemplate it in more depth—another *seed-link*.

Feeling fulfilled, I decide to leave the lucid dream and enter back into my sleeping body. I find it in my own time, still in my apartment in Paris, resting peacefully. I fall into a deeper and dreamless sleep for hours.

When I awaken, I feel more refreshed than I've felt in a long time. My travels have taken their toll. I lie still in the bed with eyes closed. *Where do I go in those dreamless periods?* I wonder.

"You go into the Void, of course," your voice cracks into the silence.

I jerk up in bed, looking around. You're standing in the doorway to my bedroom. I gasp, "O, what are you doing here? How did you get in?"

You laugh, "The usual way. You know, you gave me the key a long time ago."

I'm a bit flustered as I stumble out from under the quilt. "Uh, yes, I suppose I did. Can you give me a few minutes to shower?"

"Yes, of course. In the meantime, I'll just sit down at your desk and read what you've been writing lately while you get ready."

"OK, whatever," I sputter, scurrying off. I call back, "It's all on my laptop. Push any key to start."

When I return, you're reading the small screen intently. You say, "Very interesting to see this form of communication. I can understand now why it takes so much time to edit. The electromagnetic and microwave interference is formidable here. The air's thick with it. It's just like the interference from your mind chatter. It's a wonder my transmissions get through to you at all."

I start making coffee and grilled bread—*tartines*. "Yeah? Well, I certainly do wonder about it too. So, have you read about my adventures with Breanne and Phileina at *Sacré Cœur?*"

"I have indeed. And I have some questions."

"*You* have questions? That's *my* job!" I chuckle, flipping the bread onto small plates. I set out some butter and apricot jam. "What do you want to know?"

"First, I'd like to know what you think of Phileina and the job she has ahead of her."

I sit down with two cups of fresh espresso, *allongé*, and look at you, sitting in front of my computer. "I hope you like your coffee like this. What can I say about Phileina? She has my heart."

"She does indeed. Do you have any sugar for the coffee?"

"What? You take it with sugar? I thought you'd drink it the way *I* do."

"No, I like it the way the French take it. We *are* allowed our little differences, after all."

"Sure. OK. Back to Phileina then: It was enlightening, to say the least, to meet her. I feel very identified with her—more, in fact, than with *you* even, I hesitate to say. I don't mean that as a putdown. It's just the energy."

"Indeed. I feel the same. That's only natural. She's closer to each of us, as an incarnation, than we are to each other. At the soul level, of course, there's no separation among any of us. But please go on."

"I'm amazed at Phileina's fearlessness and maturity, at such a young age. She has insights that are far beyond my own." I grimace. "I still don't really believe that she actually *has* my heart though. It seems preposterous, even if we're only talking about the etheric body. I think I'm going to have to look at all that as just a metaphor."

"That's all right. It really doesn't matter. The important part is that you gave your gift to her freely and completely. In effect, you surrendered your life and the 'pulse' of it to her."

"That I did!" I reflect, recalling the emotion of the ceremony.

"That is sending enormous ripples out through all our incarnations. Now tell me what do you think of Phileina's role in our project? She seems cut out for a unique part in it."

"Yeah, well, sure. What I understand is very limited. It seems she will build a foundation for the whole thing. She will acquire skills and experiences during her life that she passes on to you. And she brings together the Sirian energy as well, with Invm's participation. She has quite a responsibility ahead of her."

You add, "I feel the affect of her life in me—even now—as she probably feels your life in her. From your perspective, perhaps it's more like conjecture, since you don't have the cellular memory."

"Ah, but I do have it. And I feel it," I retort. "That is, if the etheric heart has any cells in it. I don't really believe that story, mind you."

"*Touché.* Now, for my next question."

"You're going to insist on asking me more questions?"

You sip your drink with a satisfied sigh, "You know, I don't coffee this in my own time, but it feels good here, to bring back the old memories. So, yes, questions. Please tell me what you felt when we saw the grand spectacle of incarnation."

"Hmm. You mean, what the soul showed us? I haven't really had time to think about it. This is a good a time, I guess. Let's see. First of all, that spectrum was enormous. The Life within our soul is much greater than I realized. I mean, with Source, I take that vastness for granted. I never looked at the soul that way. I've had many, many conversations with GS over the years. I've gotten to know her almost like a pal. That was always very casual. This, however, was very different."

"I too have never seen all the incarnations displayed that way, all at once. It was dramatic and inspiring. What else?"

"Well, it seemed like we were at the very center of all those incarnations. I don't know if that's really the case, but GS said we're currently in a time of accelerated transitions. Oh, and let's not forget—Phileina is the first *awakened* incarnation of the lot."

You interrupt, "And we are performing a bridging function for all the other incarnations? Right? Our three lives are in fact *central* to the whole in that respect. So, it's possible we are right in the middle of the linear progression. It seems that those lives extend far beyond the Earth experience. That would be interesting to explore someday."

You put your cup down and stare at me. "Now, the real question I have for you: How do you interpret your dream of Mars in Paris?"

I stare at you. "That's what I wanted to ask *you*. I'm not sure what to make of it. There certainly are references to Mars in this city."

"I understand. Maybe if we try a different approach. Let's join forces for a moment and answer the question together." With that you push our cups out of the way and take my hands in yours. At once, electricity flows across to me. I feel our minds come closer, our hearts embracing. In fact all the chakras are in communion with each other. This is a total energetic link. Because the heart chakra is central, I also feel the presence of Phileina near.

To my surprise, my voice speaks for both of us. *It's the seed-link opening.* "Mars and Paris have a relationship that is little understood. It derives from ancient times. But it is *here* that the Roman god Mars felt his last strong presence on Earth—in the temple on Montmartre. His religion was passing. Rome was shifting toward Christianity. It culminated in a violent clash with the new, emerging belief system.

"It turns out that Mars was, in effect, *cursed.* He was buried alive in Paris— sent underground, into the *underworld*. In the end this could only be temporary, and he would eventually have to resurface. That dream and the imaginative story of the underground was a vision of his re-emergence into the upper world. Mars is transformed now."

As we hold hands, the voice in me continues, "The presence of the 'unknown' was naturally instrumental in creating the resurrection ceremony. According to its nature, that presence remains inscrutable; so we can say little of its intentions. Nevertheless, we can feel it everywhere in the dream: It was the initiator for lifting the suppression, breaching the gates of the underworld. Through the portal granted by its presence, the curse was broken.

"The fact that Mars was here, buried in the psychic fields of Paris, made this locality an attractive vortex for military conquerors, kings and emperors over the ages—not to mention a *führer*. It kept a seething presence of conflict and protest turning in the underbelly of the city-state. St. Denis, first bishop of Paris, refused to die on the butte of Mars, as the legend goes, even though beheaded by the Romans here. He could not share this site with the Roman god. Throughout the long history of this city, there have been repeated rebellions and upheavals.

"Concomitant with the unrest and militarism, however, there has always been a Venusian presence in the city as well. The Romans, too, brought Venus here. They believed Mars and Venus were destined to belovers, that they would in fact be married. Venus in Paris was responsible for the arising and attraction of great art, beauty and expressions of love and romance here, in many forms over the centuries. Together the two powerful, attractive-yet-unreconciled forces provided the impetus to make Paris a vibrant, passionate capital of the world.

"Greek and Roman history tells us of the interweaving of names and essences. This is also the heritage of Paris and its seasons: March, the heart of spring, is the namesake of the Romans' favorite god. And spring has long been the season both for making war and making love. Throughout human history, love and war have been commingled. A relevant example is the story of Helen of Troy: A young Trojan prince, prophetically named Paris, instigated that costly war when he kidnapped Helen, the wife of the king of Sparta. It was Paris who assassinated Achilles (an incarnation of Mars) by shooting him in the heel with a poisoned arrow. Archetypes have long memories.

"The conclusion in the dream, that merged Venus and Mars—finally concluding in the marriage—fulfilled what had first been proposed in Roman times. It was the destiny of Paris to see this accomplished in its years of awakening. Hundreds of years passed as karmic rebalancing prepared for the merger. At last, as this was accomplished, Paris became the locus of harmony far and wide, for male and female, intellect and intuition, art and enterprise, love and courage."

My voice falls silent and you let go of my hands. You sit back and continue to look me in the eyes. I try to digest this information and begin to wonder. I get up from the table and ask, "O, what's this got to do with me writing this final book? In fact, why did I end up writing it in Paris? How do these stories of Mars and Paris relate to the transition from my species to yours?"

You answer, "An obvious question, after all. First a little more history: Apollo, as you know through your dealings with the muses, has shepherded our entire work together. The sun god was also called Musagetes, *leader* of the muses. What you may not know is that in Greek mythology he was an elder brother of Mars, Ares. They were both sons of Jupiter and Juno. Venus— Aphrodite in Greece—was the daughter of Jupiter and Dione; she was half-sister to both Mars and Apollo. The charge given to Venus was love, beauty and fertility. Mars received the charge of the warrior archetype, plus the taming of wild nature; he became a male expression of fertility. Apollo's archetype was the synthesis of music, literature, prophecy and light—the Sun.

"This story and the transition between our species will become clearer as we proceed. We will unfold the metaphor of transformation, particularly with an eye toward the new role of our old friend, OM."

Then I remember an image from my dream. *I saw Mihelo and Omis descending from the light in the clouds.* I ask, "So, what has Omis got to do with all this? Why was *he* in my dream?"

You wink and answer, standing up from the table, "For that I feel we must go and talk to Omis again. Come." You reach out your hand to me and I feel the old familiar electricity.

Letter Seventy-Six
Apollo's Palace

As our hands vibrate, we materialize back at Omis' mansion on the Sun. Immediately, I think of Apollo—the sun god, the oracle of oracles, the chief of the muses. I know innately that this work is *his* work. The muses have always been with me in writing it, in transmitting and translating it. And where the muses are, so must also be Apollo. Now I know that without him, none of it would have come about.

Just now, amazingly, we are all still seated in our chairs in front of the grand house, of the grand Old Man. I look over at you and B and Invm, then at Omis in the form of OM. He reads me like a book—a very quick 'read', I'm sure. I blush, knowing that he knows what I know, what I've experienced and written—and *thought*.

OM smiles like a Cheshire cat and says invitingly, "So, you want to know about Apollo, do you? I suppose you want to hear about the gathering of night as well."

"Well, I don't know. I hadn't thought about that as a question; and I've never heard of a 'gathering of night'. But if that's what you want to talk about, it's fine with me."

Omis' expression doesn't change. With all of us attentive, he commences, "Apollo prefers to perform his work out of sight, behind the curtain. But he enlists many of us into his business. For instance, whenever you invoke any of the muses, you invoke him—and you agree to work within his sphere of influence, tacitly. That is the key: He is never overt, yet always present.

"I must say, however—almost as a warning—that to play with Apollo is to play with fire. He is quite literally the *sun god!* No fire in our world is greater than his fire. His appearance can *inflame*. He usually speaks in riddles, to confuse—and safeguard—the unwary mind. He will deflect or even mislead those who come to him inappropriately; his guidance will be deceptive."

I interrupt, "Then I must ask, OM: If he is inspiring my writing through the muses, there is a real risk of my presenting confusing information—perhaps even misleading. Is this the case?"

Omis answers as though he anticipated my question. "Of course you are presenting confusing information. Have you not felt this yourself?"

"Well, yes. But I don't want to *mislead* people."

"Don't worry. You won't mislead anyone more than yourself. And each reader will do that for him or herself. Your frequent doubts in the face of our teaching speak to your misapprehensions; you question everything about this work. We knew you would when we took you on. Yours is a necessary stage of transition out of ego. Doubt can be useful; it is a destroyer of false beliefs. Most human beings reading these letters would not identify with their message were you not doing this, feeling their doubts and skepticisms, reflecting their misgivings, and misleading yourself, as they also are.

"All this serves an important purpose. These transmissions are not to be taken at face value alone. The reader must always be willing to pass beyond the interference of ego in order to open and receive. She or he must be willing to dig below the surface and find the real messages embedded there. As much as we say that awakening is coming for everyone in the next decades, these writings themselves are *not* for everyone!

"You yourself are also one of the 'readers' of these letters, by the way. You have always needed to read and reread what you've written in order to understand. You are part of the human audience for our message. As you read, look beneath the surface; read between the lines and inside the words; *feel* more than think about what you read. The *meaning* is on many levels. And remember, you provide the final synthesis and meaning for *yourself*, out of your own being. Creating meaning is your task.

"Apollo—in addition to being the sun god—is the poet, prophet, riddler and oracle extraordinaire. He lives continuously on the brink of creativity and of the unknown—that presence you yourself have encountered recently. He receives the raw transmissions from Source, and steps them down for us all. When we angelans are studying Source, at the edge of the Threshold, we are gazing into Apollo's eyes. His wisdom, interpretation and illumination are what we seek. He translates the initial impulses out of the Void directly to us. He does the same for anyone who would honor his decree: 'Know thyself!' This is his very first riddle: Indeed, what does he mean by 'know'? And just who is 'thyself'?

"He communicates with us *all* through riddles. It is his way of insuring that listeners will take the transmissions into their hearts and not just their minds. The nature of an oracular riddle demands that the receiver delve within to discover the truth. This is why we call it *revelation*. Riddles protect both the message and the receiver of the message. They carry us through portals to our inner being—where peace passes understanding—where we know our true place and capacity. The central challenge, in the end, for all beings in incarnation is to solve *the riddle of their own lives.*

"By virtue of Apollo's place in the bosom of mystery, he *must* be obscure and potentially misleading. For those who would hear his words, they must examine their motives and inner constitutions. They must know themselves intimately, in the heart, as formlessness itself. Otherwise, they run the risk of taking the oracle's surface words as 'truth'. This is where the greatest danger lies for being misled. The *self* does the misleading, of course—that 'self' that we are instructed to 'know'. The real truth cannot be written, heard or spoken— from anyone's lips, to anyone's ears. Words, lips and ears are *mind forms*. The real truth is formless."

I interrupt again with a concern. *I just can't help myself.* "So, how can there by value to what I'm writing? It's just words on paper, after all."

"Value and truth are two different things. There is much of value in these books. But there is *no truth!* The value lies in the *stimulus* to seek the truth and to find it within the reader's heart. All readers must take on this mission for themselves. The *value* lies in the call to awaken, to find the pointer and portal that suits the capacity of each individual heart.

"The *truth*, I will repeat, is the purity beyond thoughts and words. It resides in those sublime and formless realms that preserve the sanctity of soul and Source. From that pure power center, it reaches out into your world and makes impressions upon your manifested forms. Those impressions, for better or for worse, are often mistaken for truth—hence your religions, with their dogmas and inadequate representations of 'truth'.

"Even though Apollo is a trickster—a 'coyote' in the sense of native spirit-uality—it is of great benefit to seek him out humbly, with wariness and aware-ness. It is wise to reveal him *within* yourself and to know him as he is. It is also wise to know his potential for deception. This approach keeps you on your guard, alert, engaging heart more than head, weighing—with sensation—the truth within what your ears may hear.

"It is not that Apollo actually seeks to mislead and deceive humans. Hu-mans bring their own deceptions *with* them into his presence, as part of their un-evolved nature. According to this nature, they digest what they hear through the mechanisms of ego and thought. It often results in confusion and defeat, babbling and shallow belief. The worst is that such people have taken what they *think* they heard—believing it to be *the* truth—and turn it outward into the world, preaching their distorted interpretations as the 'word of God' or 'divine transmission'."

I nod in agreement. My mind wrestles with another anxiety. "If Apollo is so important, why haven't I been told before now about his role in this pro-ject—that he is actually the initiator of the whole thing?"

"You *have* been told, in the way of Apollo—in riddles and inferences and mystical clues. Nothing is direct with the sun god, except his physical light. And in that too, one must be careful against over- or underexposure. His influence is always presented in turns and spirals and reflections in mirrors. Look back at your own introduction in these books. You credited the muses from the start, did you not? Whether or not you knew the whole story, there was a *reverence* in your relationship with them. And you know that the muses are but expressions of Apollo. You have indeed invoked his guidance continuously. And now that we near the end of our cycle together, you are discovering the deeper layers of the riddle that has been guiding us all along. It is perfectly natural, apollonian."

I look around at you and B, wondering what you think of all this. *Were you both aware all along? Was I the only one in the dark? Yes!* I turn back to Omis. "All right. I accept this relationship with Apollo. But what does it really mean to the project? What difference does it make in the end? I have never actually understood where the information was coming from or how it was being transmitted. Will knowing that this Greek god is part of it clarify anything?"

Omis stirs in his chair and looks out at the golden mountains. I feel he may actually be looking at Apollo out there. It is as though the greater expanse is actually his *interior* space, his palace. He speaks slowly, precisely, "I have come to know and love this divine being. He shines into my world with each ray of light. He imbues my essence with its vitality and light. He is the *substance* of my feeling and appreciation. Knowing his presence reveals the inner workings and structures of consciousness to me. This is the difference he makes. It can be the same for you. His place and presence can make all the difference in your awakening."

I turn back to you and B. "What do you have to say about this? I take it that you knew about Apollo all along. Can you help me understand what's going on?"

Invm answers to my surprise. Everyone turns to him. "Perhaps my view can help. We have a different aspect of Apollo in our solar system, Sirius. But it is really the same being. Apollo's twin soul is our sun god, if you will. She is the *sister* god, goddess, as you would say. Note, however, it is not *religion* when we use these words. Rather god and goddess are titles, related to function and degree of advancement in evolution.

"The same mystery nature of Apollo prevails within our cultures. However, we look differently at mystery. Ours is more 'scientific' I would say. We see mystery as the 'prime elementary particle' of manifestation; it distinguishes form from function. Thus, for example, it is the link between chemistry and physics, between the microscopic and the macroscopic, between one quantum state and another. It constitutes the 'missing link' in evolution. This 'mystery' presence explains to us why the simple addition of a few atoms of hydrogen to any given molecule, microscopically, produces radically new attributes at the macroscopic levels. It is why, when you put two volatile elements together, such as sodium and chlorine, you produce a salt that is safe to consume.

"Among the worlds of Sirius, we study this 'god' endlessly. Nevertheless, we have yet to discover codifications of her behavior. We accept this as demonstrating the limits of science and of knowledge itself. There are presences in the universe much more profound than systems of intellect. Apollo's twin, in our worlds, opens the path to wonder and imagination. Without her influence, ours would be a dry and humorless society."

After a moment's pause, we politely chuckle at Invm's admission. I smile at him; then I look at you next. "O, do you have anything to add?"

"You know me too well. Of course, I have something to add. Apollo for me is a rather *distant* force. I do not feel him as a continuing presence, except as the vital unknown and, of course, a manifested form of the formless sun. But I have long felt his occasional influence—the presence of mystery—in our project.

"When I have discovered new aspects to the project, such as when you and I found out OM's role in the future, I recognized it as Apollo's handiwork. I did not reveal that to you directly, however; I sensed that revelation would come in its own time. And it has. In that way—Apollo's way—the revelation would be more resonant and embracing."

Next I look at B and ask, "What do *you* know of Apollo? Is there a more direct contact for you?"

Instead of answering with words, Black smiles. She reaches across the table, touching my hand. I'm reminded of the time we met in Jerusalem. Without warning, B and I are again descending into the blackness together; the floor has dropped out. She grasps both my hands and stares into my eyes. Wind is whipping us as we fall.

True to her manner, she says, "I will *show* you what I know. We're heading to the edge of the Threshold, the closest we can come to the Void without entering it. All this was discovered while we were trying to understand the realm of the angelans. It is Source gazing at its most refined."

Suddenly we make a turn, two turns, three. It reminds me of Breanne cutting down the alleys of Montmartre, one after another in rapid succession. We seem to be turning and twisting, but at the same time we're plummeting into the abyss. Now we're flashing through other dimensions. We enter one space, make a hard right turn, then—blink—we enter another space. It seems as though we're jumping galaxies and even universes in a mad scramble to outwit the Threshold itself. A tiny hole opens and we slip through.

Suddenly we're zooming down to a planetary surface, skimming along the shoreline of a beautiful, purple ocean. The night sky is a deep blue-violet. Stars, in great profusion span the dome. Another quick left and we're racing up a valley. The river below is broad and still, reflecting the stars above. As we continue, the valley narrows into a deep ravine. The stream is now a raging torrent. High mountains rise on both sides of us. At last, we climb steeply up one slope and jump into yet another dimension. *I never knew you could do this kind of dimension jumping!* The mountains are still here, but the colors are slightly different. We stop!

"Here we are," she says triumphantly.

The dark sky is just beginning to crack with light along the horizon, out beyond the far peaks. The darkness in this dimension is deep crimson; the tiny streak of light is yellow-orange. It slowly spreads to the sides. *The sun will appear soon,* I anticipate. The sky now lightens more, gradually creeping up the wall of night. Then, almost imperceptibly, the yellow streak squeezes into a point and flashes blue-silvery green. Gone. I feel a sense of deep mystery. *I've never seen a sunrise like this.*

"Watch," she whispers. *How could I not watch?* My eyes are riveted on the edge of this world. Suddenly I'm aghast. Out on the horizon, there is not one sun, but two! Dual orbs of brilliance are cutting above the horizon simultaneously, side by side. They are as glorious as any sun rising has ever been. Then it all freezes. The rising has halted with the two stars sitting squarely on the lip of the world.

As I watch, the stars begin to move again, but in the reverse direction. They're setting! In perfect synchrony they sink below the horizon again. Their shared aura remains, but the orbs have disappeared. B looks at me to take stock of my awe. It is probably heightened by the orange glow all around my face.

She says flatly, "That, my friend, is Apollo and his sister!"

I sputter a word or two, "Wow! Thank you. That was truly awesome." Digesting the impact as best I can, I choke out, "Now, please explain."

B responds excitedly, "This never ends. Here in this spot, on this planet, in this dimension, there is always the rising and setting of these two suns with a period of darkness between—the gathering of night. And this is only the physical expression. If you slip into the under-dimension, you will encounter yet a deeper mystery.

And so I do. *Slip away!* The world above fades, and I appear to be sinking below its space. Here I feel an enormous flush of warmth and welcome, coupled with anticipation—a pleasant form of uncertainty. Immediately a question is pressed into my mind from the inside, from the *feeling* inside me. It is a simple question, rather like a riddle: 'Will you now *un-know* your self?'

Without a thought, my answer bubbles out, 'Yes! If you insist.'

At once, I'm in a chamber of sorts. It has strange metallic golden walls that are constantly in slow motion, transforming around me. They are solid at one moment, transparent at the next. Through the transparency I can see star fields and galaxies; they too are moving, turning across the firmament. When the walls turn opaque, large holes remain randomly-placed in them. Through the holes I peer into the endless Void behind all space. The holes close and open, in a seemingly random succession. Soft musical chords echo in time with the movements.

Now into this space, two bright orbs of light enter, one on each side of me. An inner sense tells me that these are the *hearts* of two suns—one from the Earth system; the other from Sirius. Here is where the two hearts meet. I am in the dimension of *star hearts*. It is a blessed space of incomprehensible love and compassion. The two star hearts are directing their attention toward me. They 'glow' a message of sacredness.

I reflect on their message; it is an injunction. My sensibilities shift and broaden. Somehow, bizarrely, the two globes of great power are *deferring* to me. They are addressing me with something verging on adulation. They show a deep awe at my presence. This seems preposterous to me until I truly feel their impressions. They are telling me *I am Source*. They are looking to me as the center of the Cosmos. I laugh—from the center of my being. The laughter continues. In opening to mirth, joy and bliss well up and penetrate my awareness. Instantly, I know what they know.

In a flash of truth, I realize I *am* Source. I am following the injunction: I'm *unknowing* my self! Any whiff of a separative conception—as in selfhood in the world of men—has been sucked away in my laughter. *I simply am—Am.* My presence looks out upon its creation: First, in this place, I see the sun gods I have authored. I appreciate their reverence for me. I return their praise and adulation. *There is only one of us here. We are one.* No words separate us—no thoughts—into speaker and spoken to.

Awareness. Great, glorious awareness of creation and manifestation proceeds ever out from here, from the Star Heart Chamber. All creation is one. The duality is one. It never really departs from this Void space. But I see how it works: The sun gods inject the creation with a riddle. A simple decoy is cast upon the energy flow outward. The Great Illusion is born of this riddling: *"The*

One is not one. The 'not' and the One are two. The two and the 'not' are one. Knowing becomes the not-self. Unknowing becomes the Self." Out of sheer frustration with this riddle, the whole universe trembles and convulses into accepting the Illusion.

In this mind, I look out upon my little life on Earth. I see all the lives of my soul, projected out. I see wholeness within the illusion. I see that everything is its opposite and inside out; there is no separation truly possible. Nothing leaves this space of Oneness; nothing separates. It's all just a *dream* of separation.

Then I see my soul inside its group of other souls. I see that group subsumed within a greater group, a galaxy of soul clusters, and the galaxies of clusters are endless, eternal—synthesis and progression, stage-by-stage, level-by-level. Each higher, finer and deeper level is a step toward Oneness, toward *amness*. But it never reaches that objective—not in *form*. All the while, it has never departed from the Oneness that it seeks. *The awakening precedes the seeking!* The illusion has never departed from reality. Form has never left the formless.

I see my story, my time on Earth. I watch the unfolding of the transposition project with all its layers and players, who are already *me*. I see my time in Paris. Phileina and Breanne shine like stars in a tiny firmament. I see the masculine and feminine of an entire culture—entire Europe—embrace and unite in the forms of Mars and Venus. All is swallowed up in levels of expression. All is clear and resonant unto itself. I see now Apollo and his twin in Oneness. I appreciate. I am infinitely pleased.

I taste the mystery in my throat and swallow. In this act, I begin to shrink back into my incarnate, little self. Slowly. Infinitely. I move upward, toward the surface; I'm reversing the passage by which I came here. I gather up B and we sweep back out. Instantly, as though nothing had ever happened, we are at the table again, just beginning our journey, just now touching hands, just now remembering. The vision of you and the others on the veranda of the sun blinks a few times back into stability, into what it was before.

Letter Seventy-Seven
Invoke the Void

Omis flashes his angelan form for a moment, as if to re-establish his presence. In that same moment, I see through the illusion of this mansion on the Sun. The roiling sea of fire shows itself in all its fearsome grandeur. It is what we're all precariously suspended above. The illusion of solidity swiftly returns, and all is calm. Omis looks serenely around the table at each one of us before he speaks, as if nothing had happened.

"Now you have a picture of Apollo, my friend. But, I must remind you; this is only one face that you have seen. There are many more. He is a most awesome and complex authority, and impossible to know in his entirety."

Omis hesitates, knowing I have a question. He nods, and I start, "I witnessed a most powerful presence on that little trip with B. In fact I saw into the root of us all. I knew my being to be the Source itself. The question I have is this: I want to know what lies between here and there; how does it all actually manifest into form? How does the system of beings—gods, angels, angelans, humans, etcetera, come about? What is the relationship between Apollo and the angelans, the archangels and the Solar Logos? Is there some kind of hierarchy built into it, behind it?"

Omis replies, "As we have told you before, there *is* a multi-dimensional hierarchy. It is not physically based, nor does it employ tactics of control and manipulation, as in the hierarchies of the human world. It is intrinsic in the expression of *Conscious Evolution*—embodied at each stratum of collectivity and individuality. What you have also seen is that this evolutionary hierarchy is a grand illusion, a structure created by the likes of Apollo, to mask the reality. Without the mask, there is no differentiation, no expression. It is all 'smoke and mirrors', to use a human term—the greatest 'trick' of the greatest trickster in our dimensional systems.

"The illusion is not in opposition to reality, however. It compliments reality fully; it *fulfills* reality—as the breath fulfills the being, as the cut jewel fulfills the raw mineral. We are all aspects of Source—and, yes, we *are* in fact Source—as you have seen. Source allows these aspects to exist in expression, so that the jewel may be exposed. A master jeweler must cut the diamond into form. He must etch Life into the illusion. That would be Apollo!"

I continue, asking, "But what is a 'god' anyhow? Why are we using this terminology? Are we a reviving a pagan religion?"

"Apollo is not a Greek god. That is how you have come to think of him. But this too is just a riddle of cultural evolution. Apollo is a mask, a face, if you will of the 'Solar Logos', which in turn is a mask of Source. In other spiritual and philosophical traditions, other terms have been used. Both 'god' and 'logos' are names applied to offices and functions in the hierarchy of spiritual being. These names have been applied in a religious sense, true, but that is not how they really are.

"I know that you and many readers blanch at the word 'hierarchy'. Allow me to explain it for you. The word derives—thank you, Orange—from the Greek, meaning 'sacred authority'. What defines 'sacred' is the overarching inclusiveness and integrity of being that attends this organism; what defines 'authority' is the essential *authenticity* of its presence.

"To answer your original question and give you some examples, the Solar Logos, is the being who embraces and *includes* all lesser individualities in the solar system. These 'lesser' beings are actually essential components in the *form* of the Logos. They are on the path of evolution toward becoming as the Logos is. On etheric levels, each planet has a Logos—Greek for 'sacred word'. It is the word of expression and creation from Source, and through Apollo.

"True hierarchy is a product of all-encompassing levels of being. The souls of each of us—to continue with examples—includes the incarnate forms that you have witnessed projecting into the world; the soul is, therefore, a level 'above' us in hierarchical terms. The oversoul is composed of multiple souls—another level 'up'. The planetary logos includes multiple oversouls, and so on.

"On your own individual level, you include the organs, cells, molecules and atoms of your body. They are 'lower' levels of hierarchy, included *within* your individual form. 'Upper' and 'lower' are words that might also mislead. You might want to substitute words like 'larger' and 'smaller', 'older' or 'younger'.

Omis continues, "As a human, your emerging awareness rejects the concept of 'hierarchy', and rightly so. It is a corruption of its authentic meaning. If a form is not truly inclusive in essence and practice, it is a false hierarchy, a *sacrilege*. O would point out that the sacredness has been *stolen* from it; that is how the word 'sacrilege' came into being. Such a hierarchy is an artificial contrivance by human egos to centralize control over others and increase separation from Source.

"This has been necessary over the course of human evolution to maintain order in societies and to stimulate awakening. It was used to introduce humanity to a basic understanding of *collaboration*. But as the whole of evolution comes awake, these structures are no longer necessary; they are counterproductive. The only valid hierarchies for you now are those based on autonomy, compassion and inclusiveness, or as the Parisians would say it—*liberty, equality and fra-*

ternity. You are centered in Paris for these last transmissions to gather this three-fold essence—to observe the fusion of yin and yang, war and peace, love and power.

"Apollo, the trickster oracle and 'deceiver' of Greek mythology, was characterized by dissociation and disguise. The riddling nature of his approach is a careful design. It is intended to preserve the sanctity of his prophecies. His relation to the hierarchy of spirit is integral with the Solar Logos, but he makes no claim on it. Rather he prefers to remain free to facilitate his revelations."

"Why does he want to disguise his connection to hierarchy?" I ask.

"Because the structural nature of hierarchy binds the awareness to a form. Apollo's true nature is to dispense with *form*alities. He dislodges our minds and turns us inside out, instilling questions in us that reveal our destiny. If he were to emphasize a position in the hierarchy, his focus would become structural and formal. Others have that role and function, not him."

I open my mind and try to absorb what he's saying. "So, is Apollo, the sun god, the *same* as the Solar Logos?"

"He is one face of the Logos, not the entirety of that being. He is the 'charioteer', in Greek terms. He brings forward the light out of darkness each day for the world's illumination. He manifests the intentions of the Logos at a very high level. All of us, at whatever level we operate, are 'cells' in the corpus of that great being. All our lives, our comings and goings, are governed by its vast life force and purposes. This is the divine creature in whom we 'live and move and have our being'."

I say, "You mentioned something called the 'gathering of night'. I saw such a gathering demonstrated on the journey with B, but I don't really understand what it means. Can you explain?"

"Let me defer to B on this matter. She has had more recent experience." He looks over to her with gravity.

B responds, "Omis, I doubt that I have half the understanding of this that you do."

"Approximately half, yes," he chuckles. "But please go ahead. It will be good to hear your voice put this to words."

"All right then. What I have observed and have heard in my studies is this: Apollo is tasked with revering the dark origins of creation—the 'night', in a word. This is in keeping, indeed, with his elusiveness and obscurity. Symbolically, the sun goes into night after each day on Earth. It is reborn each morning out of the darkness, rested and recharged. This, of course, is only from a planetary perspective. Yet the metaphor is important. It is testament to how allied our source of light and Life is with the underworld and the Void. Though the Solar Logos represents illumination, its roots are in the deep, dark stillness.

"The 'gathering of night' is an intentional approach to the essence of form-lessness—to *gather* it in. It is a conscious honoring of the Void, and an entreaty to draw up wisdom out of the pre-manifested depths. To 'gather the night' is to invoke the Void. The *unknown* is a highly active presence in this endeavor. There is no telling, at any given moment, what the wisdom of the Void actually is. To call it forth, one must utterly surrender to it. We know how dangerous that can feel. Any particle of fear lurking in your mind can be exploded into an agonizing upheaval.

"There is a second meaning to these words, as well. A 'gathering of night' can be a special kind of *meeting* of comrades during the darkest hours before dawn. Plato suggested such night meetings as a form of worship toward Apol-lo. The participants would gather and sit in stillness as the night was ending. I must say, however, the purpose of these meetings remains a mystery to me. Omis, would you please take it from here?"

The angelan smiles and bows his head. "The purpose is simple. And I would recommend an exercise to anyone who has sensitivity to stillness. Hear this: The hour before the light reemerges from darkness, and indeed the *three minutes* just before, are teeming with extraordinary potentiality. This is the most creative exposure to the Solar Logos and Source there is.

"The practice I recommend is to sit with a small group at the end of the night, after having slept well beforehand. Find a location where you can see the rising of the sun on the horizon. A mountaintop would be ideal, but any place with sufficient eastern exposure will do. Sit in stillness, as souls. Invoke a shared soul presence with the others in the group. Enter into a silent compact among yourselves, to honor the presence of the unknown and to invoke an opening to the Void in your midst. Surrender your separative natures to the will of Source. Let go and gather in the essence.

"You will, in this exercise, be creating a portal into the Void at the center of your shared, soul group. Continue sitting in silence and Oneness as the sky begins to lighten. The instant before the sun breaks the horizon, forces will flood through the vortex you have opened, through your joined soul center and into your hearts. You will become vessels of pure creative wisdom in that instant. Take it into your being like breath. Breathe in the energy of the Void with lungs of fire—etheric lungs of *chi* energy. Take as many silent, deep breaths as you can before the sun actually appears. When its face crosses the horizon—when Apollo rises—the seal is set. You have taken into your being the wisdom of darkness. You have, as a group, 'gathered the night'."

I gasp, almost out of breath from listening to this. "Omis, that's beautiful. I had no idea. What B and I observed on the edge of the Threshold was exactly that, only I didn't realize it in my mind at the time. I can't wait to try this myself."

He partially winks and smiles. "I think you're ready. However, it takes serious preparation, finding others who are interested and available at the given time and place. Nevertheless, I wish you Apollo speed."

Your voice now enters the conversation. You have been listening appreciatively and intently this whole time. "And so, Omis, would you explain what these souls have in their midst once the sun finally rises?"

"A very good question. They are left with 'a very good question' in their midst. It is the fire of the *unknown* in the belly. There is no telling beforehand how it will manifest. That, my friends, is the treasure of it. But I assure you, it will be powerful and pure and ready to be acted upon. The group will know, in its heart, what the mission and immediate destiny are. There may be no words spoken. You may simply look at one another, knowingly. You will have, within you, a living paradox—the knowing of the unknown. This is the time for sounding the 'AH' chant; it is the sound of opening and invocation."

You continue, "Can one practice this alone, without the others?"

"Yes, you may attempt this alone, but a much greater amplitude comes about from the linking of two or more hearts, at the soul level. This linkage can indeed be done at a distance, but the timing of the sunrise may vary, depending on your position on the planet. There is a special magic in the instant of the arrival of the sun god; it is more than symbolic. If you and your partners are in different time zones, the synchrony of the sun crossing the horizon is more important than the time on your clocks."

You ask, "What about the reverse of this procedure? At the end of the day, when the sun disappears for the night?"

"Another good question. This is the time of withdrawal into the Void. It is equally sacred and may be honored. This is not the time for a *gathering*, however, at least not in conjunction with Apollo. It is a time of dissolution and dispersal. One best practices that exercise alone, in deep reflection and appreciation for the passage of the light that has just terminated. This is the time for sounding the 'OM' chant—the sound of completion and integration."

I interrupt. "I once witnessed the 'green flash' at sunset—on a beach in Mexico. It was a special moment for me. I don't know if it's relevant here, but it certainly comes to mind whenever I think of sunsets."

Omis grins. "It is indeed relevant. You know that green is the color of the heart and of nature itself. Seeing the 'green flash' is an invitation to appreciate the completion of the day in your heart, as an opening into the depths—even into the Void. There is a similar but much rarer event in the morning, an instant *before* sunrise; it may be witnessed on exceptional occasions during the 'gathering of night' ceremony."

"Well," I gasp. "B and I just saw that!"

Omis stares into my eyes and grins. "Isn't *that* a coincidence!"

I laugh and continue, *"Touché.* So, could you please summarize? Why does Apollo go into the night and the Void? This is only from our perspective on Earth, a planet, after all. Out in space there is no sunset."

"Ah. But there is," Omis replies. "Night is continuous there. Light exists within the eternal context of darkness. Space is the eternal Grand Night. All light issues forth from it. You can sense this in your body and being, if you pause for a moment and contemplate the question, 'Where does light come from?' Just as form must derive out of formlessness and sound out of silence, light must come out of *lightlessness.*

"Your scientists have recently discovered dark matter and dark energy, estimating that it constitutes most of the mass of the universe, even though it cannot be seen or measured. This empty darkness is the formative principal in all of creation. You ask, 'Why does Apollo return into the night?' Isn't it obvious? He knows where the power is."

Letter Seventy-Eight
Surrender to Oneness

"What about my other question?" I persist. "How does Apollo relate to the angelan evolution and the archangels?"

With another magnificent flourish, Omis rises into his angelan form. His grandeur is astonishing in this sudden movement. His glistening, transparent wings spread wide and return to his sides. "For the answer to that let us invite Mihelo and Gavrea to explain."

Suddenly the floor falls away, the mansion dissolves into nothing, and we mortals are hovering in perilous form above the surface of the Solar Logos. Our eyes are protected, so we can actually see the surface. Fires spew upward toward us in streams of incandescent fury. You and the others are much calmer than I. As terrifying as it is though, I must admit it's one of the grandest sights I've ever seen. The colors are wonderful and constantly changing—all various shades of gold and yellow and orange. Out of the molten sea, two forms suddenly appear far below and sweep up beside us. While the surface seems close, it must be thousands of miles down. Mihelo and Gavrea have never looked more resplendent. They take positions on either side of Omis, holding as firmly as two mountains.

From the gigantic fire at our feet, hissing sounds and smells of scorching dryness invade my senses. Thankfully, I feel only warmth, not the true temperatures of this place. The three angelic forms, hovering together before us make a thrilling spectacle. Such an audience is rarely granted to humans or vigilans. *How is it that we qualify?* I wonder.

Gavrea answers my thought, "We have waited long enough to address the evolutionary chain behind us. Your only qualification is that you are *human* and *vigilan.*"

Omis, as host, announces his intentions, "My teachers, we would hear your wisdom on a matter concerning Apollo. How do you say we are, in relation to him?"

Now that I'm paying attention, I can see differences between the forms of the archangels and the angelan. The archangels are more 'heavenly' to use an insufficient term. They are larger, taller and more gossamer; transparent. The skin colors are different as well. Omis is darker. I can't help asking myself a silly question I might have asked long ago. *Why do they have wings?*

The answer comes immediately from Mihelo. "We do *not* have wings, dear human. *You* do. You have them in your mind, *imagining* what we look like. Our true form is unintelligible to the human intellect. Your race has invented the forms you currently perceive—as a translation of reality. Our auras become *wings* in your interpretations. That is fine with us. If your imagination did not do something like this, you could see nothing at all."

"I'm sorry, Gavrea, for bothering you with such an insignificant question. I didn't really mean to verbalize it. It was only a thought."

Gavrea answers dispassionately, "Thoughts—when precise—are a means of communication for us. We are pleased to answer any sincere question you have."

"Well, in that case, there's something else." I cough. "Are you saying that I'm just making up your wings in my mind—and Omis' wings too? How can I know what's real?"

"You know, friend, that no *thing* is real. All forms are generated between a projector and a screen. If it is 'reality' that you would know, you can truly receive it only through the stillness resident in your heart. Stillness equals emptiness. All forms have the Void within them. The essence can thus be touched. This is 'embracing the emptiness'. By contrast, embracing the *form* has been humanity's lot and limitation.

"The fact that you are here with us, suspended over the surface of your Sun—and not being instantly vaporized—is also testimony to the non-reality of form. We are sharing with you our powers of embracing the emptiness in order for you to bypass the effects that would 'normally' befall you in this place. Because we live in the state of *bypass* and timelessness, being here is 'normal' to us.

"Now, we have come specifically to answer a different question. This we shall do before taking you on a little journey. Stop. Do not ask 'where'. The question we will answer now pertains to the relationship between angelans, archangels and Apollo? We are here to share an understanding with you. This relates to *our* destiny and yours."

Mihelo speaks, and as he does, the aura around him glows with alternating patterns. I sense inwardly that these patterns are a visible projection of the thought-forms behind his words. If I could understand *that* language, words would not be needed. *And neither would the wings!*

He begins, "Apollo is who *we* really are—as a race; that is, as two races, three, four and five. Oneness has differentiated us into these numbers. There is only one, yet there are five. To explain further, your race is called human, ours you have called archangels and angels. We have in our midst also the races you know as angelan and vigilan.

"There is an overarching *race,* according to this terminology, that is only one. That race is Apollo."

My mind squints at this, not getting what Mihelo is saying. I finally shake my head. "I'm sorry. What does that mean? Apollo is a *race?* How can he be a race? Do you mean he is a member of another race?"

The archangel continues, as though I hadn't asked, "Apollo is our creator and benefactor and our destined evolution. In the timelessness, it is already accomplished. His being is *our* being. As angelans and archangels take the next step in the evolution of their species, we merge. I believe you have heard this before. We merge into one species. That species is a summation of us; its name is Apollo."

I still don't get it. What is he saying?

"I am saying that both our species—the angelans and the archangels—become one. That *one* is named Apollo."

I finally begin to put my mind around the idea. "So, your two whole species become just *one individual being?* Is that it?"

"Precisely. His being is *plural*—a multi-souled entity—the next level of 'hierarchy' to us, as it has been explained by Omis. Apollo is the *divine directorate.* He encompasses us with his form and we are immersed in that expression entirely. Within him we live and move and have our being. In timelessness it is already done, hence he appears as an individual 'god' to those below. In time, however, evolution must proceed according to its nature; thus you see us as distinct species.

"Apollo represents our destiny as well as yours, as your awareness matures through the vigilan race and then the angelan. In time, that is a very long period. In reality it is now. It is already done."

I feel this idea gradually sinking in. *But it seems very bizarre to me.* "Are all the Greek gods like this? I mean what humans call 'gods'."

"All gods, as conceived by humanity are archetypes and thus collective in nature. However, Apollo is unique. He is also the 'hierarchy' for the other beings you have called 'gods'. This includes the one known as Jupiter. That is the paradox of the 'son becoming the father'. It also renders much more substance to Apollo than was thought in your times and before. But we are not here to change your society's thinking on this matter. We state it now merely to assist you and your circle of friends to enter more deeply into the mysteries."

"So, please help me understand how the writing of these letters happens, given that Apollo seems to be at the center of it. Did he generate the project? Does he direct my inspirations, my actual writing?"

Mihelo makes an adjustment in his countenance before answering, as if he is opening a new page of information to download to us. "The answer to this is 'yes' and 'no'. There is a presence within Apollo that is intimate at each level of manifestation. That is to say, he is *immanent* within you and his energy flows out into literally every action that can possibly take place for you. His energy is, therefore, being used by you, by Omis and O, by ourselves, to perform the work we do, to make the projections we make. Apollo is also *eminent,* and transcends entirely the world of forms as you know it. From this angle he is quite removed from the details of our activities on this plane—as you are removed from the activities of the individual cells of your body."

"All right—*immanent* and *eminent.* I like that. Alice Bailey used that combination of terms in referring to divinity. But I'm still not really appreciating what's going on here. I'm writing these letters, with inspiration coming from *somewhere*—from the muses, I've always felt. Apollo directs the muses, so he's sending this inspiration. Right?"

Mihelo smiles. "It is simple from my view. From yours it will sound complicated. The inspiration is drawn from many sources. This is the function of the muses. They do not follow 'orders', as such, from Apollo. They take his impressions, his desires, and manifest them into ideas, thoughts, suggestions and images for the likes of you—and for anyone else that has ever been inspired to be creative.

"The function of the muses is to reach out in all directions, to locate resources for the intended projection, and then to synthesize these into a 'gift' of insight, delivered into the heart of the individual creator. That individual must then take it from there. She or he must bring the inspiration of the heart into the mind and body—through resonance and coherence; that is, the mind must be synchronized with the heart and body. The inspiration will thus finally be manifested.

"You have many layers of potential misinterpretation in such an exercise. This is why any artist, poet or prophet—any practitioner of creativity—must acquire skills. True skills lie, not in the hands or eyes alone, but in the coherence of heart and head. This has been your role in drafting and consistently reworking the substance of this project."

I nod, understanding at last. "That explains a lot to me. So, please allow me to summarize this, to ground it for myself: Apollo first sets a course for a given desired manifestation—a potential project. Then the muses, acting under his purview, get creative in their own right, going out and finding relevant resources and influences to give form to Apollo's intention. They then massage that raw material into an inspiration, and slip it into my intuition, my *heart*. From there it's my job to get still and *feel* the inspiration in my subtle body. Finally, I take it up to my mind. But that can't be done without 'coherence'—a resonance between heart and mind and body. Do I have that correct, Mihelo?"

"You do. And these are the basic mechanics behind the inspiring of any artist, scientist, or teacher—any creative being. No individual has ever *created* alone, without the benefit, guidance and support of the muses. This process works so much more smoothly when made *conscious* and appreciated. The 'unconscious' ego can be creative at times, in an imitative way, but when it is, this is only *temporary* at best."

Gavrea now speaks again. Her voice is mellow, in noticeable contrast to the fierce environment below us. "We come to you from deep awareness ourselves. The gift we would bring into your being is the gift of *depth*. Our service to you is to connect you with the heart and the full being of presence, which is none other than Source. This too is Apollo's mission in your lives. He brings the light out of the darkness—and returns it there, fulfilled. He brings knowing out of the unknown, and the fullness out of the Void. And he returns it, fulfilled, into the Void. It is the cycle of supreme empowerment.

"We are all *of* the Sun. We live at its behest in all our means and ends. But it is not only the sun of day and illumination. It is the sun of night and dissolution, as well. Out of these roots are expressed all the shadows and light of dual creation. They are yours, in your entirety. As you live and follow the path to revelation—and solve the *riddle of your life*—you bring *us* into your world. We archangels live at the edge of Oneness—at the very edge, in Apollo. It is likewise the edge of the commencement of duality. These two are one.

"Surrender to Oneness, we say. In this act of pure and ultimate contrition, you elevate your soul to its natural height; you return it to its natural depth. In this act, you acknowledge that you are at one with Source, at one with the Void, at one with the Now. Oneness, likewise, surrenders to *you* in the same moment. Surrendering renders the realization of Oneness. The awareness and revelation of Oneness is nothing other than Oneness's acceptance and its surrendering to itself."

I hear my voice once more with a question. "Please give me an instruction, Gavrea. Tell me how to solve the 'riddle of my life'. I realize right now, for the first time, that this is just exactly what I've been troubling myself with as long as I can remember. It defines what I feel has always been missing from me, what I have always longed for. I've always sought a true purpose in my life"

"You speak truly, son of Apollo. The riddle is the Life. It is the *longing* for Life, for consciousness! While we cannot—nor can any being—reveal this ultimate riddle *for* you, we *can* show you the way you may do it for yourself. First, you must ask for guidance. This you have done, here and now and forever. Done. Second, you must accept your *sole destiny* as the solving of this riddle. But this is a paradox of the greatest magnitude, for the riddle is what you *are*. You cannot find the answer to the riddle without already knowing and *being* the answer. Third and last, you must see the beginning and the end as the same. Where you have come from is where you return, finding that you have never departed. This is *awakening*.

"To solve a riddle is to *read* it from beginning to end, and from end to beginning. Read it from inside out and outside in. This third step results in a decision within your heart to have the answer and the solution—the *reading,* if you will. Once you know you have your decision in hand, head and heart, you will walk through the doorway opened by the riddle of your life and be free. You will know what it has been to be incarnate in a form. And you will surrender to freedom."

Silence falls with a rush and hissing sound, dropping into the fiery, turbulent sea below. Above us is the night and stars and planets—the lives of all the creatures in the solar sphere. I float in acceptance of this tableau. I accept that I am the riddle of my life. I am one small part of the great scheme that lays eternally all around me, around all of us. And yet in accepting my small part in this, I must accept the *whole* of it—inside me—as well. The smallness is irrelevant. It is the 'part-ness' that counts. *I participate, therefore, I am.* Therefore Oneness is.

Letter Seventy-Nine
Open Opportunity Essence

Suddenly we're hanging in raw space, out some distance from the Sun. We may be in the orbit of Mercury, for all I know. All of us are still together in a circle, floating. I can now see each of our auras, shining brightly, like bubbles of light. *Something about an audience with Apollo seems to make a person shine.* It also seems that our auras themselves are protecting us from the vacuum and frigid temperatures of space.

Mihelo now projects a large transparent ring of golden light around the group with a movement of his hand. Its surface touches each of us, shining and sparkling like bubbles in champagne. He speaks, "Now, it is time for a little journey." My curiosity peaked, my thoughts go back to other journeys you and I have had. He continues, "It will be a journey into time. The transposition aspect will be familiar. We propose taking you to two places that you have perhaps never imagined going. And it will be to both places *simultaneously*. This means that you must *bi-locate.*"

My mind races suddenly, unaccountably giddy. I begin to feel fanciful and high. *Are we going to the center of a galaxy? No, we've been there, done that! Hah, maybe two galaxies at once? No. Will it be the bottom of another ocean? I think probably not.*

The archangels, monitoring my thoughts, seem amused at my internal lightheadedness. Gavrea says, "You are correct that it is none of these destinations. What we will do is take you 26,000 years into your future and 26,000 years into your past, both at the same time."

We sit in stunned silence. *What? How?* Then I decide to ask a dumb question. "Why?"

Omis answers, "Because it is the natural fulfillment of our project. We have known for some time that this was a multi-generational effort. I now, this moment, understand for the first time that those generations have spanned the length of 52,000 years on Earth. I sense it is time to become familiar with our far-distant brothers and sisters."

We look at each other around our glowing circle. I stare for a long time into your eyes, then at B's gleaming face. I sense this may be the last journey we make together. *Do I actually see an expression of excitement on Invm's face?* The Sirian is very focused on the substance of the golden ring that links us all. I'm sure he's analyzing it with his mind—plus a strong measure of heart coherence too, of course.

Our circle keeps its silent communion. We are pulled together closer, slowly, in stillness, until our auras are touching, overlapping. With this direct contact, I feel an alignment and a resonance. Each of our chakras is linking, one with all others. An energetic network has formed within our etheric bodies, weaving around the circle. The angelic creatures take up most of the space, I note, due to their size. But it feels comforting to have them looming so large with us—like elder siblings. *Of course, that's exactly what they are.* The peace and stillness in them is profound, like I've never felt in myself, not even with the vigilans. They truly *know* how to be still.

This weightless hovering is not so bad once you get used to it. I begin to settle down, extend my arms, and look farther out, across the sun and into the abundance of stars in the Milky Way—arguably the most beautiful view anywhere in our solar system. I vividly recall the trip you and I took with the angelans to the center of it all. A brighter point of light in the distance catches my eye. I know in an instant, it's Earth. It calls to me—home. *The sun may be home to these angelans and Apollo, but Earth is still the place for me.*

"*Be still!*" I hear Gavrea's voice in my mind like a command. But it's also an affirmation and an invocation of my own deepest silent being. It is the presence of the still, small voice in us all. We are each being drawn even deeper into this stillness.

Whispering aloud for all of us to hear, she continues, "There is no limit to stillness. Your finite mind thinks otherwise, I know, dear human. But stillness is not just a shallow phenomenon, not just a flat emptiness without sensation. It has an infinity of potential in its belly. It is a deep, living well of *open opportunity essence.* Stillness can be lived! It is the root source of all sensation. We shall peel back the layers of it now for you. Deeper and deeper you will feel our way into it."

We are very, very still. No thoughts come. Awareness grows like a raging, blooming flower, full of color and tenderness and fragrance. It spreads through our group like a tide, lapping at the shores of our shared appreciation. It reveals itself over and over again, each layer with more profundity and intimacy and sensitivity. I am looking into this peace with the eyes of angelans, indeed with the eye of Apollo. I know these are his realms of experiencing and exploration.

Omis' voice rises slowly to our ears out of this emptiness that lacks nothing. I understand the need for this voice, yet part of me sees it as an intrusion on the purity of the livingness. My own grating voice would sound a hundred times worse right now. The angelan says, "Invm, we would ask you for your skills to be applied for us all now."

The Sirian looks startled, being pulled back from deep meditation. "What would you have me do, Lords?"

His use of the word 'Lords' surprises me. *I'm beginning to use my mind again. Or is it beginning to use me?* But I know Invm's word is totally appropriate here. It is not uttered out of flattery or religiosity. There is none of that in him. It is a simple reflection of fact. If there's anything I know about his race—they deal in *fact!*

Omis answers, "Your talents have aided us for many decades in our work together. You know the forms of geometry-in-space that we, ourselves, are far removed from. We ask you to read the energy coordinates we will give you. Place them into the geometric grids you know so well. It will be an exercise of enjoyment for you, I'm sure."

Invm tightens his lips into a Sirian smile and nods respectfully. The rest of us radiate our respect to him. He replies, "At your service, as always, Omis. Show me the coordinates please."

With that, a space opens into our midst. It is a visual manifestation revealed directly out of the stillness. It's a *form* of stillness, if that makes any sense. In the space, we see shapes and lines coming out of nothing, wheels and disks overlapping in great complexity. The quantity of detail is enormous. It looks, to my imagination, like a thought-form for a huge mathematical equation—too much information for my poor mind. I look at Invm with great admiration as he dives into comprehending the display.

He asks, "You would have me plot a course between *here* and here—and *here?*" He points to three different places in the array.

Mihelo answers, "That is precisely it. Bring these three worlds together in the geometry and we will take care of the rest."

Invm takes on a form of concentration I've never witnessed in anyone. His eyes squint and almost unite—into one eye. *Where have I seen that before?* He uses his hands, too, to trace trajectories and project his thoughts into space. As he does so, the wheels and lines begin to move inside the vision. It's as though we're seeing embryo galaxies in miniature move across the Cosmos and across time. New, bright lines and circles appear temporarily, apparently as guides to the Sirian's calculations and mechanics. At last he stops and looks up to Omis and the archangels.

"I believe this is what you've asked for," he states simply.

Mihelo says, "So it would seem. Well done. Now we will bring in another essence to provide the vitalization. Hold still, everyone."

Hold still? Aren't we already doing that! I don't even move my eyelids. The stillness radiates up to us, out of its lair in eternity. With it, there is something else—a sense of bright peace. It is like a sunrise out of the Void, the night giving birth to the day. We are all taken over by it. We become it, like we are the day itself, shining mystery into the newness. This is Apollo—*directly!* He is grand and glorious and full of the knowing of all destinies. This is where we're heading on the long, long path of evolution. And yet, it is already accomplished in this moment. There is no separation and cannot ever be, not here and now, as long as this sacred moment lasts. *Forever!*

My mind reaches out at this feeling, tentatively, wishing it could participate or even contribute something. Unfortunately, there is no hope of that. The best my mind can do is to bow down, through a sacrificial act of transparency, and allow the space to reveal its own self. *I wish I could take this moment back with me into my world and life. And I can,* I realize. But it will be in measured proportions, superimposed upon the long, long path of evolution.

Apollo's presence electrifies the group and the geometry that Invm has arranged. We find ourselves in motion now, sweeping into the circles and disks and lines of light, set against the dark, empty backdrop of creation abroad. Whirling and turning, aligning and connecting, we move as if we are gears in a cosmic machine. The intricacy of our shifts and pauses, turns and returns, is far beyond what any of our minds can grasp, even the angels.

Divinity is in us. I feel like we've moved right onto Mount Olympus. Our location has definitely changed—and something else. There is a splitting of our presence. It is not a separation though; it is a new kind of wholeness. We are completely aware in both parts of ourselves. This is *bi-location,* conducted by the gods!

I feel the Earth beneath my feet suddenly. Gravity. It seems so hard and heavy, having it back all at once. *Where am I? Where is everyone else?* There is no one around me—just the Earth and an empty sky. Gavrea's voice echoes from an invisible distance. She is sending us forth on our mission. "You will each have your own, independent experience of this visitation, though you will be together in essence—and in voice at times. Go now, and enter the form of two worlds. You will be guided by us—through your hearts and minds—to know what it is you find."

I turn and look up at two Suns, superimposed upon one another. I see two Earths in the same way. The landscapes of each are present in my senses at one and the same time, like a three-dimensional double exposure. *This is beyond strange!*

Letter Eighty
The Future Now

I'm standing in a meadow. Rather, it's two meadows at once. They look similar in a way—just enough not to drive my mind crazy. But one of the meadows is in the mountains, by a lake. The other is at the seashore, with mountains rising up in the near distance. The two suns are in identical positions overhead, with just a slight shift to enable me to see there are two. *So, how is this going to work,* I wonder.

The answer comes swiftly, softly. *"Enter into each, as you choose. Use your 'other' awareness to find the choice-point."*

I feel my mind stepping into the background, willingly. It doesn't want to go insane. Another kind of mind steps forward—*manas! I remember this.* It chooses the seashore. This image comes forward now with the *manas mind* and I feel like I'm actually here. The other world is a shadow in the background. *Manas* experiments. It chooses the second world now. The image shifts to the mountain meadow by the lake. I am now *there!* My normal 'little' mind reacts. *Awesome!*

The wind stirs and I see ripples through the leaves of nearby trees, At the same moment in a far distant time, almost as a daydream, I see ripples on the ocean waters. It is a very calm sea. My mind enters, and I hear it saying, *This may be difficult to write. Manas* streams an answer, *"Relax, we will find a way. A way will find us."*

"The first step is to distinguish the two times," it says. Immediately, I sense the way to know—the time that is *past* has a slight blue tint to the light. The *future* time has a rosy cast. I look around at the mountain landscape; it is blue. *So, here I am 26,000 years ago. Why am I here?*

Out of nowhere, I hear your voice. I look around, but I see no one. You say, "I'm in the same space as you. Only we each seem to be experiencing it *alone.* I suspect the others are here too, but I haven't made contact yet."

I answer, "Well, this is just like the old days. I recall it was a long time before I ever actually *saw* you."

"Yes. It's different now though. We are each in the same place, just *seemingly* alone. Let's do a little exploring. Look out across the lake; there's a building. It looks like a temple."

"Where? Oh, way over *there*. Yeah, maybe it's a temple. Shall we go and have a look, oh invisible one?" I chuckle, feeling that strange giddiness coming back.

Before we can move, I'm suddenly in the rose scene, by the ocean. But I'm looking in the same direction across the lake. I see an island with a small structure on it. I say, "O, are you with me here?"

"Yes. I shifted at the same moment."

The moment? But are we really in the moment, here in the far future? A little doubt stirs in my *little* mind, and I ask, "Speaking of the moment, O, how is it that we can be in the Now and be 'time traveling' too? I know you've explained this before, but I think I need a refresher."

"You *think?* Of course, the mind wonders at that. I guess we have time for a little explanation, while we walk. I'll say it a little differently this time." She falls silent for a while. "It will be a bit tricky, so please pay attention: The only point of being *in the moment* is to be awake and grounded in *reality*. When we say the future and the past don't really exist, it is only to trick your mind into allowing you to be awake, to realize the presence of being. Once you're living the presence, you don't need the trick anymore. You *are* the moment."

"Well, OK, but what happens to the past and the future then?"

I continue to walk along the shore. You resume, "They enter the moment with you. They actually *do* exist! Bear in mind, however, that existence itself is *not* real; it's part of the illusion. All actions and situations, relationships and creations—all forms—'exist' within your being, the Now! They are there—past, present and future—from the earliest first-incarnation baby crying to the last dissolving incarnate master, leaving the Earth plane forever; they all *exist* at once. Recall what we experienced with the soul recently. For it, all the lives are simultaneous, happening at once, *right now.*

"The soul experiences millions, trillions—in fact, uncountable numbers— of actions of all those incarnations, all at once, in the *timeless* way. Such is *bi-locating!* It's *multi-mega-locating!* That's too much for any incarnate mind to grasp; we have to use the 'other' awareness to appreciate it. So do you. For our finite comprehensions, all those actions are placed into logical, sequential frameworks by the soul, in relation to each other, in relation to the worlds they inhabit. These play out in what we call *time*. The Source is timelessness; it is the non-manifested moment.

"There is nothing wrong with time, as a form, or with traveling through it. It's just not *reality*, that's all. *All* form is illusion. In terms of immersion in time, the so-called *present* is just as much of an illusion: To illustrate, just try to find the so-called present time. It's always *gone* when you look at it—never there, even for a split instant. However, when looking at any timeframe, we are still in the Now. We cannot be anywhere else. You know this. 'Now' is our consciousness looking at and using time. Our presence is always now, even while we play the 'time' game. It's an illusion, yes. *All forms are illusions.*"

I interrupt, "I see what you mean about this being a little tricky to understand. I feel like I'm drowning in information again. What about the problem of not living in the moment? This seems to be a major obstacle to humans. We're always worried about the future, or fretting over something that happened or didn't happen in the past."

"Living as though 'out of the moment' was simply a matter of mistaking the *form* for the reality. Identification with form is again the issue. Focusing exclusively on the future or the past—or on *time* at all—is an escape from *presence*, orchestrated by the ego. Ego cannot breathe the air of presence; ego will do anything to avoid it. However, our transposition project is not about avoidance. We are *honoring* the past and the future—from the perspective of the Now, from presence. It has nothing to do with putting the ego in control.

"There is no argument between time and the Now. There is no argument between formlessness and form, or between reality and illusion. They each have their place in creation. Each of these pairings is just another kind of bi-location, if you will—of Oneness in duality.

"Your current spiritual teachers frequently emphasize 'living in the moment' because it is time for you to wake up and see *through* the form we call time. It is not because time is evil. Time is just a form, like all other forms."

Your presence stops me for a moment. "Here's a little exercise: Give time its due. Look at every 'moment of time' as a *worthy* form, informed by Source. Apply your consciousness directly to it."

"What do you mean by directly?"

"I mean embrace each simple action with focused attention and intent. Be aware of yourself in the action. Do not look outside the moment for satisfaction, either in the past or the future. Each moment, taken directly and with consciousness, is a statement of full Life energy. In this exercise, you honor both the greater moment and the lesser. In it you will find the peace that passes understanding, the timelessness that passes time, and the presence that is eternal."

I catch myself gazing out, absently trying to understand the structure on the island; my attention has wandered. I bring it back and think of your 'little exercise'. I apply myself *directly;* all my senses are alert again, recaptured from my wandering mind. A renewed expansiveness enters. It is just a humble moment; yet it is filled with abundant energy. "All right. I think I get it. But thought is not the *way* to get it. Right?"

"Exactly. Allow your feelings and sensations to *get* it."

I pause and breathe deeply, feeling the inner peace rise up inside. "Let me just put it in my own words, to remember it better. You're saying reality is timeless and formless: That is the Now, the Moment, true being. On the other hand, the illusion—the world of form and action—takes place over spans of time. But we can actually appreciate both at once. And it's important to realize this every second, in each action we take."

"That's it. Where humanity got so confused was in forgetting about reality and identifying with the world of form. You took that world to be the *only* one, and to be *real*. That is the error of your ways. To correct that, all you need do is realize you are living in the moment, always, that you actually *are* the presence and the Now. *That* is awakening; it is how you bring down the Veil between yourself and the soul."

Another thought slips in. "But humans have always been religious and spiritual. We were not totally forgetting reality were we? Haven't we always looked for divinity, sensed it somewhere?"

"Yes indeed. But you still turned it into a *form*. You could not grasp the formless. You projected gods and God out upon the universe, as *separate* from you. You could not see yourselves as the essence of it all. Your egos would not allow it—not, at least, until *now!*"

I reflect in silence for a moment, then say, "So, we are now 26,000 years in the future *and* the same in the past. And it's still right now!"

"You've got it," you reply freshly. "So, what do you say we go out to that island?"

"How? Are we going to walk on water?"

"I don't think so. There's a boat, just over there." You point down the beach. *How did I miss that?*

Letter Eighty-One
Wealth

My bodies, in both worlds, begin to walk down to the beach—one along a mountain lake, the other along the calm ocean shore. In the rosy 'future world' there is a boat. In the past, there is only a narrow footpath leading beside the lake. I climb into the small craft. It's a simple, smooth oval shape, seemingly made of wood, yet formed from one piece. It has no visible means of propulsion—no motor, no oars. Shrugging, I climb into it from a small dock.

I whisper to you, "O, are you in the boat now?"

"Not yet. I'm just looking around. Did you notice the pebbles on the beach? They seem to be made of clear, colored glass—all of them."

I look back and realize what you're saying. "Wow. No, I didn't notice. I guess I'm not *in the moment* as much as I thought. The beach is beautiful, now that I really look at it. It's like a stained glass window on the ground in tiny smooth pieces."

"All right," your voice comes in. "I'm in the boat now."

"So, what's next?" Before the words are out of my mouth, the craft is sliding effortlessly away from the shore, under its own power; we're heading directly toward the island. *Does someone know we're coming?*

The islet is about a kilometer away. As we glide ahead, I study it, hoping not to miss another obvious detail like the pebbles. I see a grove of tall trees and a small knoll behind the building. The structure is a composite of several domes, one of which is nearly a sphere. It has a number of windows of various shapes that harmonize nicely with the design. A large opening is carved into the near end.

The boat settles up next to another dock. I hear a faint clicking sound, as if something has locked us into place. "Shall we go?" I ask.

Your response surprises me. "No. Let's wait to be invited. I have a sense that someone is coming."

Just then I'm put back into my other body, in the blue world. I'm walking along the path to the temple. You affirm that the same has happened to you. With faint impressions of the boat 52,000 years away, I look ahead at this other scene with its old, old building. Columns, not unlike in Egypt, stand tall and noble. Yet the design seems like a combination of styles. The weathering on its carvings speaks of great age; one statue is broken.

"O, who is doing this to us? Why are we jumping back and forth?"

"It must be the archangels. They want it this way for some reason. I guess it's showing us the linkages between the two time periods. There is a phenomenal amount of similarity overall, don't you think?"

I nod, though you can't see me. "Yeah, for sure. Let's walk to those pillars up ahead. It looks like a gate."

There are two carved stone posts on either side of the footpath; at this point the trail starts an ascent to higher ground. There sits the temple. Clearly it has seen better days. What were once gardens surround it on all sides. The place looks abandoned. Vines and weeds grow everywhere, covering sculptures and small structures. Some have fallen down or are leaning precariously. Wild flowers grow in the mix and offer splashes of color. The walls of the main building are also clad in vines. Nevertheless, the sight has beauty. Beneath the vines I see colored glass like jewels in the walls; they are windows. I stop at the pillars and stare, entranced.

"Shall we wait here to be invited in?"

"Yes. Let's sit down on that bench by the gate. I have a feeling about this too." You pause and reflect before continuing. "We're supposed to prepare ourselves in some way."

"What do you mean? How can we *prepare* ourselves when we don't know what to prepare *for?*"

"We can be humble and wait in this outside area. I would advise being silent and still. Let's see what comes to us. Remember, the unknown."

I accept the silence and sit with the invisible you. With no vision of you and no conversation, I feel completely alone in this place. It seems very far away from my world—26,000 years away. I breathe and relax, gazing out at the land. The mountains rise up in splendor over foothills. The snow on the high peaks glistens in brilliant sunlight. Misty valleys descend below the plateau that cradles the lake. I sigh and begin to meditate. A breeze picks up dust and sends it into small whorls across the track. The whorls come in our direction briefly, and then fall back to the ground, losing their transient form.

I wonder at the humble, dusty trail that leads up to such a grand temple; it's a juxtaposition of opposites. The bench is just planks of old wood—hardly what I would expect here. My ruminations lead off into thoughts about disparity of incomes in my world for some reason. The image of a recent memory comes to mind. It was in the airport in Paris.

"I finally can't resist breaking the silence, and whisper, "O, while we're waiting here, I have a question. It's bothered me for some time. How do you handle wealth in your world? I was at the airport recently, in the duty-free shop; there were bottles of cognac for sale for 3,000 € each. I was shocked. Who buys such things at airports? How differently they must look at money from the way most people do. My world has so many, many poor people and such a small minority of very, very rich people. It doesn't seem fair or balanced to me. Have you worked out better systems, in your time? How do deal with wealth and money?"

You reply, also whispering reverently, "Indeed we have. Many in your day have dreamed of more balanced sharing of resources. We have achieved it. But it is not something we set out to do, surprisingly; it is, frankly, an *after effect* of who we are. We wanted to redistribute wealth among the population at large. Our intentions have been to be free from our own inner inequities. That would be freedom from ego. It was the biggest imbalance in your world, as you know—the biggest hoarder of wealth. As long as ego reigns, there will be a comparatively small number of individuals who work and struggle to control those beneath them; they will then claim the largest share of the resources. This is, of course, one of the prizes ego seeks—control, separation and in-crease of itself.

"What our species found out, as we opened to our real consciousness, was that the most important, most vital richness anyone could possess in this world was keenness of appreciation. In my species, the wealthiest one is the one who *appreciates* the most! What happens to proprietary wealth in this situation is that it becomes much less relevant to our identities. It becomes a *footnote* to appreci-ation, not the *headline* of a vast empire of acquisition.

"In your world, wealth was tied to your sense of identity. 'I am my wealth,' was your common understanding. That is one definition of ego, of course: *iden-tification with form.* If you believe you are solely a form, you will *act* like a form, and seek to enhance yourself by amassing *other* forms. Those who are identified with money acquire monetary riches; it is the definition of their existence. They seek to enhance and fulfill themselves by relentlessly gaining assets, by having more of what they see themselves to be.

"Of course, if the definition of *who you are* is 'one who acquires more', you will go on seeking more possessions endlessly—or at least until you change the definition. You will always desire more forms to have under your control, within your greater form. You will unconsciously be seeking to bring them into your being. But you never reach the limit—because there *is* no limit under this definition of self. 'More' *is* the definition.

I respond, "So, 'wanting more' condemns us to *never having enough.*"

"Well said. It is a self-perpetuating curse, a kind of poverty of power. The more one has, the less one will be *complete.* Each new acquisition is a proof of ultimate *lack*. It means that more things are still *missing*. Lacking and acquiring more are opposite sides of the same coin. The ego always believes something is missing. In building elaborate frameworks around what it thinks is lacking, it actually contributes to its own lack.

"In the same vein, if time happens to be your focus, then there can never be *enough* time. You will try to get more of it any way you can, as in taking it from others. If it is property or possessions, or money or sex—whatever—there can never be enough, by ego's standards. Ego would have to go out of business if it allowed 'what is missing' to be filled in. It won't allow that, so it perpetuates the feeling of lack. But our species did the unthinkable. We found the very thing ego was missing most. And then we filled in that ultimate lack."

You let the statement hang in silence. I wait, wanting to ask the obvious— what was that *ultimate lack?* But I hesitate, needing to examine my own motives. *Am I asking as a form of acquisition, to fill a lack?* I realize, my ego *does* want me to ask. I observe, and let its urge pass. In that moment I see how slow and constricted ego really is. My heart awareness, by contrast, is fast and free. At last I inquire, "What did you find to fill the lack?"

"I thought you'd never ask," you laugh. "It's so simple. It solved any and all problems we had, regarding disparity in wealth and possessions. It put ego out of business. It was simple. The ultimate missing element was the *moment* itself, and our *presence* in the moment. Once we found that, we filled in what had been the missing for millennia. It was the *whole* puzzle!"

"Simple presence did that?" I query.

"Simple and deep, authentic presence. This is who we really are, who *you* are. This came roaring out of the depths of our genetic codes, our psychic molecules. We, and you, evolved into truly appreciative beings. We started with ourselves, each one. Every individual turned on to the understanding that he or she is *free* within the moment, *equal* to the moment, *at one* with the moment: *Liberty. Equality. Fraternity.*"

"Sounds good to me," I reply, shifting on the hard bench. "But what about a few more details from your world, if you don't mind. Are there still rich and poor people Do some people have enormous wealth? Is there still a middle class?"

"We all have enormous wealth, my friend. And we are each poor. But there is no middle class."

I wrinkle my eyebrows. "What can that mean, 'you are each wealthy *and* poor'?"

"As you were told earlier, we each give meaning to our lives. We create what it *means* to be wealthy. We create what it means to be poor."

"But why would anyone intentionally create poverty in their lives?"

"Ask Saint Francis; ask the wandering sadhus and sadhvis of Asia; ask anyone who has placed their life and faith totally in the hands of presence. History is full of renunciates who intentionally took vows of poverty. There is an exquisite freedom that comes with casting your fate upon the universe. It is the ultimate acceptance that the universe is *conscious* and is indeed *beneficent*. This we practice in our lives. Along with it, you will be surprised to know, we also practice great personal wealth."

I shake my head, not understanding how these things can be compatible. "But how does this work out in your actual living? How can you be both wealthy and poor? Those are contradictory opposites!"

"Opposites *unite* in paradox. In paradox lies Source. Source is the ultimate *wealth*. It is *everything*—and everything's creator. The Void is ultimate poverty; it is the absence of everything—the foundation of *naught*. We actually *do* practice this level of awareness in our lives. I know it's hard for you believe that we have such a degree of collective and individual sincerity in our world, but we do. Each nation has its own unique expressions for this, of course, and its own forms of appreciation. But this lies at the absolute root of our awakening.

"We, as a species, view formlessness as our true identity, and we see *form* as the way to express that identity into the world. The physical expressions come naturally into the course of our lives. We universally experience periods of great wealth, interwoven or alternating with periods of zero possession. And our lives are made up within the flow between these poles.

I interrupt, "But you said there is no middle class."

"Yes. By that I mean there is no established form or structure in our societies that stays in the middle. The 'middle' is not a class for us; it is merely a transition between the polarities of extreme wealth and poverty."

This is disturbing to me. I wrestle with what you're saying. "I really thought you would tell me that everyone had reached a mellow level of reasonable wealth. From what I've seen, you all appear very comfortable, with plenty of creature comforts. I'm having a hard time processing what you're saying about poverty."

"By poverty, I in no way mean 'misery', if that is what's bothering you. You have seen me with a house—the one with no roof. That house will be gone soon. Once our project is completed for this cycle, I will move away and wander for some time around the world. I will give up my properties, positions and possessions and be *free*. It is the only way we can practice *equality* of expression in our world. It is the way we find and give meaning to *fraternity* with our fellow women and men."

"Does someone *make* you do this? Are there governments that force you into poverty in order to keep you enlightened?"

You chuckle. "Of course not. We each *must* do this, yes, but not because someone makes us do it. We do it because it is our nature. We want to know and experience all sides of our nature. To be without possessions is a humbling and exalting experience simultaneously. We adore humbleness in ourselves; likewise, we love our exaltations. We flow. This is the way to truly be in touch with nature, creativity and vitality."

"Then what happens?" I ask.

"I continue. In the cycles of my life, I will return eventually to wealth once again; I will have a home and garden again, with all its many aids and comforts. In our world the saying 'easy come, easy go' is taken as a way of life. It is our faith in *practice*. It works for us. But then, our world is a safe place for such a practice. It has no rampant, irrational fears; there is no one looking to take advantage of our vulnerability as in your world.

"Each individual has her or his own way of doing it, of course. Some spend decades at one extreme of the other. Some pass through the cycles in a matter of weeks. Others have developed ways to experience both at once, in a continuum. That requires some real imagination and wisdom. What we all gain from this practice is a complete understanding of one another and of ourselves. We know firsthand how each perspective feels and what it offers to the other. This way, we embrace the totality and abundance of our individual lives and in the life of the whole. It is the best medicine for openness and sharing that a society could ever have."

Letter Eighty-Two
Linear Fashion

Inside the pause of our conversation, I suddenly hear a deep bell tone—one lonely toll. It comes from the tower above us, in the temple. I rise and face through the gateway. In this action, I find myself abruptly back in the future, seated in the boat, in the rose-tinted light. A figure is emerging from the dome structure. It's a woman, small in stature, perhaps only a meter tall. She's wearing a bright green body suit, with several, long, golden scarves cascading from her shoulders. She strides across the distance and directly up to me; then she extends a hand.

"Let me help you out of the boat, kind friend. Thank you for coming all this way. This is a great day for us."

I take her hand, but turn aside and ask you, "Is this happening for you too?"

"Precisely the same thing," you acknowledge.

Our host looks quizzically at me and asks, "Are you speaking to someone else?"

I waver. "Well, yes. I'm not alone. But apparently you see just one of us at a time."

The small woman smiles and says, "Yes. I see only you, but I sense there are others. Very strange, don't you think?"

I laugh. "Very strange indeed. Say, how is it that you speak my language?"

She replies, "Oh, I don't. But, you know, we have technology for that. And I'm sure those who sent you do as well. Would you please follow me into the concrome."

"The *what?* That word didn't translate."

She looks back over her shoulder as we walk toward the building. "That's probably because you don't have them in your timeframe. I will explain once we're inside."

I hear your voice next to my ear. "I have an intuition that she means 'inside' quite literally."

We step up to the opening. It has no door, or at least no covering. She twists her hand in the air and motions me to enter. She proclaims, "Welcome to the concrome."

As I step inside, the scene switches again. I find myself standing between the pillars in the blue world. A figure has emerged from the temple and is walking down the path toward me. He's wearing long flowing white robes, looking rather Arabic; and he wears a headscarf. He is my height, with dark, olive skin and—yes—long blond hair. His appearance startles me. This, coupled with the repeated switching of time zones, is unsettling.

The man extends both his hands and touches my elbows. "Welcome, kind friend, to my world. I have been awaiting your arrival for several years. Please feel at home here, and follow me into the Temple of Urmat. It is a haven for the long-distance traveler. It is well that you understand." *Is he using a translation device too?*

I walk warily, not sure when the next time switch might occur. Then I hear your voice, "I've just discovered the way to see these shifts coming: It has to do with a build-up in the field of presence that keeps us here. Each time we reach a threshold or a change point, the flow of energy gets supercharged."

This time, as the man from the past shows me the door to the temple, I sense an intensification of energy, like an electrical surge. When I step through the door, the pent-up energy releases, and the rose future comes into focus. I stop and say to you, "OK. I've got that part. I can sense when it's about to happen. Is there anything we can do to control it or stop it from happening?"

Now I hear Omis' voice overriding yours. Time seems to stop. He says, "Yes, there is. We assumed you would understand without explanation. Our mistake. There is no need to shift back and forth like you've been doing. It would be far more productive to have your experiences either in a linear fashion or in a fully balanced bi-location.

"When you feel the energy building up, you need only to ask it to disperse. The field may be treated as a conscious participant. It will respond to any request you make. It can also assist you in balancing the two worlds.

"You may prefer the linear approach, in which one experience is complete before you enter the second. However, there are advantages to the simultaneous *balanced* method, if you can manage it. The direct experience of bi-location will give you more direct insight. For one, you will see into the intimate linkages between past and future through your presence. If you choose this approach, I would suggest that you start by focusing on the energy fluctuations O has identified. I leave the choice of approaches up to each of you, however."

I speak, "All right, Omis. I know which one I want. I'd like to take them in sequence, one after the other—linear style. And I'd like to do the *past* first, just because it's more logical to me. My brain is scrambled enough as it is. How about you, O? Which will you choose?"

You reply, "I will take the simultaneous method. I feel I can handle it now. And I want to have that awareness of both at once. I feel it is important to know the bridging function we play."

Omis comments, "Bear in mind, since you two are choosing different ways to process this, your communication will be somewhat limited. You will still be able to make contact with each other from time to time, but not constantly."

"All right. I'll put up with that. But before you go, Omis, I have one more question. What happened to B and Invm?"

"They have chosen to refrain from contacting you for the time being, for private reasons. It seems they're discovering deeper soul connections and would desire a space to explore that. We are very pleased by this development actually."

With that, Omis is gone and I'm fully back in the blue world, immediately stepping into the temple. The white-robed man hasn't heard my conversation with Omis. He ushers me down a long hallway of polished granite. A lighted room is at the far end. We walk to the threshold and I look across. The 'presence' energy field intensifies and I know this is an opportunity to make the switch again—if I wanted to. *Let's stay here,* I announce inwardly. At this, the energy releases.

In the room, several torches are hanging from sconces along the walls. The walls are stone, lined with carvings, tapestries and bookcases. Rich carpets are on the floor. It's a very comfortable space. In a way, it reminds me of the office where I met GS. The torches give a warm, welcoming light. One large stained glass window is centered on the far wall. In the middle of the room, sits a thick wooden table with a few open books and scrolls on it. Under the books, I notice a large manuscript and a stylus lying nearby. It seems that this man has been writing. Perhaps my arrival has interrupted him.

I look at my host and start to introduce myself. He responds somewhat stiffly, "All I need to know is that you are the one prophesied, the one from the next cycle in the future. You have come at the appointed time, just as foretold. My name is Krotos of the Ufrad. I am the only remaining scribe. I was appointed to document the journey our civilization has now completed—the ending of an era. You are here to bear witness to my work. Welcome, brother."

"Thank you. I don't want to disappoint you, but I'm really not sure *why* I'm here. You seem to have a better idea of that than I do."

His face reveals confusion. *I'm sure he'd prefer to believe I knew what I was doing.* With a sudden influx of inspiration—probably from you—I say, "But never mind that. I am indeed a person from the future. Please tell me your story."

Krotos relaxes his expression, and turns to his manuscripts. He pushes the books and scrolls aside and picks up several loose strips of paper, shuffling them together. He points me to a chair beside the table. Then he pauses solemnly and stares at the papers, as if feeling the story they might be ready to tell. I sit down, never taking my gaze from him. His eyes are sad. I realize how weary he looks. Finally he says, "I am the last, you know—the last of my kind. I have carried these books and this manuscript here to the Temple of Urmat to archive them. I'm just coming to the end of my work."

I look sympathetically at Krotos. "I'm drafting a manuscript myself, and I'm about to come to the end of it too. We obviously have something in common. I can empathize with what you're feeling."

He looks firmly at me for a long moment and says, "I truly hope that that is *not* the case. If you can *empathize* with me, it means my efforts have been in vain. I have seen much that I hope you never have to see. I have traveled a path that no one would choose. It has led past the utter destruction of the world I knew." He sighs, pushing back the hair from is wizened face. "But let us get to our purpose. I must tell you the story, and complete this mission once and for all."

My host takes the manuscript away from the table and sits down. I shift my own chair to face him. Now the energy field intensifies again. I see, in my bi-located self, that a similar conversation is about to begin 52,000 years from now, with the small woman in green. It is a temptation to switch over, but I resolve to follow my original plan. I ask the field to disperse; it does. I remain in the blue world.

Letter Eighty-Three
So It Might Seem

Krotos, unaware of my inner processing, begins his recitation, "Our great civilization, as I have explained, has come to a catastrophic termination. All our large cities are now buried—swallowed up by Earth and ocean. Mountain ranges have fallen and seas have risen. I alone, of the scribes, have survived to tell the story. Millions of people have perished in this upheaval. Sadly, we have no one to blame but ourselves. We failed to heed, or even *hear* the warnings. There were plenty of signs, such as the unprecedented extinction of species around the world and the change in climate everywhere. We witnessed enormous political upheavals and divisiveness. Wars! We ignored and denied the ancient prophecies, until the last hour, when it was too late.

He takes a deep breath. "Our culture rose to great heights. It spanned fifteen thousand years, in many incarnations. Unfortunately, one of those 'heights' was a perverse insensitivity, especially concerning the past and the future. And most importantly, we lost our sense of *presence*. We cut ourselves off from our own nature and soul. Many of my compatriots realized, at the end, what was happening. By then, nothing could be done to escape our fate. We paid a great price for our hubris and our defiance of the spiritual dimension. We lost everything our ancestors had worked and struggled for over thousands of years."

Already I can't resist interrupting. "But you yourself are a product of that civilization. There must be others..."

"Oh yes, there are a few left," he admits.

"That means your society must have had some redeeming qualities."

"It's true, there were many qualities of our civilization worth preserving. Perhaps some of it will be handed down. But those of us who remain are few, and poor in spirit now. We, who understood the significance of the times and the great cycle, were always a small minority. We were derided as lunatics, as deluded by our beliefs in the records of the past. We were never a critical mass in my world. The time was not right. That, apparently, was not our destiny. Perhaps your time will be different. I hope so. I wish you better fortune." He says this without conviction.

I look at the aging monkish figure more closely. His face is etched with a lifetime of harsh strokes. This lifetime is weighing him down, disempowering him deeply. I speak. "My time! Yes. We're certainly in the thick of it right now—even as I write. Many people believe it's too late to avoid destruction or reverse the trends toward global ruin."

He looks alarmed. "That is not good news. We had hoped that humanity would find some maturity in 26,000 years!"

I wonder how much to tell him. I shrug and say, "I think we may have changed a bit since your time. Many of us feel we are on the path toward a new and evolved species. But there is still the majority who refuse to see the immanent collapse. They are deniers.

"Other strong negative forces exist as well. One is composed of those who *believe* they mean well, while their cynicism eats away at their awareness. They are *identified* with their negative perspectives and don't even know it." I continue my lecture, somehow inspired. "There are others who seem hell-bent on retreating into some semblance of better times in the past. They see the world changing, but their answer to it is to retreat and reject evolution. Very few actually realize the greater cycles our civilizations follow.

"And yet, at the same time, there is a completely different dynamic at play. I've been fortunate to be taken into the future—many futures. The picture, from there, looks much more encouraging." *I still have my doubts,* I sigh to myself. "There are apparently alternative futures—some are evolved and awakened; others not. Now I'm in the past, and you're telling me civilization actually *did* fail. I've read about such failure, but it was so long ago, it seemed so hypothetical and lost to history. You're telling me it really *did* happen to you?"

Krotos shakes his head and bends it down. "Your times do not sound hopeful either. It seems humanity is cursed to repeat its failures. Certainly the calamities keep repeating through history. Why hasn't your society heeded the warnings we left for you, or at least the signs in nature?"

I squint and ask, "Warnings?"

"Yes. We left them in obvious places around the planet—on walls of temples and pyramids, on stone monuments, buried in catacombs and caves. We also introduced them into stories that could be orally transmitted to you down through the ages. Have you not found these messages?"

"It's not that we haven't found some of them," I reply. "The basic problem, I think, is with their age; they're too old to be believed by most people. 26,000 years is a long time! Our 'modern' societies don't respect the wisdom of the ancients. We believe we're much more advanced than anyone before us. In this regard, humans are destined, I'm afraid, to disregard the lessons of the past. We seem to have to repeat former mistakes in order to learn. And at the same time, we keep *not* learning." I find myself beginning to feel rather depressed, explaining these things to Krotos.

He grimaces. "What you say does not comfort me. The one hope we still have is that, perhaps, during the next great cycle—long after we are gone—civilization would return and be more successful. Our hope has been that you would learn by our errors. It is for that reason we have left our warnings and guidance for you. It is for that reason I am here at all. This is our *last* hope for the future. But it is not *our* future; it is yours."

I ponder his words. "You know, as I just said, the problem seems to lie in the distances of *time* itself. People can forget a lot in 26,000 years. They can develop along far different lines than one might imagine."

Krotos asks, "But your people know at least, don't they, that Earth cycles repeat?"

"I'm afraid not even that. Well, yes, we know about some cycles—yearly and monthly ones, the seasons and so forth. Our scientists tell us about cyclic ice ages and comets revisiting Earth. But we haven't yet, as a whole world race, understood the larger cycles at play—stellar and galactic ones. We tend to think the only important events are the little ones that happen during the time span one person's life."

He responds, perhaps trying to give me encouragement, "But these galactic cycles *do* happen on Earth. That's exactly the problem we faced and failed to address in my time. You may still have time."

I can see this is just going in circles. *Cycles, I guess.* I decide to interrupt our negative spiral. "Truly, it is *not* too late for my world. Not yet. So, please tell me now: What are the most crucial lessons I can take back? Can you boil it down to just the essence?"

He doesn't hesitate, but speaks directly, "It is just what we've been talking about. First, be aware that the cycles do come—the same ones that have repeated every 26,000 years, and lesser ones every 5,000 years, throughout Earth history. There are other *longer* cycles too. All of these must be appreciated. The society, as a whole, needs to appreciate its place within these cycles.

"The awareness of the grand successions is key because their impacts can be *predicted*. If you study it, nature will reveal itself; it will show you how to prepare. Second, I would advise you to put your own houses in order, both as a society and as individuals. Be centered in your own true essence and destiny. Wake up! Third, work *with* the events that come attendant to the cycle; do not fight against them."

I realize what he has just told me is at the heart of your 'three suggestions'. His last point grabs my attention. "Please explain more about that one. What do you mean 'work with the events'?"

"Surely, you know what I mean—you're from thousands of years in the future! It is a matter of listening to the messages of nature. As the Earth heats up, as it does every 5,000 years—and even more, every 26,000—society needs to understand and take actions to lessen the suffering that will descend upon its people. As solar winds increase and activate the electromagnetic poles of the planet, society needs to monitor and balance its systems, people need to monitor and balance the energies within their own bodies in the same way. As the oceans begin to rise and the Earth begins to move, you need to establish sites of stability and mobility. As other species go extinct, read in it the message to your own species.

"But alas, I know these are costly measures to act upon preemptively, especially if you no longer honor the prophecies, and if you think they are mere fairy tales. This, as you can see, is the path *we* chose. The costs are infinitely greater in the end, if you take no notice of world changes. In our case, the price was the life of our whole civilization. Right up to the end, we kept pushing away appreciation of our state; we kept aggravating the natural calamities instead of mitigating them. It was as though we suffered a disease of blindness to the evidence before our eyes.

"We too had ancient teachings and warnings, handed down through the millennia—from the end of the last great cycle. A few of us knew how to read them, but we too found it difficult to believe their accuracy. Then hubris and defensiveness arose and took control. It is sad to hear the same thing happening in your time. Is there no advancement of awareness? What have your leaders and teachers been doing over all those centuries? Isn't twenty-six millennia enough time to learn a simple lesson?"

I answer, "Well, I don't know your society, but I would hazard a guess that there *is* advancement. There is now an opening to wisdom in both our worlds. Otherwise, we would not even be speaking to each other in this place. A certain proportion of the people—in each of our times—is open to this wisdom. The question is, 'Will that proportion be large enough to sway the whole?' Unfortunately, the ruling systems become stagnant and seem only to close down what needs opening up.

I watch Krotos' reaction for a moment before continuing. "The teachers from *my* future tell me that two things happened to my civilization: They say that our whole species had to *die*—entirely. In the end, we failed to make the changes needed for our *fitness* to survive. But at the same time, we *did* survive—in a *new* species! The changes happened in spite of our ego, in spite of our mental stagnation. They happened within our hearts and our bodies—at the most fundamental levels."

I stop here and reflect. A sudden flow of intuition comes in from you, and from our soul. I realize there is a need to encourage Krotos somehow. I start, "It seems that we have been put together to compare notes, to perhaps learn from each other. And perhaps something else too."

He looks me in the eyes for the first time. "I would say that that is so. I knew of your arrival. It was foretold in a very important prophecy."

"So, are you saying you're the *last* survivor on Earth?

Krotos smiles grimly. "No, but there are not *many* left. My community is about 200 people. We know of only three other small communities within a month's walk from our village. It is very sad. And yet we *are* 'survivors'. Each of us has struggled much to come here. We escaped the lowlands, the endless fires, explosions and eruptions, the ravaging seas and devouring Earth, the starvation, disease and chaos."

"Are you bitter?"

"No, actually. Not me. But some are—and with good reason, I would say. The times have been extremely hard—savage and deadly. However, there has been beauty and joy in places, at times, too. Our community finds, for instance, much solace within itself. We have rituals inducing us to retreat within the essence of our collective selves."

I look deeply into his eyes, offering something from my own inner essence to him. "Tell me more."

"We practice the 'going within', inside the heart—into oneself and into the group heart. The community has a soul—even if the individual does not. We can enter into it; it is our refuge. This practice has replaced all religions. We survivors have seen that the old religions did not help. They stood against our evolution. They stood against our *survival*. Now we have turned away. Yet we still have our spirit—in the community. It is more alive than we are.

"I am here at the Temple of Urmat, not as a follower of this faith. I'm just *using* the space. The followers of Urmat are all long gone. But this place is inspiring. It feels sacred. Just look out at that view."

I turn and look though the tall, narrow window. I can see through clear sections of glass, out at the open space. Beyond is a wide valley, falling away below, under sweeping mountainsides. The sun is low in the sky now, casting rosy orange light and shadows across the rugged terrain. It is indeed beautiful.

"Well, Krotos, yours is a difficult story to hear. I'm very sorry for your civilization. It seems such a waste."

"The Great Fall is now seventeen years behind us. It's not that long. So, we all still have vivid memories."

"Tell me, what do you see in the future for your community?"

"We do *not* see a future. We think only of retreat. The only future we have known, after the Great Fall, was this one—your arrival and our meeting. And now that has been fulfilled. I suppose we will fade away. Most of us are old. The children are few, and we all lack initiative."

"But don't you want to start over, to rebuild a new civilization? You can't just lie down and die."

He looks wistfully at me. "Ah, but we can. You don't know how it has been, how badly we have been beaten down. We have lost the drive to rebuild. All our energy now must be directed at bare survival."

I query, "This seems very strange to me. You still have the survival instinct, but you choose not to use it *creatively*. Are you going to use it only to defend yourselves and retreat more deeply? Is that what you're saying?"

He stops and ponders for several moments before replying. The silence is deadening. "Yes. That is correct. Why should there be another way? It seems natural to us—we are finished! We've been destroyed physically, psychologically and spiritually, alas. We are beyond repair."

"I can't believe that. There must still be a spark in you for starting over. Surely, your 'going within' ceremonies tell you of compassion and creativity. Besides, the world, after you, did come back to life *eventually*. It rebuilt its civilizations. I am here as a result of it, after 26,000 years."

"Yes, I understand. And yet it took you all that long time to come back and find us. Our sacred texts foretold you would do this. And you have. But you have also told me that *your* civilization is failing too. I can't see any point to it after all. We have even less purpose now."

I nod and smile at him. "So it might seem. It would also seem that your sacred prophecy must have had something else in mind—something other than just you and I sitting down for a sad little chat. There *must* be a bigger purpose; I have to believe that. Wouldn't that make sense?"

He pauses again, taking in my idea. His eyes seem to brighten just a bit. Stuttering, he slowly repeats my words, "S-so it might seem."

Letter Eighty-Four
Intrinsic

The field is suddenly so intense I can't hold my place anymore. I must let go of my focus on Krotos. He fades into the distant background as I watch. The 'presence field' itself is giving me encouragement to move on—and, perhaps, return again to this man later. In a flash, I am with the small green-suited woman again. We have just entered the concrome together, 52,000 years later. Rose tint. I smile. *I hope this side is a bit more cheerful than the last!*

She introduces herself as 'Treema'. "I am guardian of the Destiny Well."

"Is that what a *concrome* is?" I ask, trying to recall what we had talked about before.

"This is where the Well is located, yes. But the concrome is more than that. My language technology is telling me that the name 'concrome' comes from words you would be familiar with in your own time; it means 'with color'. Does that make sense to you?"

"Hmm. Yes. But what's so colorful about it."

She continues, "Come in and see. The concrome is a *centering vortex*. My people come here to go within—through the layers of color inside. I suggest we follow this course right now. It will assist our communication—that is, if *communion* is desired between us."

I hesitate, not wanting to jump into anything so fast. "I've just arrived. Can you tell me a little more about yourself and about this place first?"

"But 'entering communion' is the *real* arrival. It is much more authentic than words would be."

"Well, just tell me one thing first. Is *your* civilization dying?"

She laughs in a jolly burst. "What? No, not at all. Where did you get such an idea?"

I sigh. "Well, I've just visited a time 52,000 years ago. The world there was falling apart. They lost everything. I was starting to wonder if that happens at the end of every great cycle."

"Ah, I see. Well, every cycle is both the same and different, from what I understand. But I really can't tell you much without the communion. *Ahem.*" She points into the interior of her dome.

"All right then. What do you want me to do?"

She takes my hand, like a child would, and pulls me along behind her. We move into a dimly lit room, though it is no ordinary room. It's more a coexistence of open and closed spaces. The overall feeling is wide openness. However, within the dome there are also many partially visible partitions. I *detect* boundaries within the space that are like large bubbles, intersecting with one another.

I follow the small woman into one of the bubbles. She points into a dim, shapeless interior. "Please. Take that station. I'll take the other."

I walk toward a hollow opening. As I touch it, I'm immediately turned around and pulled into the space, reclining as if in a chair. But basically, I'm just floating in the air. I look around and try to get my bearings. The ceiling is black. Everything is dark—yet the familiar rose tint prevails. There are many other 'stations' inside the dome; they cascade off on multiple levels, above and below us. As I look at them, they seem to stare back at me. They recognize that I'm looking, and return a slight pulsation.

Treema has reclined beside me and looks over with a welcoming smile. "I guess you've never done this before. Just relax and wait for the colors."

At first there is nothing—no sensations or vibrations, no *colors*. Nothing. It is like entering the Void in a way, though I'm not falling. Gradually, I sense a kind of halo around me. And yes, it has color—a moving, pastel rainbow effect. The halo makes a pale circle wrapped horizontally around the bubble. Now it turns slowly up until it is vertical and starts to glow. I feel radiation penetrate my awareness.

Gently the halo separates into two, then three and more halos, each a different color. It stops dividing at seven. They arrange themselves around me at different levels, and there is a striking resonance with each of my chakras. The rings are linking to my whole chakra system—the green halo for the heart, blue for the throat, etcetera. Now the rings send down a beam, making a *visible* connection to the chakras.

I look over at Treema. The same thing is happening around her. I can see spheres of light inside and through her body, connecting to the halos. Chakras and halos are all linking up. Our two sets of halos next expand out until they merge with each other. At last there is only one set of seven halos around us both. The colored beams of light stretch down to each of our bodies independently, still interconnected. I sense Treema's halos resonating with mine. There is a kind of scan in process—up and down our bodies.

Finally, all the chakras have been scanned and registered. Abruptly, two out of the seven rings glow more brightly—the heart chakra and the crown. *These are our strongest linkages,* I sense. They are the chakras we will use for our 'communion'. At this same instant, in the background, I can feel a connection with Krotos open up—far back in time. I know that he and I have used the root chakra and the solar plexus for *our* communion. The feeling of this tells the whole story. It makes total sense to me. *That's how we did relate!*

Treema suddenly jumps up out of her 'chair' and smiles down at me. "That's it. We're done. Are you ready?"

I recline here for another minute. The feeling is so relaxing and peaceful, yet energized. It's like I just had a chakra massage, *inside* my body. At last I get to my feet and look down at my hostess, a good two feet shorter than I. She smiles endearingly. I realize what the 'communion' means now; it feels like she has spontaneously become closer than family!

"Wow. I'm impressed, Treema. How did this happen?"

She motions me to follow her, but remains silent. The silence wraps around me like a cocoon. Then comes my answer. *I know this.* It works by locating the most fitting chakra and sub-chakra connections between two or more individuals and setting them in motion. The motion is synchronized spinning. But only the positive emotions have been stimulated.

Treema senses my elation and gives me a caution. "This feeling of euphoria is common at first. It wears off after a bit."

"I must admit I feel quite 'high'."

"That's not surprising. But it's not an *artificial* high. Whatever you feel right now is purely authentic between your own being and mine. The purpose of this alignment is to promote the most efficient and productive intercourse between people. Since it uses our own true essence and authentic nature, there is nothing *false* about it. It cannot mislead us."

I try to get a little more serious. "You know, Treema, when I was in the … Say, what do you call that thing we were in?"

"That's the *concrome*. Not the entire concrome, mind you; that was just the entry port for it. The 'together-colors' instrumentation can assist us with many exercises. For instance, if you wish to solve a complex mathematical or engineering problem, you could set that intention, and then use it to link with your colleagues—probably between the single-eye and throat chakras. Or you might use it by yourself to align particular energy centers within your own body."

"Thanks. That clarifies things. When I was inside the concrome, I saw my energy pattern with another person—Krotos, the man I met 52,000 years ago. How did that happen?"

"Since it was a very recent contact, you were drawing it out of the cellular surfaces. Did you have a particular problem with the man?"

I wonder for a moment. "No, not really. I just don't think we had the best connection. I would like to have had a concrome there when we talked. I saw, for instance, that he and I were relating through the root and solar plexus chakras. That doesn't seem like the best connection. Our conversation was pretty gloomy."

"It's not surprising. Didn't you say his civilization had just collapsed? That could make a person rather grumpy. But you were both intuitively aligning your energy centers the best you could. For that situation, you came up with those two centers. It sounds natural to me. Of course, you can perform these alignments without our machine, if you know how. And everyone knows this in rudimentary ways. We all use the chakras to make connections in our environments all the time. The concrome is just a way of doing it quickly and accurately."

"Thanks," I mumble. "That just gave me an idea for later."

She grabs my elbow and pulls me forward again. "Come now. Let's go to a meeting room."

We walk out onto a spiral ramp, lit softly from below. It heads up to another level in the dome. When we arrive, there is a wide-open panorama before us. The top of the dome has peeled open like the petals of a flower. The view is breathtaking; the calm sea reaches back to shore. The mountains behind are sparkling in the sunlight. I see no other signs of habitation.

Around us, on the platform, is a small garden with trees and a fountain. Plants and benches are arranged through the space, with an occasional small table. This, apparently, is the 'meeting room'. It has the same invisible boundaries as the space inside. I stand for several minutes, just absorbing what I see. *There is nothing artificial. Even this structure fits perfectly here.* The beauty comes out of its authenticity. As I contemplate this intrinsic quality, I go deeper and find that it is indeed inside *me. I am intrinsic! And so the beauty is* in *me—in the eye of the beholder.*

Treema says, "I hear your thoughts, dear friend from a former time. They are beautiful. Please come and sit beside me." She motions toward one of the benches—a couch really. We sit together, shoulders touching very naturally, as though we have known each other for a lifetime. The seat is comfortable, molding itself to our forms. I am aware of our chakras connected—the crown and the heart. Violet and green light swirls around us.

I feel Treema's presence through the connection of energy and luminance. The colors add definition and focus. Her thoughts are right next to mine, closer than our shoulders. I feel her appreciation. She looks at me with the most compassionate eyes, but says nothing. No words come to my mind; it feels abnormally blank. Precious emotions are stirring through my whole body. *How is this happening?*

Treema tells me—without words or thoughts—that it is only the continuing effect of the concrome alignment. *"Allow it to be as it is,"* she says in a purely emotional language, in my heart. *"Be intrinsic."* A barrier that I didn't know I had has dissolved. She begins our communion.

Impressions begin flowing quickly between us; it is a *quickening.* I suddenly know many things 'without having to learn them'. I think of Phileina's comment back in Paris. I know that Treema is very appreciative of my presence because I am representing my epoch to her. Her generation has profited much from the guidance we left behind in our time. It was apparently maintained intact in archives for 260 centuries. Many humans, as they became vigilans, left records concerning the Great Storm. There were explicit instructions and warnings about how to move through the transition smoothly—more smoothly than *we* had done.

Early in Treema's time, a kind of council was formed—a congress—to prepare for the influx of galactic energy from Hunab Ku and elsewhere in our twin solar systems, Earth and Sirius. Portals were intentionally created all over the world and people—vigilans—were taught to use them to great benefit. Collectively and individually, the peoples of Earth and of the planets of Sirius synchronized. They made a joint crossing into the new cycle under full conscious presence. This had never been done before in the long history of Earth. Treema has been the scribe for it all.

With the practices built on our collective instructions, Treema's Great Transition has become an event of magnificent beauty and creativity. The cyclic energies are finally being put to use as a galactic blessing, a rebirth of mammoth proportions. It seems that awakened humans had gathered together a massive record of our times, including all our mistakes and triumphs. We left the instructions for portals and for bridging the transition. Together we calibrated the barometer of our Great Storm.

I sit and absorb this insight from Treema's people—vigilans of the 260th century. The sunset is marvelous from our perch in the meeting room. It sets in both fast and slow motion before our eyes. An eternity is passing within this moment. We sit together for hours, exchanging our understanding and the peace that surpasses it. Night comes and the stars are spectacular. The aurora dances along the horizon as if set to some great, silent music. We are both entranced by the stillness.

Letter Eighty-Five
Vesica of the Gods

Much more silence passes—intercourse with stillness—but at last I hear a voice. It's Treema's. She says softly, "You, my friend, have an idea to bring closure to this experience. I recommend that you place it in the outer world with your voice. Activate the throat chakra now."

Strange, I think, *I have to be* told *to communicate through speech.* "Yes, Treema, I will. Here's my idea: To bring you and Krotos together and bridge the distance between you. But as we both know, this has been our destiny all along. The *three* points of history will converge and bridge amongst themselves to leverage even greater awakenings in each age and cycle—and *within each moment in time.*"

I pause to appreciate the depth of this last realization: Each hour, minute and second is affected by the influence of our leveraging. At any point, in any time over the past 52,000 years—and, yes, hence forward—we humans and vigilans now have access to the expanding consciousness of evolution in a way like never before.

I resume. "We are part of a grand leveraging of awareness by itself. Having been unleashed, *Conscious Evolution* is expanding, lifting up the past, present and future. It is unending and always beginning anew. *Conscious Evolution* is now available to all beings on Earth. The opportunity and blessing is beyond any finite means of measurement.

"Our bridging among the three transition periods will create one, fused system for posterity. The effect will be enough to give counsel to many other such periods. *Conscious Evolution* is present in a way that will convert the Great Storms of future cycles into unprecedented opportunities for the planet and system. I can't begin to imagine such expansion, but it is already beginning now, with you and me, Treema."

She looks at me with great confidence and power. "You have come here as a catalyst for evolution—as a *portal.* Your willingness to come, representing the last of your species, is a catalyst between Source and *Conscious Evolution.* I knew intuitively your coming would be a spacious event. I thought of it as a validation of your species' rebirth. It has indeed been that. Yet, the surprise gift you brought was the trigger to this *quickening* in all our hearts. Thank you, dear brother from the past. This is truly a vision from the heart, the *eye* of the heart."

I return her gaze, and stare into *her* eyes, across hundreds of centuries. The magnitude of our shared presence reveals an underlying—intrinsic—

resonance. I can't resist a kiss. Our lips touch tenderly. In the magic of this kiss, the world suddenly bursts open. We're falling. Our bodies rush into darkness, emptiness. From blackness something is coming, rising up at intense speed. It is our planet, a *new Earth*.

The distance closes fast upon us. In and instant, our feet slam upon the surface of the planet with full force. But instead of annihilation in this collision, there is suddenly a magical stability. Powerful forces have met. A grand presence envelops the Earth in stillness and bliss.

Out of the fierce and silent chaos, Mihelo, Gavrea and Omis arrive, wings rampant, auras radiant. You, B and Invm appear beside them. *Everything is happening so fast.* My authentic being takes hold of my mind: I simply notice and let go of resistance. We are all now together, majestically, on the plateau at the Ends of the Earth.

The scenery has changed since my last visit. Trees and shrubs have grown up along the river; a small village is tucked away in a narrow canyon; children are playing at the water's edge. The whole landscape looks intensely peaceful and alive.

Mihelo speaks, his voice booming, "We are together again in the presence of the Earth. You have visited this holy place before. It grows holier with each intention we set. Let its ground bear witness to the sky that brings us here."

I see the rocky shores and mountains, the rolling ocean of our previous time here. It is still a dynamic atmosphere, charged with the enduring afterglow of the Great Storm. The archangel directs his eyes at mine. There is an infusion of mystical substance into my mind. All the normal tendencies toward random thought and commotion are frozen into hard crystal. This mind-ice shatters and falls out. Stillness incarnates in its place. My mind is, at long last, totally empty! *Manas* enters my presence like never before—fully.

Mihelo directs, "Now create! You have had the vision. It is *yours* to manifest. We all stand together here to assist. But it is *you* who will now act. Draw out your authentic essence onto the shores of this world's dimension."

I don't know. What can I do? The doubts and false humility try to regain a foothold, but *manas* commands, *"Not this time!"* I flip my old fears over into appreciation of the unknown, of authentic, intrinsic action. *I am* ready! I stand beside Treema, holding her hand. She is smiling and ready too. I thank her pointedly, profoundly, through our chakra connections.

Now I turn to the sky, to the sun, to the sun *god*. I call on Apollo, with my little, yet universal voice. It is a powerful voice—*the still,* small *voice.* "Apollo, come to our aid, I entreat you. Our mission is worthy and commanded upon us by destiny—*your* destiny. We would link the great ages within our gathering here today. We would join 52,000 years of time into one timeless moment. Come to us!"

Without any waiting, everything changes. The air is electrified, irradiated with full solar power, engulfed in golden luminance. It sparks and flashes. Its molecules are astir. We breathe in this air and are near swooning. With Treema's hand in mine, I stand firm. Apollo is here!

No words come from the sun god, but we all know that a question has been asked, It is, "What would you have us do?"

I pause and reflect. His use of 'us' triggers an inspiration in me. *Thank you muses!* I answer in words, "I would have you and your counterpart, your twin sun, come together. Form, please, oh sacred beings, a grand vesica piscis. Form a portal between and among us. Join and weld together the past, present and future ages into this moment. Come forth, sister of Apollo!" *I'm hearing her name as 'Isis' in this moment.*

Immediately, two enormous, flaming rings form. They stand vertical—one in front of us, one behind. Fires swirl within their bands. They're so bright as to barely visible to incarnate eyes. They imprint our very souls. With sizzling tumult, the rings slide together. They overlap precisely, creating a pointed oval—a vesica *of the Gods!* We witnesses are standing right in the center of it, cohering its essence. The vesica takes on dimensionality on the plateau at the Ends of the Earth. It embraces us fiercely.

From a long, long distance, through a near endless tunnel in space we see the form of Krotos of the Ufrad. His tiny form grows closer, until he is with us in the vesica. His first reaction is total bewilderment and awe; he crouches and trembles. I touch him on the elbows with my hands, greeting him as he did me. When he recognizes me, he relaxes a little. But he's still utterly confused.

"Have they taken you as well, my friend?" he stammers.

I chuckle and smile sympathetically at him. "So it might seem—but actually not. Let me introduce you to our company." I go around the circle and name the individuals for him. He is in unqualified disbelief at the assemblage, especially the archangels and Omis. He keeps bowing involuntarily to everyone. Gradually, however, he begins to realize that his fortunes have changed. The universe has just opened up to him.

Krotos finally musters the courage to ask, "Where am I? How did I get here?"

"I summoned you," I answer. "With help from the archangels. Oh, and did I introduce the sun god, Apollo ..." my voice trails off. *I think I'll just leave it at that.* I continue, "We're in a place called the Ends of the Earth. It's a sub-dimension, used at the end of every Great Year.

"You know that I am from 26,000 years in your future. Well, Treema here lives 26,000 years in *my* future. That puts *my* time transition right in the middle."

He looks a little bolder as he says, "Three in a row. This is beyond anything I've ever wondered about. But I still don't understand why you've brought me here. What are your intentions?"

"We want to ask you to join us in a little project. Well, not *little,* but it *is* relatively simple. It is focused only on the brief, intense periods at the cusps of our great years. We want to create a new set of instructions for the generations that are to come."

I continue, "If we put all three of our platforms together, we can make a profound statement for *Conscious Evolution.* We can construct a pattern of understanding, as a guide for ages to come. Our three times represent the entire spectrum—from unawake to awakening, to awakened. Together, they present the whole story of evolution becoming conscious at a critical point for the Earth. In this manifestational *triad,* our message will be greatly empowered."

Krotos ponders for several moments. Finally, he speaks. "You have heard the story I told of myself and my people. We have been disheartened and defeated. I was resigned to dying a slow death in my village. Virtually my whole civilization has disappeared."

He is clearly wrestling in his mind and heart for a way to express a new feeling. At last he simply falls very quiet and looks around at all of us, wondering, pleading.

I look at Treema with hope and ask, "What if we took Krotos into the concrome?"

Letter Eighty-Six
Adieu

Gavrea's soothing voice rises to our ears. "That won't be necessary. We can perform this function here and now for you."

Instantly, our chakras are glowing visibly through and beyond the skin of our bodies and our cloths: Krotos, Treema and myself. The vesica cell ignites with energy around us. I feel its qualities of love, light and power. Bright arcs curve out from my body to Treema's, thence to Krotos—the heart, the crown, the root chakra and solar plexus. Soon all the centers connect. *We are like multi-colored, electrified spaghetti!* The light flows together into us; our auras merge into a single shape that fills the vesica from the whole group. We ourselves have become the lens.

The light of Apollo and Isis converges now upon our lens. Behind them is the presence of Source itself shining out like a bright grin of God. I sense, too, the Void. It is holding the space and formless substance of our projection in its infinite sway. *All of this is entirely metaphorical,* I know. *But how else shall I express it?* We are together, all.

Our communion is complete. We share a common destiny now and a common intent. It takes only a short time for us to share everything we need to, as scribes for our ages. There is a message from the Apollo beings as well. It is entirely contained in the word 'allow', but there is so much more to it beyond the word. We *do* allow. This word is now synonymous in my awareness with the Solar Logos. We take it in and let it go.

All the lights gradually dim and fade. The auras return to normal and the vesica dissolves. We are left standing on the plateau in silent awe. I turn to Krotos and bow, as you and the others look on in deep appreciation. "Thank you, brother. How do you feel?"

He looks around, obviously pleased and invigorated. "Everything has changed. I had no idea this kind of energy could be available to me. I thought I was a hopeless case. Thank you, dear friend and comrade. I know now that we three share a rare bond. We have been scribes for passages of great stimulation, Great Storms, at the 'end times' of our ages. I am exalted to know this, in my heart and throughout my whole being. Thank you each."

He looks up at the angelan and archangels. "I must return now to my own world to change the course of my life. I will look not at the end time, but rather at the *beginning* time. I will work to rekindle the flame of destiny in myself and in my compatriots, to renew our understanding of history. Even though you and Treema are distant from us, you give us a reason to dislodge our hope-lessness and despair. Perhaps changes in us will produce a legacy of change in the coming millennia. This seems to be a course of new meaning for my life—a way to embrace the future rather than deny it."

"So it might seem," I offer. "So it shall be."

Omis' voice comes in behind us. "So be it, dear friends. *Amen*."

Mihelo and Gavrea say simultaneously, "We affirm. This is the meaning of 'amen'. It is the affirmation of angels."

I turn back to Krotos and grasp his shoulders with my hands. He looks gratefully into my eyes and slowly dissolves out of sight—back to his world—right as I hold him. *A very strange feeling,* I register. I drop my arms to my sides and look next to Treema. She is smiling boldly, joyfully by my side. She looks up into my eyes and tears begin to flow on both our faces. We have bonded well across time. Our communion continues. It will never stop, no matter how far apart our times are. No words are necessary. We too embrace. We share our tears. It is a holy moment. Then, like Krotos, she dissolves out of my arms, into her far distant time.

I feel the emptiness left behind in the space of departure of these friends. The empty feeling is a face of the Void, a hole in my world. Here is the true presence of us all. It is endlessly deep and whole. And yet, in this moment, it feels so hollow and sad. I rejoice in the sadness. The sliver of a memory makes me reach into my shirt pocket. There, I find the tiny flower Phileina gave me, it seems like a thousand years ago; it's still fresh.

I sigh, turning to Mihelo, and say, "Archangel, you didn't prepare me to feel so much during these meetings. How is it that I could develop such deep feelings for these individuals, so quickly?"

He answers, "You create all meaning in your life. You create the feelings. We gave you the opportunity to be creative. You seized that opportunity. Emotion is a natural outlet for the flow of energy-in-motion. You have moved a great deal of energy today, in a very short time."

I ask, "Does this mean that we humans will have an easier time getting through the Great Storm now? It seems like a whole lot of stuff got cleared out—broken down and swept away. Will that translate into my world as mani-fested events?"

Gavrea replies, "Yes indeed. You are currently living in a year that has been predicted to be tumultuous, a grand turning point for humanity, and a rebirth of eternal proportions. Those predictions now will come forth in form for all to see. This year—2012—is a *beginning*, as many of your wisdom teachers are now saying. The *end* has already passed, through the portal; and you have passed with it. The Storm will continue to play out for a while, in the coming few years and months. But it will be obviously waning, losing its strength, as all storms eventually do. The collective ego will progressively lose strength, as there is no longer any need for it. There is no longer any place for it in the pantheon of your Earthly counselors."

Omis speaks. "The divisiveness in the world will also diminish as a result of your work here. Others, from many faiths and teachings, have invisibly participated in these events. And, of course, you know it is not *you* who have done this. You are just a *metaphor*. Let your ego process that!"

I smile. "Yeah. I might feel like taking some credit, but I know that's impossible. What I have done is only to tell a story—a script. I am a scribe. Nevertheless, I love the work I do. My ego is actually 'proud' of it—in spite of the fact that it means the passing of ego; it is condensing down to where it came from. My pride will pass and dissolve back into the greater field of appreciation."

Omis prompts me. "Where is that?"

"Well, you know, it's in my own little fragment of Source, my soul, my God Self. That's where the ego came from, a very long time ago. It has had a job to do, and it's done it well—a little too well at times I'm afraid. Now it's going into retirement. The French would say, into 'retreat'. I wish it well and Godspeed. It will merge into the soul, taking what it has learned in the world of experience over many lifetimes."

"Well said, friend. You are on the road, and close to crossing the bridge that leads into your next species. You have just described the secret of the ego. Ego has always been a surrogate for the soul. It has mimicked the essence self in every way it could find. Its efforts to dominate and control have been mirrors of the soul's dominion and power. Its efforts to protect and defend you have been facsimiles of the soul's will and freedom. Its actions to separate and divide you have been the soul's way of alerting you to the realities of union and Oneness. The Veil is lifting: the curtain is rising on the next act of your play. Enjoy it, friend. You and your friends have come a long way to arrive in its presence. This will be the performance of lifetimes!"

"Omis, I suddenly feel you're getting ready to depart from us. Am I right?"

"Yes. You've heard enough from me. There will, you well know, be other encounters as you live out your futures."

I wince. "I don't want another parting right now. I will miss you when you go. Can't you just stay on for a little longer?"

"Well, since you asked so nicely, I will tell you one more story before I go. First, though, let us bid *adieu* to our hosts and great retainers, Mihelo and Gavrea. Thank you, mentors and collaborators."

The archangels fold their wings and auras in upon themselves and radiate a profound blessing into us all. It is like we are living within their smile. They look sharply at each other and disappear in a flash.

You look over at B and Invm, who have taken on a quiet glow ever since they began to find things in common. *Speaking of stories, I'll bet there's one there.*

You say to them, "There is so much to be thankful for and appreciate. You two are like Mars and Venus to me—bright stars in my sky, warriors of fierce love and peace. You two have given me a renewed sense of convergence for our two star systems, a crown of achievement. And Phileina, your offspring, is the priceless gem in that crown. Thank you for always coming into my life on Earth and for being near to my soul in the ethers."

Omis shakes out his wings and condenses down into his OM form. He walks over to a rock that sits on the plateau. It must have fallen here when the arrows of the avatars flew this way. He sits down and stares out for a long moment at the great ocean.

Letter Eighty-Seven
Destiny Well

Our old friend, OM, turns back to us and smiles. "I will tell you the story of Treema and the Destiny Well."

I sigh happily. "That's great. I was afraid we would never know about it since Treema's gone. I forgot to ask her."

"Well, I have known Treema for a number of incarnations, as it turns out; these memories are just returning to me now. Treema has a level of insight that I've rarely seen. She has always had a passion for exploring destiny—her own and others. Several lifetimes before this one, she managed a small enterprise you would call, perhaps, a 'travel guide' service. She was very good at what she did. People came to her from all over the planet to get advice on explorations—of almost any kind."

OM looks at me and says, "You and O are from the same 'explorer clan'. This is one reason you felt such an affinity with her. Well, Treema had known about destiny, but only what the average vigilan would understand. She knew it resided inside every person and that its power lay in the Now, not in the *future*. But that's a little tricky. Even vigilans can slip into assumptions about destinies and futures.

"Some people came to her just wanting a vacation in an unusual place. Others wanted a full adventure into the unknown. Whatever the desire, Treema studied her clients thoroughly before signing them on. She turned some visitors away—say, if the spark of the unknown was not shining brightly enough in them, or if they did not share a passion for the required depths.

"You might think that soul passions are resident in all vigilans. And it's true to some extent. The soul is much closer for them than for humans; the Veil *has* been lifted. But incarnate forms come in a wide variety of styles. While mystery and the unknown influence the essence field, not all vigilans want to *explore* it—just as they do not all want to be Source-gazers. But for those who are destined explorers, the soul's incarnate field offers endless potential for discovery. And, as you have heard from your own soul encounters, this territory keeps expanding, deepening and evolving.

"As for any given soul, the *style* of expression for its forms remains consistent throughout all its incarnations. This is natural since, to the essential self, all those incarnations are simultaneous. What the soul chooses is, of course, orchestrated from deeper hierarchical levels—the oversoul and beyond. Its composition derives from the vast network of Life and spirit. Out of this elegant system comes an arrangement I have called the 'soul clan'; it is an arche-typal theme.

"For Treema, as for you, this theme is 'exploration'. It means that she was forever being drawn into the spiritual vortex that her soul had placed just be-low the surface of her outer life. The vortex attracted her and she followed it, life after life. It led ever deeper, and thus did her experience and her passion build.

"When clients came, she would first evaluate their resonance and deter-mine the particular soul clan. She would assess other attributes of the client's deeper being. She used numerous techniques and instruments in this evalua-tion, which finally manifested into the device she called a 'concrome'.

"Though explorers were her favorites, she did accept clients from other clans; these particularly included the clans of the 'founders', the 'illuminators' and the 'seers'. They each provided her with the practice she craved: delving into the mysteries of the Cosmos. Every soul is open to clan sub-themes, so she had clients from all walks of life.

"In the course of Treema's multi-lifetime avocation, she accumulated ex-perience with many groups of souls. Each project was an adventure into mys-tery for her. Gradually, through the intensity of her focus, a silent *new* presence began to come forward, to be born up through her collective appreciation. It quietly gelled into a life form of its own. Without quite realizing this, Treema simply followed the pattern she had established for her work. Secretly the si-lent presence enabled her to move into alignment with it.

"It was not until one particular client came with his unique request that her perspective changed. She realized finally what her work had invoked. The cli-ent at this time was me, in one of my farther ranging incarnations. You see, I am a member of the explorer clan myself. My own soul had sent me to Treema on a specific mission. It was simple enough to be profound. I asked Treema to take me on a trip into the very heart of exploration itself. 'What in the soul,' I asked, 'drives us to look ever more deeply, ever farther within?'

"She was excited by this challenge, and took me on at once. We began working together to formulate a specific 'adventure'. This was her way of de-scribing a given client's project. As we worked and played together, we both began to sense that silent, invisible presence that she had attracted. It grew stronger with each session, until, finally, it began to communicate with us. Its voice was coming from the same depths we were attempting to plumb. It *was* those depths in an ephemeral incarnate form.

"Once we realized what was happening, we redoubled our efforts to an-swer my original request—'what is it that draws us into the depths?' Now, with a face on this presence, the question became 'what draws us into *your* depths?' The presence itself was, in fact, the answer. As we gradually got to know it better, we found that it constituted a portal. It was, and is, an opening into the areas of our essential being where destiny itself is formulated. The presence revealed that it was the incarnate vehicle for what we came to know as 'soul exploration'—that is, exploring the *soul* itself. This was and is the Destiny Well.

"Our adventure project changed everything for Treema. This was no longer just her *business;* it had transformed into a true *calling* and a service to her entire species. This lifetime for me was also a turning point; it was where I originally encountered the idea for the time-transposition project. As we entered the depths of being, we learned to slip through the time stream. There, the Now becomes the empowering agent of motion."

Omis stops and looks at me, inviting my response with a sigh.

"So, that's what a *Destiny Well* is. How does it work?"

The angelan is ready to answer. "It works like any well: It is an opening, tunneled into the depths, from which one extracts valuable resources. It's like a *tunnel* into the soul, if you will.

"There are infinite layers of meaning and sensibility within the soul. They're like rock strata in the Earth, through which a physical well can be drilled in order to find water, oil, or other precious materials. Each layer contains something of value, and the well may only go so deep as to locate a specific resource. However, the deeper you go, the more valuable the riches. So it is with the Well of Destiny. With proper guidance, the visitor can find and align with the most vital essences."

I ask, "Why would that be? Why would the soul hide these things from us?"

"Because the soul is intrinsically mysterious; it is allied with the unknown, the inimitable Source and Void. It wants us to find out for ourselves, to explore and create our own *meaning,* to become *resourceful.* Resourcefulness means 'revisiting Source in full measure'."

"Tell me what you mean by *destiny,* Omis," I ask. "I've heard Orange's take on it, but I'd like to hear it from you, especially as it relates to the Destiny Well."

OM sits silently for a moment and allows the presence of this place—the Ends of the Earth—to arise around us. I feel its energy. *"This* is destiny—the *Now* you feel here, *flowing forward.* Destiny is a *sensation* more than a concept. It is the immediacy and power of the moment. Paradoxically, it is also evolutionary momentum and potentiality. It is the thrust of manifestation. O will tell you that the word 'destiny' derives from Latin, 'to establish, to make firm'.

"Destiny is all of these things. To put it into a form and definition, I would say 'it is the full program to bring spirit into matter—from authentic being into *synthetic* action—that is the action of synthesis.' It is your forthcoming nature—what you become right now. Destiny is the essence of forms you are ideally suited to manifest in any given moment."

"So, it seems that destiny is the *engine* behind what we experience in the Now."

"Yes, you can say that."

"One more question, please. Treema said she was the 'guardian' of the well. Why would destiny need guarding?"

"There are many answers to that question. I would say 'guardian', in this case, equals 'guide'. Treema doesn't *guard* the well as much as she *guides* visitors in its use. Without such supervision one could enter into dark catacombs of the soul and be utterly lost inside those mysteries.

"Let me say, finally, about Treema: She was able to establish, through her discoveries and her long-term service to the vigilan world, a regulated means to enter one's own soul and discover some of its precious properties—the Well. These treasures could then be brought back to the surface for the profit of one and all. She has left her mark on this world, and upon both you and me, now and in the future. This is *her* destiny."

Omis stands abruptly and takes his angelan form, one final time. He is taller and more resplendent than ever. Gold light cascades around us onto the plateau. He simultaneously looks us each in the eye—the heart eye—and says, "From here, I trust you can find your way home. God speed."

With that, he raises his wings high, stretching up to his full measure. His form suddenly sweeps upward and around into a stream of glistening mist in the air. Omis *is* the space now. He is both here and gone.

Letter Eighty-Eight
Open Space

"So be it," you say in a formal tone, a crisp and respectful voice.

Even though I know his presence is still here, I can't help but feel a terrible vacuum, a *hole* in me—in my heart. The plateau looks strangely empty and still. The ocean is too flat, the mountains too far, the sky too dark. We all stand still together, appreciating the emptiness.

You look to Black, Invm and me and say simply, "This might be a good time to return to Paris."

I chuckle and nod in agreement. "I'd completely forgotten we're being 'televised'. Yes. It seems right to go back there." I look one last time at the Ends of the Earth; its tranquil vitality has returned in fullness.

The four of us stare out at the plateau. It stretches to the mountains and up through the valley cutting through. The beautiful river rolls down through the trees and past the village, over the cliff; it drops as a waterfall into the sea. The ocean is serenely calm, under an empty sky. Above is the golden sun. I look at it with new admiration and bow my head to Apollo. I wonder at his mysterious presence in all our travels. At that moment, the world falls away, and we're gone.

Instead of Paris, however, the scene that materializes is Invm's laboratory. All is dark inside. The facsimile of our solar system still floats in front of us beyond the glass partition. We're in the same positions we were in, standing on the plateau. Our eyes gradually adjust to the dimness. I look at the model solar system and marvel once again at the beauty of the energy patterns.

Invm says, "I will accompany you all to the station. Come."

B stops him, reading his intent. "You won't be coming to Earth?"

He replies with the thin lips I've learned to read as a smile, "The gravity, dear one—it would be too much for me. And besides, the three of you have business there that does not include me. We will meet again elsewhere."

She looks disappointed for the briefest second then regains her composure. I've never seen such a 'human' side of B, even if barely noticeable. I find it endearing. She bows her head slightly to Invm and immediately begins moving toward the door. We all follow.

Out on the street, the low gravity is amusing; we take slow, loping strides, and have mounted the hill at the edge of town. Everything looks exactly as when we arrived. The settlement below is nestled below its bleak, dusty hills. A red desert of canyons and chasms winds off toward the empty horizon. I turn back and awkwardly shake Invm's hand. I look him straight in the eye and say, "You are still a mystery to me, friend from Sirius. But I would have it no other way."

He smiles stiffly and puts his long, thin arm on my shoulder. "Your species is quite a revelation to me. I have come to appreciate the richness of *human* emotions—still present in the vigilans. I like them after all. We Sirians have much to learn from you. As a representative of my species, I honor and thank you reverently."

After a long pause and a deep breath, he adds, "And I am glad to have been your father once, however briefly that may have been."

The four of us take in the deep feeling that surrounds that simple statement. I feel heart centers linked and iridescent again. A memory of Treema sweeps past. *I wonder if she feels this?* Black and Invm take a last moment together, staring into each other's eyes. Touching hands, they part in silence.

Without ceremony, we step into our transport alcoves. Instantly, we're translated into beams of electric light, flying across space. The laser lines move us swiftly away. The brief transfer at diamond points passes in meditative silence. Fifteen minutes later, we're standing on the gravel of the *Champs de Mars* under the holographic *Tour Eiffel*. My dream of Venus and Mars makes me appreciate its beauty all the more. I look up at the night sky around the gleaming edifice. There is the laser line, leading out to Mars. As impossible as it seems, we have just traveled across the solar system on that thin pale thread. I take a breath. The stars are bright. And so are my memories.

Now, you, Black and I start our walk back across the *Pont d'Iéna* to the amphitheater. We enter through the arcade and I look up into the sky again. The great *scenari* is visible, spread up against the stars. The audience is still immersed in the display. Thankfully, we're able to pass through the aisles without being noticed. There seems to be lag time in the story above. In it, our figures are still on the plateau. We enter our section, nodding silently to our friends. Green touches your hands and stands to kiss you on the cheek.

We recline into our seats and look up. The final scene with Omis is just concluding. It's good to see the angelan again for a moment. We hear him telling about the Destiny Well, and watch ourselves listening; it all seems so real and unreal at the same time. *How can I be watching myself up in the sky, re-enacting these impossible visions?*

Omis' words close out the final scene. "From here, I trust you can find your way home."

As the sky goes back to stars and space, silence hangs in the air. Slowly, almost sleepily, the crowd begins to applaud politely; gradually the applause grows louder. People look around at us from all sides, with approving smiles and bows. We look at each other in amusement; I feel a little embarrassed. I turn to you and whisper, "Thank God, we're not on camera anymore."

You, for your part, are soaking it in unabashedly. You are simply, fully, receiving the appreciation. I ask, continuing to whisper next to your ear, "So, what now, O? What's next?"

You finish waving at those you know, and turn to me. "Well, now the congress *really* begins. The theme has been set and the participants here will move into dialogue groups around the arena, as well as other places in the nearby neighborhoods."

"How do they know which group to go to?"

Outside our group space, the crowds are beginning to move through the aisles. B answers my question, "It's all quite spontaneous. Anyone can sponsor a group on any topic related to the overall theme. They then gather people around their space and begin to talk about it. Later, all the groups will be brought back together to share what they've learned."

"That sounds like a meeting style from my time, called Open Space."

"Indeed. It is that. We've evolved it a bit, of course."

"I'm pleased. My friend, Harrison Owen, created that technique. He would be pleased, too, I'm sure."

I ask, "So, please tell me again what our *theme* is. I guess I missed it."

You reply, "The theme is how *Conscious Evolution* has empowered the transposition. We are here to explore the ways vigilans and humans—everywhere, in any timeframe—can continue participating in this expanding awareness. It's fitting that we reflect back and evaluate what we've learned—and how we've changed history."

"We've changed history?" I wonder. "How so?"

"Yes, we have. I do not mean you or me, or any individual has done this. But, collectively, we have shifted the flow of consciousness through time, by infusing more *presence*. We've helped make time transparent, and revealed the space behind it. All our work has been based upon the inspiration that reality stands behind all illusion, and that formlessness will shine through any form."

Green has been listening; he adds, "It's the same as Oneness showing through duality, through the complexities of the outer world. Our little group here has played its part to inject *your* world and the world of your children with this new perspective. It is what some have called 'a new Earth'. We *are* your new Earth; our society is what you all aspire to in your hearts." He pauses for a thought. "Well, you still have *free will,* of course. You will choose what seems best to you. But I'm certain it will resemble what we have evolved."

I turn my gaze around the group. They have all gathered around us, standing, listening, ready to go out into the congress. I feel profound appreciation for our group, in ways that words cannot convey. Presence is smiling through them, each and all together. There can be no end to the revelations within us, within all the focused minds and hearts in this assembly. I recall you saying that nearly all vigilans on the planet are focused here now. They are attending to the exploration of *Conscious Evolution. I wish I could say the same of humanity. Perhaps some day soon.*

I raise my eyes for a moment, out to the sky and plane below—the plain of Mars and the Eiffel Tower. People are dispersing into their dialogues, out on the plain, in cafés and bistros, and in small spaces everywhere—*wherever two or three are gathered together in appreciation.* The conversation is only just beginning. I feel myself in each of those spaces, spread out through the consciousness of this new species, reaching out into unknown territories with an eagerness that refreshes and exalts my heart.

You stand and stretch, then offer a hand to pull me up. As our hands touch, that old familiar magic enters me. This time there is no holding it back. It is full force presence, from you to me and around the group. It is *high electric.* I cannot deny the effect you have on me. This time there is no resistance. Our shared authenticity is a solar fire. In its space, I feel the Great Storm that has raged inside me these last years clearing into a blazing, solar crystal calm.

It seems for a moment you were about to say something else, but no. I realize you have never stopped speaking inside me. Every word in these books has been *you* coming through my voice and thoughts, my pen, and through the actions of others. I hear you everywhere. And it's not just *your* voice. It is the still, small voice that carries the word, the Logos into each our lives. It is the silent, radiant voice of our Source. *Apollo.*

END

Epilogue
Why Souls Love the Earth

"Souls bring love to the Earth. It is their primary mission here," you are saying . I'm sitting on the porch of Judy's house in Asheville. I'm back from Paris. It's drizzling rain on a late spring afternoon. I've only just driven in and I'm adjusting to the peace of a sacred space. *How can you be talking to me already?* I mumble in my mind.

"Shall I wait for a better time?"

"No. Now is always the best time," I decide to reply. "Thanks for showing up. You know I can't resist you."

I look around, but do not see you. This is just the way we began years ago—*your* voice coming to me from deep within my own. Now I remember the sentence at the close of the last letter. It has been your voice—inspired by the still, small voice of Apollo—always impressing my words and sentences. *If there has been any wisdom in the story I've written, it would be rooted there.*

"I am here," you say. "I like your phrase 'now is the best time'. Though I know you meant it casually, as with all forms one can look more deeply. Now, of course, is *no time* at all, and yet that makes it the 'best time' paradoxically; it is the *center point* of time. So, tell me. What do think time *is,* my friend?"

"You're asking me? Haven't we been over this a hundred times before? Isn't time just a *thought*—a fiction of our minds? It's a passing form."

"It is; and yet it is not. All things are their opposites in the duality world, as you know. The relationship between 'passing' and 'passage' is the key."

"OK. What do you mean then?"

"Time is the 'passage' through which all 'passing' forms move. It is the grand inside-out portal into now. Therefore, in duality, all forms become *passages* both in time, and *into* time. Souls use these passages to enter the Earth, and to create the likes of you and me here. They do this out of love for the space and purpose of this plane. They extend love into us because that is their nature. They project themselves into 'passing time' and 'time passages'—out of *love.*"

I ponder for a moment. "Just how do you mean 'love'?"

"Love is *God.* It is divine nature. Source. Love is everything you can name and not name. It is everything you can do and not do. It is all there is! In duality, love is seen to be just an *aspect,* a mere face of the deity, or an energy presence. But these are only perceptions. We can describe love in many ways, even in terms of its opposites—fear or hatred. However, no description or perception can contain all of the true essence. Love is the ultimate, perfect, formless 'container'; it is also that which is *contained.* It embraces all creation. Love attracts and merges all, binds all in its *boundless* domain. We talk of love, trying to capture an understanding of it. We say it is this or that, as I am doing now. We try to place it into a form, to put conditions on it. They do not fit. They never can.

"Love is Oneness. It is the Void. Paradoxical to what I just said, there is no 'container' for love. There is no *form* or separation of it into this or that. Love is not separate from truth or beauty or God. *Love is not separate.* And yet we treat it as though it can be differentiated. We must, if we are to use our minds in this world—in speaking and writing and imagining.

"Souls love the Earth because they know their place—in both realms. They also know us, the projection, as *we* are. They embrace the two—from the One. This is true love—embracing duality from Oneness! We, on Earth, are forms incarnate. We have broken off into the Illusion in order to be projected here, to perform roles and functions in the great game of evolution. We cannot do this without a base from which to live and move and have our being. That base is love. It is soul. In its bridging and form taking, soul comes to know duality. It takes on a dual nature, which bestows its *twin* quality, wisdom."

"Wait. Please explain," I interrupt. "How is wisdom a *twin* of love? I've always wondered about so-called 'love-wisdom'."

You answer, "Love is *intimate knowing.* So is wisdom. The distinction our minds perceive hinges on the nuances of 'intimacy'. One side of this metaphorical 'hinge' swings into profound, personal closeness; the other swings toward the depths of integrated intelligence. Both definitions merge when we contemplate 'intimate knowing'. Love places emphasis on the *intimacy,* while wisdom focuses on the *knowing.* As one, they employ an identical power in nature. Such is the duality of Oneness."

I ask, "The soul has duality?"

"Ah, but of course. You know about 'twin souls'. You know about the dark night of the soul, and the bright solar angel. You know that the soul is the bridge between two shores, linking heaven and Earth."

"Well, yeah. I guess that means there *is* some kind of duality."

"As love-wisdom—via the soul—approaches the Earth plane, it creates the game of *yin* and *yang.* Love's presence encounters 'objects' of love. Wisdom meets particularized, objective knowing. *Projected* Oneness transforms into *indi-*

vidualized duality. In terms of *projection from Source,* the soul becomes a lens for all sacred properties shining into us.

"So, why do souls *love* the Earth?"

"First, they are the embodiment of that love within themselves, in their ethereal vastness as well as in their particularity. Second, their destination, Earth, is itself a personification of love. Though this planet has seen long periods that were most *unloving,* remember, everything *is* its opposite. Therefore, that which is 'unloving' is a disguised form of *love.* I remind you that opposites are the extreme poles along an axis that unites them wholly, as one. Looking from beyond duality, the *true* Earth is a prime vehicle of the divine Logos. *Logos* is the 'word' of planetary life and compassion. That word is 'love'.

"Third, since the mission of souls is to inject compassion and integrity into incarnation, they inject love into us. So, to say that 'souls love the Earth' is actually a three-way redundancy. It's the same as saying, 'beings of *love* bring the energy of *love* to the embodiment of *love?*' 'Being, energy and embodiment' are the answers to the question 'why'."

I shrug, amazed at your words. "OK, since you put it that way…"

You smile and continue, "From another angle, we can say that souls are drawn to Earth by their empathy for a place of such struggle, pain and turmoil. They enter here as the cleansing, purifying agents of *Conscious Evolution*—even as their incarnate forms create all manner of mayhem. Souls look upon our planet as a *birthplace* for love. That is to say, Earth is the lowest plane—the ground—on the *in*voluntary arc of spirit, coming into form and matter. It is the densest physical point of all. Thus, it can become the launching platform for *rising* again, up through the *e*volutionary arc. It is the base for rebirth and renewal.

"In the greater scheme, soul embodies the prime intention of the Solar Logos: to redeem consciousness in matter, to lift it up from its 'fall' into separation and obscurity. It seeks to fulfill the destiny of a truly *peaceable kingdom* on Earth.

"The ultimate mission of the soul within our planet and within all species—mineral, plant and animal—is *transcendence.* Under its auspices, all species move into expanding awareness and appreciation. At the end of the long progression, we step off the Earth at last, into the eager, welcoming Cosmos. Our forms transcend themselves into formlessness and freedom. This is mastery of incarnation. Thence we come to embody wisdom, love and ascendancy, ready for birth into ever greater mysteries."

Finally I ask, "O, this is all very illuminating. But why are we talking about souls right now?"

"Look back at the other epilogues. *We always return to the soul in the end.* For incarnate forms, it is analogous to returning to Source. We come full circle when we return to the soul. But for me, speaking personally, I talk of the soul because the soul *talks to me*—of itself and of the One Self.

"There really is only *one* soul, after all. It presents itself to us as many, just as our own forms paint us as *separate* from one another. This is illusion, of course. But, in the end, it is a *useful* illusion. The soul comes forth in these epilogues, to speak *through* us, in order that we will see *through* the mirage, in order that we *use* the illusion and not *be used* by it. The soul would have you know its presence behind the words and spaces of these letters. It would have you know its pure love and wisdom."

You fall silent at last. I do too. In fact, I have put the writing aside for a night, and it is now a beautiful, sunny morning in the mountains of North Carolina. As I sit appreciating the deep, heart energy of Judy's place, you resume your words in me, "Now, we have a guest who would like a word with us: My mentor and your future mother is here."

I'm surprised by this announcement, but I welcome it. I sense a sudden shift in the energy field. It's like the angelans are condensing down a form for my mind. B's voice comes through at last. "Welcome back, dear friend. You have been with us to the edge of it all, eh. What an adventure! Now you're back on solid ground. Breathe deeply of the place you stand."

I accept the presence of Black into my psyche. Memories of Breanne come to mind whenever I think of her. "Ah, B, thank you for all you've given me—and *will* give me. I'm glad you're here. By 'solid ground', do you mean Judy's farm or just being back in my own time?"

"I refer to the *place* more than the time. This Carolina-mountain space is essential and magical for your spirit. You know, of course, it is *my* place, as we have silently let you know. As for the time, it can hardly be called 'solid' for *any* human being.

"The ending of eras is always very *porous*. Humanity is slipping and sliding through the cracks in time right now. Insubstantiality is replacing any material solidity you may cling to. Get comfortable with the *illusion* of things, and you will pass through this time more smoothly."

"What do you mean 'comfortable with the illusion'?"

"See the illusion for what it is: All *forms* are insubstantial. Learn to see reality behind the curtain of form. Illusion is another word for 'formless'."

I ask, "I've heard you vigilans talk about this often enough. But just what are we supposed to *see* when we look *through* the form?"

"I can tell you what you *won't* see: You won't see another form. There is no *form* behind the form. Formlessness looks like *nothing at all* to the mind's eye. To look *through the form,* is to look with the heart's eye. All actions, all thoughts are forms. 'Seeing through' is a pointer to the *secret* within form. Its transparency can transport you into pure sensation, beyond form, beyond the senses. This is where the *five* becomes the *one;* it is what we have called *transposition.* Our five senses are built upon the one and only fundamental 'sensation'— which is *presence.*

"To your mind this will forever remain a mystery. For the heart, however, *presence* is as pure and natural as breathing. When we say 'look through into the formless,' we invoke the Void into sensate, waking consciousness. We invite you to accept your innate, formless identity.

"Remember, reality is formless; it is no *thing.* What your senses tell you about reality is not the truth, not real; senses report only the world of form. When we say, 'look through the form', we are asking you to perceive reality itself, truth itself. *Know that you are real!* The outcome of such perception is *awareness of presence.* Presence cannot, of course, be an *object* of perception—that would make it into another form. But with a simple twist of realization, you can drop the thoughtform and know, intimately, that *perception and presence are one.* This is what we are talking about when we advise you to look into formlessness."

B continues, "Now, here is the 'secret' of form: *Death is your ultimate teacher.* Learn from death that your earthly identity is nothing but a form. You know that all forms pass away—into formlessness, yes? *You* are passing away as we speak, in this instant, tomorrow and the next day. Find death before death finds you. This is the secret of looking through the form into the Void. Know now that you are a passing form."

"Whew. That's intense. I'm going to have to contemplate the whole thing later—in a *seed-link* perhaps. I just can't swallow it all right now. It sounds right, and I do appreciate what you've just said."

B replies, "Yes do put it in a seed-link and ponder it later. You will find a universe there to explore." I sense she is winking at me.

I clear my throat. "So, I must say, I *am* feeling more formless and insubstantial than ever these days. Forms seem less and less dense to me. Time is accelerating; events are blurring together; friends and relations are dying; chaos and danger are rampant in the world—in politics, economics, religion; my body is showing signs of wearing out. Nothing lasts: I just spent three months in Paris, and it was over in a flash."

B continues, "This is just the way it is for you. Appreciate and learn to love the passing parade of forms and affairs. Being able to appreciate the *insubstantial* is a gift. *The more you can see through, the more you can* be *through!* The unformed is your true foundation. It's what lasts amid the constantly changing form world. All that comes and goes is mere *coloring* on the canvas of Life. The consciousness in you that 'sees through' to the formless Source is the enduring essence. It survives when all else disappears.

"And so, in this context, I would speak to you briefly of my project—*Life of Source*. I mentioned it earlier, you'll recall. There are a number of references to it in what O and Omis have told you. Here's what it is: Source is a presence that is very much nearer to your experience —your life—than you have ever known before. You might say it is 'rising' into your awareness. It is available now for all, like never before. Life and Source are meeting in a creative crossroads of expression."

"Huh?" I stammer. "What does that mean?"

"The crossroads is synchronicity. Our new project will actively employ synchronicity and seed-links. The objective is to form an etheric structure at the edge of formless space. It will be a 'chamber of readiness for seed-links'— an *incubation lair,* if you will. Within it, the seed ideas will precipitate wisdom out of the formless space. Our task is to consciously create the chamber by filling it with our seed-links and synchronistic encounters. It will be a repository for transduction of intelligence.

I break in, "I don't understand half of what you just said. It sounds rather grand though. How would we go about creating this space and the seed-links?"

"Leave the space to me. As far as seed thoughts go, however, you have practice at this already. Think back. You've been presented with information and experiences that you could not digest at first. You bundled them into 'thought packets', with the intention to examine them later. This is how you create a seed-link. All I'm suggesting is that we formalize that process and create a conscious locus for it."

"All right, I *have* done this, but I never thought of having a *place* for them to go. Actually though, B, I'm more familiar with the *other* kind of seed-link— that someone else has given me. You and O have done this often."

"Yes. And there are yet other types of seed-links as well: Certain monuments and phenomena hold encoded information and energy signatures—such as the pyramids or the Ark of the Covenant or crop circles. There are even whole sub-dimensions that comprise seed-links, like the Ends of the Earth. They hold the essence of grand ideas.

"For storing and maturing such creations, in the cosmic scheme, there are places—some are *general* and some are *specific*. To 'seed' an idea, in general, means to put it into the *ethers*. In this new project, I would have us make it more specific, and identify a precise location in the *Akasha* for our use; this can generate a powerful multiplier effect. With the help of the angelans, we have already established the space. It is a multi-dimensional crystal vesica, located in the heart center of the Hall of Memories."

"I guess you've been busy. So, where does synchronicity come in? How is that related to seed-links?"

"The energy that creates a seed-link is 'identical' to the energy embodying a synchronicity—that is, meaningful patterns of events, ideas and forms. As the flame beings informed us, *identification* is the principle behind seed-links. The same is true of synchronicity. When a coincidence presents itself as *meaningful*, it does so by revealing the inherent *identity* of events and consciousness. Identification with Source is at the heart of it all, of course."

"Of course. But I'm a little foggy about this, B. Please refresh my memory: Why are *seed-links* associated with identification?"

"Surely. A seed-link is the essential presence of a pattern of information. That is, it is the 'identity' and essence of that information. The expression of identity is synonymous with 'life force'. It is key to our new project, because Life is the *expression* of Source. Hence, we call the program, *Life of Source*. All 'expressions'—to wit, *forms*—have mathematical codes and formulae behind them in the ethers, just as a synchronicity and seed-links have. In this project, some of us will be working with those codes. That is not what I'm asking of you, however. That will be Invm's work."

"Ah, I'm glad of that at least," I sigh. "But here comes the 'big ask'! You know, I haven't decided yet whether to participate in your project."

"I understand," she allows, chuckling. "But 'yet' is only a matter of *time*. Here is the 'ask', as you put it: If and when any of you chooses to participate in this project, your roles—in the human realm—will be quite simple. We only ask you to *monitor* your synchronicities and your seed-links; and then consciously send them to the *chamber*. Another benefit to you will be the actual *creation* of synchronicities in your lives as a result of participation. You will produce synchronistic events, just as you create seed-links. In a phrase, I would like you to begin *managing* your awareness. The project will promote a widespread growth into wakefulness."

I pause and ponder. "Hmm. That *does* sound appealing. If we agree to get involved, will you give us further instructions?"

"Yes, indeed. However, they will be in the language of the project itself. You will receive these instructions through synchronicities, dreams and other seed-links. You might possibly receive them through letters from me as well, in the manner that O has employed before."

"Really?" I reply. "Can others receive letters from you as well?"

"Yes. We have opened a new channel in the *Akasha* for this, with Omis' assistance. The channel will work for anyone who wishes to communicate. Bear in mind, however, people will have varying degrees of skill and ability in translating what they receive."

"So, if a person wanted to receive and write messages from you or from the crystal vesica, how would they go about it?"

"It's very much the same method you used in writing these *Letters:* As questions arise in your mind, simply go into stillness—with your awareness directed toward the *Akasha.* Write the questions down. Then go back to the stillness again; let sensations arise in your chakra body and take form in thought. Finally, write down the answers as they come into your mind. This is one way to download your inspirations. Feel the linkage to the crystal chamber at each step. Plant the seeds in that vessel and they will grow."

"Well, I'm not yet committing to this," I venture. "But I am intrigued. Who do you want to be involved in this project?"

"Anyone who chooses to be. You and your two friends from O's project would form the hub. But any person on the planet may join in. There is nothing exclusive about this work, let me be clear. All participants are free and responsible in their own rights to give and receive messages from Source and put them into Life, to access the Akashic chamber we create, to monitor their own seed-links and synchronicities, and to draw inspiration and guidance from them."

"OK." I nod. "So, where does this all lead? What are the project goals and outcomes? Are there any safeguards against misuse? And, again, why are you calling the project 'Life of Source'? Why not a name, like, 'Seed-links and Synchronicities, Inc.'?"

B laughs, "You humans have *so* many suspicions and questions! You are indeed a race of questioners. But we do love human curiosity. Many of the questions you will ask over the course of this project will be answered by yourselves—from within—from the *seed chamber* itself. Many of the answers will come in the form of synchronicities. As for the title of the project, it was chosen by a much deeper presence than my own. It connotes an avenue whereby Source is coming into the expression of Life in fresh, new ways. More understanding is coming to us all soon. Go within your essence to find your own answer."

"All right. But let me ask a dumb question: What *is* a seed-link really?"

"To repeat myself, both seed-links and synchronicities are expressions of Life itself, *identity* forms from Source. A seed-link is the essence of a thought. It's a condensed bit of knowing, an iconic information packet. Imaging and imagination, too, are important elements in creating an effective seed-link. Giving a resonant icon to your seed-link will give it stability and provide a key for re-accessing it later."

"Can you be more specific about icons for seed-links? How do you choose one?"

"The icon can take any form. First, sense the core vibration of the thought pattern you wish to seed. From this, the image will precipitate out. Let it appear. Once you have an icon, visualize sending it into the chamber. Let's say you want to save a sensation you've had while returning from the Void. The icon you select might be an *empty black cup*. This is a 'kernel' for your idea. Once seeded properly, it will gather nutrients around itself and begin to grow. It is a living nucleus that reaches out into other spheres of awareness, and draws information in. That is the *linking.*"

At this point I decide to put my laptop down and go have a cup of coffee with Judy. I tell her what Black has said. At once, an idea comes to her about linking with the crystal vesica. She cups her hands together in a vesica-shaped mudra. This, she senses, can be like a portal into the chamber. I think: *Exactly what B predicted—inspiration from the chamber!*

I thank Judy and go back to writing, and explain Judy's idea to B. She replies, "I remember that from long ago. Yes, hands together make a vesica; it works very well. From there, visualize the crystal inside your hands."

"I like that. I can almost *see* the crystal between my palms," I say. "OK, back now to that 'black cup' icon you mentioned. What do we do when we want to retrieve the idea and open it up again?"

"Simply visualize the cup and bring it back to your awareness. Go into stillness for a moment and center yourself in the heart. Imagine the black cup before you in your heart's eye. See it silently radiating its message up into your mind—that is, connect the heart to the forehead chakra. Allow the matured essence to return. Open yourself and intuitively explore. This may be done in writing, drawing, meditation or simple appreciation. I guarantee, new impressions will come to you if you are sincere."

"And now tell me: Just what *is* this crystal vesica you speak of?"

B pauses before answering. "As I said, it is a small chamber within the Hall of Memories; Omis and Invm have created this vessel for our use. The crystal is a simple form we can use to enrich ideas and energies we place there. The *space* inside merges with the elements we put in. Later, we will later take them out again as amplified inspirations and expressions of the Life of Source—the Life we all *are*.

"Each time we send a seed-link or synchronicity into the chamber, we nurture and mature the whole project. We create a synergistic quotient, far exceeding the 'parts taken separately'. The presence of any single idea will illuminate all the others. One caution I would advise: Be careful of judgments and polarization in this space; resistance has no place here. We do not want to introduce destructive qualities."

"Why? What do judgments have to do with synchronicities?"

"It has to do with identification, and the concentrated nature of the vesica crystal. Judgment and polarization are actions that mimic the creative amplification process, except they use it destructively."

"Who would do this? Why would anyone want to use the chamber to make *judgments* anyway?"

"As humans, you often make judgments unconsciously. The caution I give you is to be aware of the way you address the chamber—when you do address it, both sending in ideas and taking them out again. Do not do this without first entering stillness—the non-dual presence. Duality, by its nature, introduces fluctuations between negative and positive."

"All right. I think I understand." I stop my questioning and let her words sink in. *The project seems worthy enough, but I wonder if I'm really up for it.* "When would it begin?" I ask.

"Right now. Right here. Try this: Create a seed-link that contains the idea pattern for my *whole project*. Use the vesica crystal image itself as the icon. Within this icon, place your current understanding, plus the intention to attract deeper awareness into its pattern, into the whole project

"Send the seed or synchronicity into the chamber even as you may continue to explore it in real time. The more seeds there are in the chamber, the more powerful will be the magic associated with it. These will be the catalytic *glue* for the space, drawing out more power from Source into the chamber. Thus will begin a great creative sharing and amplifying."

She stops now. "That is all for this time. It's enough to begin with. Do not make this into a *chore*. Simply recall it when you have truly conscious moments in your life. Make it an active part of your authenticity and awareness. If you do this, you will find abundant returns on your investment. The greatest of these returns will be your own expanded appreciation and readiness for awakening.

"Now, I will bid you *au revoir*. It has been my sincere pleasure to work with each of you, in all the different dimensions and levels of experience we have shared."

"Wait," I exclaim. "Please don't go yet. I have another question. If it's not too much to ask, could you say a little more about Invm and you?"

There are no words for a while. I wait. Just as I think she has really gone, her voice sighs softly, "After his death in Paris, his soul returned to Sirius in the incarnation of Invm. There, his destiny became clear. At a young age, he knew he would return to our solar system, to Mars, to work with the angelans and Earth evolution. But it was a 'serious' sacrifice for him. Forgive the pun.

"Invm was born into what you would call a 'royal family' on his planet. This world, called Amrk, is lush and beautiful, with natural and technological wonders. Sirians live there in peace and grace, with abundance of opportunity for learning, development and adventure. Contemplative Sirians even go so far as to study the *psyche* of the Cosmos. They have gained understandings that Earth hasn't dreamt of yet.

"Their culture blends art, science and spirituality into one shared enterprise. Some of the more advanced scientists even explore *beyond* our galaxy, into the far, far reaches of exogalactic space. A particular focus of study for them is Great Andromeda, twin soul galaxy to the Milky Way. In fact they are assisting angelans in opening portals to Uk Banuh, the being at the heart of Andromeda. One of the amazing angelan projects is to prepare us for the grand union of our twin galaxies—3 billion years in the future. A very long-term project, to be sure!"

B continues, with animation, "Both Invm and I will next incarnate on Invm's home planet and realize the full merger of twins in our personal selves. We shall begin that lifetime as two beings, and end it as one. It will be our last vigilan lifetime before becoming angelan."

The idea of that joining sends a resonant thrill through my body. I sigh, "Amazing. Thank you. At last, I have no more questions!"

"Then let me say: The soul of all blesses your heart forever."

I feel B's presence pull back. O, I sense you near. You've been listening to her discourse all along. "It's a wonderful project B is proposing, don't you think? I will certainly be participating in it. What a great direction for us all to follow from here." I recognize your subtle overture, but I say nothing. *I don't feel it yet. I just want to stop* this *project first.*

Then I hear, "I too shall add my appreciative focus to it—in service to a good cause." I instantly recognize Omis' smooth, hearty voice.

"Omis, thank you for coming. And thank you for everything you've done for us. I'm delighted to know you'll maintain a connection here."

"How could I *not,* my friend? You are my family and forebears—and my *future!* I have known you all forever. I come here now, briefly, to impart yet another final blessing on O's project—which of course was OM's project, which was *Apollo's* project. It is finally full and complete!"

His voice takes on even finer stillness and power. "Bless you deeply, sincerely—entirely—my dear human and vigilan friends. This is indeed wholeness, in you. This is Oneness. I say to you, each and all: Now bless into bliss." These last words strike my heart. I feel they are not just a wish but also a command. The air is instantly crisper and clearer. Peace descends like a warm, invisible rain on this bright, sunny morning.

B asks one more time, "So, dear friend, what is your decision? Will you join us in our new project, *Life of Source?*"

Under the impetus of this question, a large block of my resistance finally breaks off and falls away. It feels like a calving glacier of denial. I see through the enormous hole it has left in my ego façade. Its emptiness begins to resonate with the hole in my heart; its vision is the *eye* of the heart. I see *free,* at last, what this means for my world. I see the freedom of the formless Source of eternal abundance awakening into Life.

I smile, looking around the porch, with all your energies radiant here. A gentle breeze weaves through the sunlight, through the tree branches and rustling leaves. *What a beautiful morning!* A song sparrow announces the day. I sense, without seeing, the three of you, my friends of the soul, sitting here with me in this powerful, unending moment. You gaze directly, invisibly, into me from across the circle—three beaming faces of unshakable destiny: love, power and presence. *At last the project is complete!*

My voice cracks as I speak, but my resolve is firm. "I will."

Who is the Scribe?

The information in these volumes comes through Robert, but it does not belong to him, nor is it original with him. He has been inspired from many sources, both internal and external. Over the span of his life, he has developed skills and insights useful in transcribing these messages. For decades he has worked in the fields of community development, environmental planning, documentary writing and filmmaking. He has been an agent of the U.S. Federal Government, National Park Service and a volunteer in the U.S. Peace Corps and VISTA. He has traveled the world, meeting diverse peoples, learning from their cultures and appreciating humanity in its countless forms. His commitment to our collective future—in the most positive sense—is firm and persistent. He continues to feel the presence and support of unseen, enlightened beings everywhere. So may it be for all who are open to them. We only need ask and appreciate. Amen.

Made in the USA
Middletown, DE
19 November 2024

65032976R00166